OXFORD PHILOSOPHICAL MONOGRAPHS

HEGEL'S IDEA OF FREEDOM

ALSO PUBLISHED IN THE SERIES

The Justification of Science and the Rationality of Religious Belief
Michael Banner

Individualism in Social Science
Forms and Limits of a Methodology
Rajeev Bhargava

Causality, Interpretation, and the Mind
William Child

The Kantian Sublime
From Morality to Art
Paul Crowther

Semantic Powers
Meaning and the Means of Knowing in Classical Indian Philosophy
Jonardon Ganeri

Kant's Theory of Imagination
Bridging Gaps in Judgement and Experience
Sarah L. Gibbons

Determinism, Blameworthiness, and Deprivation
Martha Klein

Projective Probability
James Logue

Understanding Pictures
Dominic Lopes

Wittgenstein, Finitism, and the Foundations of Mathematics
Mathieu Marion

False Consciousness
Denise Meyerson

Truth and the End of Inquiry
A Peircean Account of Truth
C. J. Misak

The Good and the True
Michael Morris

Nietzsche and Metaphysics
Peter Poellner

The Ontology of Mind
Events, Processes, and States
Helen Steward

Things that Happen because They Should
A Teleological Approach to Action
Rowland Stout

Hegel's Idea of Freedom

ALAN PATTEN

OXFORD
UNIVERSITY PRESS
Great Clarendon Street, Oxford OX2 6DP

Oxford University Press is a department of the University of Oxford
It furthers the University's objective of excellence in research, scholarship,
and education by publishing worldwide in

Oxford New York
Athens Auckland Bangkok Bogotá Buenos Aires Calcutta
Cape Town Chennai Dar es Salaam Delhi Florence Hong Kong Istanbul
Karachi Kuala Lumpur Madrid Melbourne Mexico City Mumbai
Nairobi Paris São Paulo Singapore Taipei Tokyo Toronto Warsaw

with associated companies in Berlin Ibadan

Oxford is a registered trade mark of Oxford University Press
in the UK and in certain other countries

Published in the United States
by Oxford University Press Inc., New York

First published 1999

British Library Cataloguing in Publication Data
Data available

Library of Congress Cataloging in Publication Data
Data available

ISBN 0-19-823770-7

1 3 5 7 9 10 8 6 4 2

Typeset by Hope Services (Abingdon) Ltd.
Printed in Great Britain
on acid-free paper by
Biddles Ltd.
Guildford & King's Lynn

To my mother
and in memory of my father
with love

ACKNOWLEDGEMENTS

From my initial awkward and naïve attempts as a graduate student to understand Hegel, through to the formating and preparation of the final manuscript, I have received a great deal of help and encouragement from many different people. Jerry Cohen gave me my first, unforgettable tutorials on Hegel, patiently supervised the M.Phil. dissertation out of which this study eventually evolved, and, more recently, made valuable comments on a version of Chapter 5. To Michael Rosen I owe a huge debt of gratitude for supervising the D.Phil. stage of the project, which was completed in March 1996. I am indebted to him for his overall direction, for a number of comments, criticisms, and suggestions that I am sure have raised the standard of the final product, and for urging me to contact OUP with a book proposal.

Raymond Plant and Raymond Geuss were my D.Phil. examiners and they made a number of challenging but very helpful comments during the *viva voce*. I am particularly grateful to Raymond Geuss for passing on to me detailed written notes on the dissertation, which have proved extremely useful in revising the manuscript. Peter Stillman also read the entire manuscript at its dissertation stage and passed on detailed comments and suggestions, which have been very helpful. Jeff Patten read a penultimate version of the book manuscript and made a number of valuable stylistic and substantive suggestions. An anonymous reader for OUP made some helpful comments on the penultimate draft. And Hans-Jakob Wilhelm provided valuable research assistance of both a technical and a substantive kind, which has improved the overall quality of the final product and helped me to come within a few months of meeting my deadline. To all of these people, my thanks.

I am also grateful to Jessica Brown, Dario Castiglione, Iain Hampsher-Monk, Michael Inwood, and David Miller for discussion and comments, and to a number of different participants in various workshops, seminars, and conferences where I presented work in progress.

While I was a graduate student, I received financial support from the British Council and then from the Social Sciences and

Humanities Research Council of Canada, and I am grateful to both institutions. I also wish to thank colleagues at both the University of Exeter and McGill University for giving me the time, space, and intellectual support to complete the project.

Parts of the book were previously published elsewhere. An earlier version of part of Chapter 3 appeared under its present title, 'The Reciprocity Thesis in Kant and Hegel', in the *Bulletin of the Hegel Society of Great Britain*, 33 (Spring/Summer 1996), 54–69. An earlier version of Chapter 5 appeared under its present title, 'Hegel's Justification of Private Property', in *History of Political Thought*, 16/4 (Winter 1995), 576–600. I am grateful to the editors and publishers of these journals for allowing me to use this material here.

AP

Montreal
December 1998

CONTENTS

ABBREVIATIONS

In references to works by Hegel, I have used the abbreviations listed below. Where an abbreviation refers to both the German original and an English translation, I give the page references for both, with the German first and the English second, separated by an oblique (/). Where possible I have used standard English translations, but I have often amended these to make them more literal or to standardize terminology. Where no suitable English translation is available, translations are my own.

References to lecture materials not published during Hegel's lifetime are made directly to the transcription from which they are taken. However, where these materials are included as 'Additions' or *Zusätze* to standard editions of Hegel's published works, I cite the paragraph number of the relevant work together with an 'A'. Thus, for example, '*PR* §7A' refers to the Addition to Paragraph 7 of the *Philosophy of Right*. I use a comma in such a context to indicate 'and'. Thus '*PR* §7, A' refers to Paragraph 7 of the *Philosophy of Right* and the Addition to that paragraph.

Aesthetics — *Aesthetics: Lectures on Fine Art*, vol. i, trans. T. M. Knox (Oxford: Oxford University Press, 1975). Cited by page number.

DFS — *The Difference between Fichte's and Schelling's System of Philosophy*, trans. H. S. Harris and Walter Cerf (Albany: SUNY Press, 1977). Cited by page number.

Enz. i — *Enzyklopädie der philosophischen Wissenschaften*, vol. i (1817, rev. 1827, 1830). *Werke*, viii. Cited by paragraph number (§).

Hegel's Logic, trans. William Wallace (Oxford: Oxford University Press, 1975). Cited by paragraph number (§).

Enz. iii — *Enzyklopädie der philosophischen Wissenschaften*, vol. iii (1817, rev. 1827, 1830). *Werke*, x. Cited by paragraph number (§).

Hegel's Philosophy of Mind, trans. William Wallace and

A. V. Miller (Oxford: Oxford University Press, 1971). Cited by paragraph number (§).

ETW *Early Theological Writings*, trans. T. M. Knox, with an Introduction and Fragments trans. Richard Kroner (Philadelphia: University of Pennsylvania Press, 1975). Cited by page number.

LPR *Lectures on the Philosophy of Religion*, 3 vols., ed. Peter C. Hodgson, trans. R. F. Brown, P. C. Hodgson, and J. M. Stewart with the assistance of J. P. Fitzer and H. S. Harris (London: University of California, 1984–5). Cited by volume and page number.

NL *Natural Law*, trans. T. M. Knox (Philadelphia: University of Pennsylvania Press, 1975). Cited by page number.

Ph.G. *Phänomenologie des Geistes* (1807). *Werke*, iii. Cited by page number.

Phenomenology of Spirit, trans. A. V. Miller (Oxford: Oxford University Press, 1977). Cited by page number.

PR *Grundlinien der Philosophie des Rechts* (1821). *Werke*, vii. Cited by paragraph number (§) except where otherwise indicated.

Elements of the Philosophy of Right, ed. Allen W. Wood, trans. H. B. Nisbet (Cambridge: Cambridge University Press, 1991). Cited by paragraph number (§) except where otherwise indicated.

SL *Science of Logic*, trans. A. V. Miller (London: George Allen & Unwin, 1969). Cited by page number.

VG *Die Vernunft in der Geschichte*, vol. i of *Vorlesungen über die Philosophie der Weltgeschichte*, ed. J. Hoffmeister (Hamburg: Felix Meiner Verlag, 1955). Cited by page number.

Lectures on the Philosophy of World History: Introduction, trans. H. B. Nisbet (Cambridge: Cambridge University Press, 1975). Cited by page number.

VGP — *Vorlesungen über die Geschichte der Philosophie*, 3 vols. *Werke*, xviii–xx. Cited by volume and page number.

Hegel's Lectures on the History of Philosophy, 3 vols., trans. Elizabeth Haldane (Lincoln: University of Nebraska Press, 1995). Cited by volume and page number.

VPG — *Vorlesungen über die Philosophie der Geschichte*. *Werke*, xii. Cited by page number.

The Philosophy of History, trans. J. Sibree (New York: Dover, 1956). Cited by page number.

VPR — *Vorlesungen über Rechtsphilosophie*. 4 vols., ed. K.-H. Ilting (Stuttgart: Fromman Verlag, 1974). Including paragraphs on 'Objective Spirit' from the Heidelberg *Encyclopaedia*, and transcriptions from Hegel's lectures of 1822–3 (transcription by H. G. Hotho) and 1824–5 (transcription by K. G. von Griesheim). Cited by volume and page number.

VPR17 — *Die Philosophie des Rechts: Die Mitschriften Wannenmann (Heidelberg 1817–1818) und Homeyer (Berlin 1818–1819)*, ed. K.-H. Ilting (Stuttgart: Klett–Cotta Verlag, 1983). Transcription of Hegel's 1817–18 lectures by P. Wannenmann. Cited by page number.

VPR18 — *Die Philosophie des Rechts: Die Mitschriften Wannenmann (Heidelberg 1817–1818) und Homeyer (Berlin 1818–1819)*, ed. K.-H. Ilting (Stuttgart: Klett–Cotta Verlag, 1983). Transcription of Hegel's 1818–19 lectures by C. G. Homeyer. Cited by page number.

VPR19 — *Philosophie des Rechts: Die Vorlesung von 1819/1820*, ed. Dieter Henrich (Frankfurt: Suhrkamp Verlag, 1983). Anonymous transcription of Hegel's 1819–20 lectures. Cited by page number.

Werke — *Hegel: Werke Theorie Werkausgabe*, 20 vols. (Frankfurt: Suhrkamp Verlag, 1970). Cited by volume number.

I

Introduction: Perspectives on Hegel's Idea of Freedom

1.1. *Freedom and* Sittlichkeit

In a striking passage from his *Lectures on the Philosophy of World History*, Hegel makes the following claim: 'For the everyday contingencies of private life, definitions of what is good and bad or right and wrong are supplied by the laws and customs [*Sitten*] of each state, and there is no great difficulty in recognizing them' (*VG* 94/80). 'The individual's *morality*', he adds, will then 'consist in fulfilling the duties imposed upon him by his social station [*Stand*]' (*VG* 94/80). Thus, 'If someone declares that, in ordinary private existence [*gewöhnlichen Privatverhältnisse*], it is not at all easy to decide what is right and good . . . we can only attribute this to his evil or malevolent will which is looking for excuses to escape its duties, for it is not difficult to recognize what those duties are' (*VG* 94/80).

These assertions together articulate a thesis that is elaborated and developed at greater length in Hegel's most important work of social and political philosophy, the *Philosophy of Right*. The thesis, which I shall simply call the *Sittlichkeit* thesis, concerns the content of the ethical norms that should guide our everyday practical reasoning. These norms, the *Sittlichkeit* thesis claims, consist in nothing other than the duties and virtues embedded in the central institutions of modern social life. In modern European societies, as Hegel argues at length in the *Philosophy of Right*, they consist in the duties and virtues inscribed in the 'concrete ethos' or 'ethical life' (*Sittlichkeit*) of three especially central institutions: the family, civil society, and the state.

The *Sittlichkeit* thesis is at once attractive and deeply troubling. Its appeal derives from the thought that practical reason implicitly or explicitly involves dialogue with others and finding reasons that are acceptable to those with whom we disagree. If, in the course of practical reasoning, we strive for some Archimedean standpoint that abstracts from human experience and relationships, then we seem to be abandoning the very connection with others that makes a meaningful exchange of reasons possible. If, by contrast, our way of reasoning is, as Michael Walzer puts it, 'to interpret to our fellow citizens the world of meanings that we share', then we at least start from some consensus on the basis of which further disagreements and conflicts can be adjudicated.[1] By insisting that the content of everyday practical reasoning is given by the duties and virtues embedded in the central institutions and practices of our common social experience, Hegel's view makes it possible to address those with whom we disagree with some hope of convergence.

The troubling aspects of Hegel's thesis are often remarked upon.[2] One problem is that the model of practical reason proposed by the thesis looks *under-determinate*. Faced with some practical dilemma, a given individual might find himself pulled in conflicting directions by the demands of the different institutions and traditions of his community.[3] Without further refinement, Hegel's model of practical reason would not, for example, resolve the dilemma confronting a young man described by Jean-Paul Sartre, who is torn between his duty as a family member to care for his mother and his duty as a citizen to join the Resistance.[4] The ethical and ideological pluralism characteristic of modern industrialized societies poses a different kind of problem of under-determination. Duties and virtues that are embedded in the practices of one ideologically defined group in a given society are unlikely to be found in the practices of all others. In a suitably Hegelian manner, the very appeal of the *Sittlichkeit* thesis—that it seeks to locate the content of practical reason in a consensus defined by our common social experience—may also be one of its greatest weaknesses: for under conditions of modernity, where 'the fact of pluralism' prevails, there may be no sufficiently thick common experience to reason from.[5]

[1] Walzer, *Spheres of Justice*, p. xiv.

[2] For an excellent discussion, with reference to recent reformulations of Hegel's thesis, see O'Neill, 'Ethical Reasoning and Ideological Pluralism'.

[3] Throughout this study I have generally used the masculine pronouns to stand for 'individual', 'person', 'agent', and so on. Hegel's notorious views about the capacities of women for free and rational agency (e.g. at *PR* §166, A) make it hard to be confident that he uses such terms in a more inclusive way. Since so much of the study is devoted to interpreting and engaging with Hegel's views, use of feminine pronouns would misleadingly create the impression that Hegel held more enlightened views about women than he actually did.

[4] Sartre, *L'Existentialisme est un humanisme*, 39–42.

[5] The phrase 'fact of pluralism' is from Rawls, *Political Liberalism.*

A second, even more worrying feature of Hegel's thesis is that it seems, at first glance, to be unacceptably *conservative*. The thesis seems to presuppose that modern social institutions are legitimate or at least that they are not seriously illegitimate or unjust. If they were seriously illegitimate—if they systematically worked to stifle human development and flourishing—then it is far from obvious that the duties and virtues they incorporate represent the content of everyday practical reason. One might think instead that, under such conditions, the 'world of meanings that we share' would be characterized by what Marxists term 'false consciousness'. And that modern social institutions *are* seriously illegitimate is exactly what many radical critics of modernity maintain. The principled opponent of the bourgeois family, the socialist critic of modern capitalism, and the anarchist and cosmopolitan sceptics about the contemporary state, each wish to deny the legitimacy of certain central forms of modern social life. To the extent that the *Sittlichkeit* thesis ignores, or assumes away, the concerns of such radical critics, it seems to involve a serious conservative bias.

A central aim of this study is to understand how Hegel hopes to handle objections of this form. How can he maintain that the content of everyday practical reasoning is given by the *Sittlichkeit* of the modern European world without exposing himself to the objections that his position is under-determinate and unacceptably conservative? My thesis is that we can make progress in answering this question through a philosophical exploration of what I call Hegel's 'idea of freedom'. By this I mean his theory of what it is to be free (the 'concept' of freedom) and his account of the social and political contexts in which this freedom is developed, realized, and sustained (the 'actualization' of freedom).[6] Hegel's lengthy discussion of *Sittlichkeit* in the *Philosophy of Right* begins with the striking assertion that 'Ethical Life [*die Sittlichkeit*] is the *idea of freedom*, as the living good which has its knowledge and volition in self-consciousness, and its actuality through self-conscious action' (*PR* §142). It is my contention that an exploration of Hegel's 'idea of freedom' can help us to understand why it is that he takes modern *Sittlichkeit* to define the content appropriate for our everyday practical reasoning.

[6] The 'idea' (*Idee*) of *x*, for Hegel, is defined as the 'concept' (*Begriff*) of *x* together with the 'actualization' (*Verwirklichung*) or 'objectivity' (*Objektivität*) of that concept. See e.g. *PR* §1 and *Enz.* i, §213.

A philosophical reconstruction of Hegel's idea of freedom can, in fact, not only help to clarify his thesis concerning the relationship between *Sittlichkeit* and practical reason but should also improve our understanding of all of the major claims and propositions of his social philosophy. Freedom is the value that Hegel most greatly admires and the central organizing concept of his social philosophy. He holds that freedom is the 'worthiest and most sacred possession of man' (*PR* §215A) and thinks that the entire normative sphere, or 'system of right', can be viewed as 'the realm of actualized freedom' (*PR* §4; cf. §29). He goes so far as to say that freedom is 'the last hinge on which man turns, a highest possible pinnacle, which does not allow itself to be impressed by anything' (*VGP* iii. 367/459). It is true that concepts such as 'spirit' (*Geist*), 'self-actualization', and 'reconciliation' (*Versöhnung*) are also central to Hegel's social philosophy and that they are sometimes taken to be the key to understanding his outlook.[7] But what Hegel means by each of these concepts, and how he puts them to use, can be properly appreciated only in the context of an understanding of his idea of freedom. The distinctive feature of spirit—that which distinguishes it from nature—is that it is free (*Enz.* iii, §382, A). The project of reconciliation involves giving people reasons to affirm the central institutions and practices of their social world by showing that those institutions and practices work to actualize freedom. And Hegel holds that individuals achieve full self-actualization to the extent that they develop and exercise their capacities for free and rational agency. The key to understanding Hegel's social philosophy, it can confidently be said, is coming to terms with his idea of freedom.

Much of what Hegel has to say about freedom is highly controversial and paradoxical and conflicts with the received opinions and assumptions of mainstream contemporary Anglo-American philosophy. The claim that a kind of freedom is realized through commitment to the duties and virtues of *Sittlichkeit* will already have struck many readers as counter-intuitive. In addition, Hegel explicitly rejects the common-sense understanding of freedom as 'being able to do as one wants' (PR §15) and instead, in a view that is widely viewed as discredited, follows Kant in equating true freedom with rational self-determination. To make matters worse, Hegel himself draws

[7] These themes are emphasized in three different studies respectively to which I am greatly indebted for my understanding of Hegel: Taylor, *Hegel*; Wood, *Hegel's Ethical Thought*; and Hardimon, *Hegel's Social Philosophy*.

attention to one of the main worries about the Kantian understanding of freedom—that it is vacuous—but then insists that his own theory of *Sittlichkeit* somehow manages to overcome this objection. He praises contractarians such as Rousseau and Fichte for making freedom the principle of political legitimacy, but completely rejects the social contract theory that they take to be an implication of that principle. He defends the institution of property as the 'first existence of freedom' (*PR* §45). And, most controversially of all, he asserts that individuals achieve full or true freedom only as members of the state—an assertion that has perhaps forever associated Hegel's name with Prussianism and even totalitarianism.

My ambition, in the present study, is to develop an interpretation of Hegel's idea of freedom that is clear, precise, and faithful to the written texts and recorded lectures of his mature period. As I will explain in this introductory chapter, it is my contention that the intersection between Hegel's idea of freedom and his theory of *Sittlichkeit* has not been well understood in standard accounts of his social philosophy and that my interpretation casts this relationship in a distinctive light. I do not attempt an overall defence of Hegel's idea of freedom and am sceptical, for reasons I will indicate, about certain parts of it. I do think I can show, however, that there is something original and valuable in Hegel's account and that some of the central elements of the theory are more coherent and less vulnerable to certain standard objections than is commonly supposed.

The decision to concentrate on Hegel's mature writings and lectures reflects several assumptions. One is that, although texts from earlier periods in Hegel's development anticipate and can help to clarify his most important mature ideas, there are also significant differences between early and mature texts that make it impossible to justify treating the entire Hegelian corpus as a unified body of thought. Over the years, Hegel changed his mind about substantive issues, such as the appropriateness of the classical world as a model for modern Europe, and about the structure and mode of presentation of social, ethical, and political theory. It is not before about 1817 that he arrives at a reasonably settled set of views about the form and content of an account of freedom. A second assumption is that there are already a number of excellent studies that take a chronological or developmental approach to Hegel's thought and it is difficult to see how much more of interest could be said here by adopting the same strategy.[8] By contrast, there is, to my knowledge, no thorough, full-length study in the English-language secondary literature of the account of freedom contained in Hegel's mature work.

For the purposes of this study, I shall assume that Hegel's 'mature' period extends from about 1817 until his death in 1831—roughly, if not exactly, the time he spent in Berlin. There is clearly some degree of arbitrariness involved in deciding when exactly Hegel's mature social philosophy begins, but several considerations suggest that 1817 would be an appropriate year at which to draw the line. It was in 1817 that Hegel published the first edition of his *Encyclopedia of the Philosophical Sciences*, which contains an extended treatment of both the concept of the will and 'objective spirit', and forms the basis of his subsequent lecture series on the philosophy of right (*Rechtsphilosophie*) and of the published version of the *Philosophy of Right*. It was also in 1817–18 that Hegel gave the first of what would turn out to be seven lecture series on *Rechtsphilosophie*.[9] There is remarkably little change in Hegel's theory of freedom from these two texts, through to the *Philosophy of Right* published in 1821, the lecture series of the mid–1820s, and the 1827 and 1830 editions of the *Encyclopedia*.

[8] Good discussions of Hegel's early development can be found, for example, in: Plant, *Hegel*; Taylor, *Hegel*, ch. 2; Dickey, *Hegel*; Harris, *Hegel's Development*; Avineri, *Hegel's Theory of the Modern State*; and Wood, *Hegel's Ethical Thought*, ch. 7.

[9] Hegel lectured on *Rechtsphilosophie* in 1817–18 (*VPR17*), 1818–19 (*VPR18*), 1819–20 (*VPR19*), 1821–2, 1822–3 (*VPR iii*), 1824–5 (*VPR iv*), and 1831. There is no surviving transcript of the 1821–2 lectures; the lecture series begun in autumn 1831 was abruptly cut short by Hegel's death. There is no longer much controversy about drawing on Hegel's lecture materials as well as his published writings and I have done so freely throughout this study. In the Preface to the *Philosophy of Right*, Hegel explicitly says that the book is meant to accompany his lectures (*PR*, Preface, p. 11/9), suggesting that he himself took the lectures to represent an authoritative statement of his own views rather than just work in progress or a series of off-the-cuff remarks. Indeed, in the light of the harsh censorship laws in effect in Prussia throughout the 1820s there are some grounds for thinking that, in places, the lectures offer a more authoritative statement of Hegel's views than do the published writings. It is also worth noting that, for a variety of reasons, we can be quite confident about the authenticity of the lecture transcriptions that we now possess. We know, for instance, that Hegel dictated his lectures in a slow, methodical style that was highly conducive to taking accurate notes and that his transcribers were reasonably conscientious about recording exactly what Hegel said. It is true that the 'Additions' or *Zusätze* based on Hegel's lectures that have been included in standard editions of Hegel's works since the 1830s are highly selective and sometimes taken out of context, but these problems can largely be overcome by referring to the complete transcriptions from which they are taken, which are now available in published form. For discussion of the relationship between Hegel's recorded lectures and his published writings, see the Editors' Introductions to *VPR*, *VPR18*, and *VPR19*; and Tunick, *Hegel's Political Philosophy*, 7–11.

Chapters 2–6 of this study each examine a key element of Hegel's idea of freedom. In Chapter 2, I explore Hegel's attempt to equate freedom with rational self-determination, asking what he means by rational self-determination and whether his view is vulnerable to certain common objections. Then, in Chapter 3, after reviewing Hegel's 'empty formalism' objection to Kantian ethics, I set out the structure of Hegel's defence of what I call (following Henry Allison) the 'reciprocity thesis': the thesis that freedom and commitment to the duties and virtues of *Sittlichkeit* are reciprocal conditions. Chapters 4–6 attempt to fill out and further substantiate the structure introduced in Chapter 3. By exploring Hegel's engagement with social contract theory, Chapter 4 develops an interpretation of the argumentative strategy of Hegel's main work of social philosophy, the *Philosophy of Right*. Chapter 5 seeks to reinforce this interpretation through a detailed consideration of one particularly important institution discussed by Hegel—private property. Finally, Chapter 6 returns to the intersection of freedom and modern *Sittlichkeit*, looking, in particular, at Hegel's claim that individuals are most fully free in taking up the role of good citizens of the state. Each chapter discusses a discrete and, I think, interesting issue in Hegel's account of freedom and, to some extent, can be read in isolation from the rest of the book. The overall account of how Hegel views the relationship between freedom and modern *Sittlichkeit*, and how he wants to respond to the objections to his *Sittlichkeit* thesis sketched out earlier, requires a reading of the whole book.

The remainder of this introductory chapter is devoted to contrasting the interpretation to be developed in the present study with some of the standard interpretations of how Hegel understands the intersection between *Sittlichkeit* and freedom. I distinguish between *conventionalist*, *metaphysical*, *historicist*, and *self-actualization* readings of Hegel's account (§1.2) and discuss the first three of these in §§1.3–1.5. In §1.6 I then give a preliminary sketch of a variant of the self-actualization reading to be defended in this study—which I label the *civic humanist* interpretation. Finally, in §1.7, I point out some of the ways in which the different perspectives mentioned above can be seen as convergent.

1.2. *Four Readings*

I am proposing, then, to explore Hegel's social philosophy through the lens of his *Sittlichkeit* thesis—a thesis that is intimately connected with the central organizing idea of Hegel's social thought, the idea of freedom. The *Sittlichkeit* thesis, as we have seen, claims that the content of everyday practical reasoning is given by the duties and virtues embedded in the institutions of modern social life. The thesis has its obvious attractions, but it also risks being both *under-determinate* and unacceptably *conservative*, and it should prove a useful entry into Hegel's social philosophy to explore how he proposes to defend it.

Looking at the vast secondary literature on Hegel's social philosophy, it is possible, I think, to distinguish four different kinds of interpretation of Hegel's position on this issue:

The conventionalist reading. According to this view, Hegel simply does not think it possible to step outside the ethical norms embedded in existing social institutions to enquire into their standing or acceptability. A good reason, on this account of practical reason, is simply a reason that has come to be regarded as compelling by a particular community at a particular moment in time. The implication of this reading is that Hegel would respond to the under-determinacy objection by pointing to pre-established norms of conflict resolution embedded in the shared meanings of communities and/or by emphasizing that there are limits in the extent to which we can expect practical reason to resolve certain kinds of ethical conflict. Likewise, he would respond to the conservatism objection by arguing that any attempt to evaluate institutions and practices 'all the way down' would be incoherent: radical criticism and deep justification are quixotic enterprises founded on a misunderstanding of practical reason. According to the conventionalist reading, then, it is not just the content of our 'everyday' practical reasoning that is circumscribed by the duties and virtues of modern social institutions; it is the content of *all* practical reasoning that is limited in this way.

The metaphysical reading. Hegel does think it possible to step outside the ethical norms embedded in existing social institutions to give them some kind of rational warrant. This philosophical activity of reconciling us to the existing practices and institutions of our social world involves seeing them as necessary vehicles for the self-realization of God. Thus this view deals with the under-determination problem by positing an external, metaphysical standpoint that can offer ordering and resolution in the case of internal conflict. It responds to the conservatism objection by holding out the possibility, in principle, of a full critical examination of the existing social world through philosophical reflection from the metaphysical standpoint.

The historicist reading. As with the metaphysical reading, this view holds that Hegel does think it possible to provide through philosophical reflection a rational warrant for the ethical norms embedded in existing practices and institutions. This philosophical warranting involves seeing the existing meanings and reasons of a particular, historically situated community as a rational response to, and improvement on, the inadequacies and insufficiencies of historically previous attempts to articulate a set of meanings and reasons. This view sees Hegel's response to the under-determination and conservatism objections as structurally similar to the response envisioned by the metaphysical reading.

The self-actualization reading. This view shares with the metaphysical and historicist readings the claim that Hegel thinks it possible to provide through philosophical reflection a rational warrant for the ethical norms embedded in existing practices and institutions. It also shares the attitudes implicit in these readings concerning Hegel's response to the under-determination and conservatism objections. What distinguishes this interpretation from the metaphysical and historicist interpretations is its account of what the activity of philosophical reflection involves. Rather than emphasizing God's self-realization, or any historical narrative, this view sees philosophical warranting in Hegel as involving the demonstration that existing institutions and practices promote, or provide the locus for, human self-actualization.

It should be clear that the first of these interpretations conflicts quite sharply with the other three. Whereas the first view places serious restrictions on the possibility of coherently reasoning about our institutions and practices, the other three readings each suggest a different kind of story which might be told about our institutions and practices that could, at least in principle, help to prioritize conflicting considerations and speak to the concerns of a radical critic or sceptic. Although it can be (and sometimes is) argued that the first view contains the acceptable core of Hegel's doctrine, whereas one or several of the other views represent 'baggage' that should be jettisoned,[10] it cannot be argued that *Hegel* adhered to both the first view and any of the other three views.

By contrast, there is no obvious inconsistency in holding that more than one of the metaphysical, historicist, and self-actualization readings captures an aspect of Hegel's position. We can often characterize a single set of facts or events using a variety of different, but mutually consistent, narrative strategies, each of which fastens upon and accentuates some different detail or aspect of the story. It is possible that Hegel views the existing practices and institutions of the modern social world as: (*a*) a necessary instrument of God's self-realization; (*b*) a rational response to, and resolution of, the inadequacies and insufficiencies of historically previous attempts to articulate a set of meanings and reasons; *and* (*c*) the context of full human self-actualization.

Nor would it be difficult to imagine someone adhering to a hybrid interpretation of Hegel's project—one that combined elements from the metaphysical, historicist, and/or self-actualization stories into a single reading. For instance, a standard view of Hegel's project combines elements of the metaphysical and historicist interpretations. The process by which God realizes himself through different forms of human community is, on this view, a fundamentally historical one: each attempt by God to realize himself through human community is progressively more adequate and complete, with the modern European community fully responding to and resolving the insufficiencies and contradictions of previous attempts. The self-actualization view can also be combined with metaphysical and/or historicist elements. Allen Wood, for instance, has used the term 'historicized naturalism' to describe Hegel's position. According to Wood, Hegel is proposing a self-actualization account of modern ethical relationships but not one that relies on a general account of the human good. Instead, the ideas of the self and its good to be actualized are always contextualized in a determinate social and cultural situation—one that can be viewed as the outcome of a historical

[10] See e.g. Rorty, *Objectivity, Relativism, and Truth*, 197–8.

process in which human beings collectively and cumulatively strive for self-knowledge.[11]

The present study will defend a variant of the self-actualization view that I shall term the civic humanist reading. In the next three sections I argue that the conventionalist reading is unsatisfactory and that the same is true of the metaphysical and historicist readings to the extent that they are not complemented by some other view. In §1.6 I offer a brief sketch of the civic humanist reading and then, in §1.7, go on to indicate the ways in which my interpretation remains compatible with the recognition of significant metaphysical and historicist dimensions in Hegel's thought.

1.3. *The Conventionalist Reading*

Most Hegel specialists do not favour a conventionalist view of Hegel's project, but it is common enough amongst non-specialists, and has sufficient independent plausibility, to deserve some comment.[12] The strongest case for the conventionalist interpretation can be made from a reading of the Preface to the *Philosophy of Right*. Consider, for example, the following passage:

> To comprehend *what is* is the task of philosophy, for *what is* is reason. As far as the individual is concerned, each individual is in any case a *child of his time*; thus philosophy, too, is *its own time comprehended in thoughts*. It is just as foolish to imagine that any philosophy can transcend its contemporary world as that an individual can overleap his own time or leap over Rhodes. If his theory does indeed transcend his own time, if it builds itself a world *as it ought to be*, then it certainly has an existence, but only within his

[11] Wood, *Hegel's Ethical Thought*, ch. 1.

[12] For the explicit repudiation of the conventionalist interpretation by three well-known Hegel scholars, see Wood, *Hegel's Ethical Thought*, 202–8; Pippin, *Idealism as Modernism*, 106–9; and Steven B. Smith, *Hegel's Critique of Liberalism*, 130–1. For a characterization of Hegel's position as conventionalist, see e.g. Benn, *A Theory of Freedom*, 173–4. A Hegel scholar who explicitly develops a 'nonfoundationalist' reading of Hegel's *Philosophy of Right* is Tunick ('Hegel's Nonfoundationalism'). According to Tunick, 'Hegel's strategy as a political philosopher' is to 'refer to ungrounded views we hold and use to test a practice' rather than to appeal 'to a criterion external to the activity of practical reasoning and deliberation', such as 'a metaphysic of history' (p. 319). Tunick recognizes that this approach will strike some people as 'but a trick, or one big circle, to justify practices by appealing to standards that presuppose the very practices', but he emphasizes that his account is offered as an interpretation rather than a defence of Hegel's method (p. 335).

opinions—a pliant medium in which the imagination can construct anything it pleases. (*PR*, Preface, pp. 26/21–2)

The assertion that '*what is* is reason' might be construed as implying that the criteria for practical reasoning are found in the practices and institutions of the existing community and that no such criteria are available outside those practices and institutions (for 'everyday' or any other form of practical reason). The claims that 'to comprehend *what is* is the task of philosophy' and that 'philosophy is *its own time comprehended in thoughts*' could then be read as assigning an essentially interpretative role to philosophy: philosophical reflection on ethical and political questions consists in looking at actual practices and institutions and discerning the meanings and norms that are embedded or latent in them. Finally, the strictures against transcending one's own time and setting up a world 'as it ought to be' fit neatly into this picture as well: if criteria for practical reasoning are inescapably rooted in actual practices and institutions, then any attempt to argue rationally in abstraction from those institutions and practices (from the 'contemporary world') would be incoherent.

Other passages in the Preface seem to lend additional support for this interpretation. The claim that philosophical reflection involves comprehension of the present is repeated several times (pp. 25–7/20–2) and, of course, the Preface closes with a famous assertion of the inevitably retrospective character of philosophy (p. 28/23). Foremost in the minds of those advocating a conventionalist reading, however, is probably Hegel's notorious dictum that 'What is rational is actual and what is actual is rational' (p. 24/20). Even if we recognize Hegel's distinction between 'actuality' and 'existence', and so avoid the mistake of reading the dictum as an unqualified endorsement of the status quo,[13] the dictum does seem to reinforce the idea that, for Hegel, criteria for practical reasoning are in some way embedded or latent in the actual practices and institutions of a community.[14]

[13] Virtually every commentator on Hegel now acknowledges this distinction and stresses the dictum's compatibility with a broadly reformist political outlook. See e.g. Knox 'Hegel and Prussianism', 18; Avineri, *Hegel's Theory of the Modern State*, 127; Wood, *Hegel's Ethical Thought*, 8–14; and Hardimon, *Hegel's Social Philosophy*, 53–4.

[14] Michael Hardimon interprets the dictum as committing Hegel to a thesis about the conditions of normative validity, which says that valid norms are rooted in the essence of the things to which they apply (they figure 'centrally in the characterization of the thing's kind and play a central explanatory role in accounting for the thing's

One response to this argument would be to maintain that there is a tension between Hegel's remarks in the Preface and his systematic philosophy, as set out in the main text of the *Philosophy of Right* and elsewhere. It is sometimes pointed out that the Preface was added onto the book at the last second and seems to have been partly designed to deflect the attention of the Prussian censors by downplaying the critical, reformist implications of Hegel's political theory.[15] This is not a very satisfactory response, however, to the extent that there are many rhetorical strategies Hegel might have used to deal with the Prussian censors besides advancing a thesis about practical reason. Instead, I will argue that there are reasons *internal to* the Preface to question the conventionalist interpretation set out above.

Let us start with the claim that the task of philosophy is 'to comprehend what is'. According to the conventionalist reading, this claim implies or presupposes something about the *criteria* of practical reasoning or of philosophical reflection more generally. A different view, however, would be that Hegel is making an assertion about the *subject matter* of philosophical reflection: philosophers should spend their time rationally comprehending the here and now rather than imagining a world as it ought to be. A claim about the subject matter of philosophy leaves open the question of the criteria of philosophical reflection—the question of what would *count* as an adequate comprehension of the present.

Support for this reading is found in the fact that, in the Preface itself, Hegel broaches the issue of criteria in a way that is awkward for the conventionalist interpretation: 'The *truth* concerning *right,*

normal operation') (*Hegel's Social Philosophy*, 58–9). He infers from this that 'Hegel's basic normative outlook limits criticism [in] that it rules out "external criticism", criticism that is not based on norms rooted in the essences of the institutions to which it is applied' (p. 80). However, Hardimon also attributes to Hegel the view that the essence of the modern social world 'is *absolutely* as it ought to be, because it reflects a correct understanding of the human spirit' (p. 74). This statement would seem to imply that there are criteria of normative correctness external to the essences rooted in actual institutions (in Hardimon's account these criteria involve the degree to which the essence of a social world adequately recognizes both subjectivity and social membership (p. 75)). The key to this apparent tension in Hardimon's interpretation may be that he is understanding 'criticism' to mean something like 'condemnation' or 'issuing instructions on how the world ought to be' rather than taking it in the neutral sense of 'evaluation'. It is implicit in Hardimon's view that Hegel *does* allow for external evaluation of institutions and practices (and their 'essences')—indeed, this is a crucial part of the project of reconciliation.

[15] For a discussion of this view, see e.g. Knox, 'Hegel and Prussianism'.

ethics, and the state is at any rate *as old* as its *exposition and promulgation* in *public laws and in public morality and religion.* What more does this require, inasmuch as the thinking mind is not content to possess it in this proximate manner?' (p. 14/11). On the conventionalist view, one would expect Hegel to answer that *nothing* more is required: to engage in practical reason just is to explore what truths concerning right, ethics, and the state are expounded and promulgated in public law, morality, and religion and to know these truths in a 'proximate' manner and not in any deeper way. But, instead, the passage continues with a very different answer:[16]

What it needs is to be *comprehended* as well, so that the content which is already rational in itself may also gain a rational form and thereby appear justified to free thinking. For such thinking does not stop at what is *given*, whether the latter is supported by the external positive authority of the state or of mutual agreement among human beings, or by the authority of inner feeling and the heart and by the testimony of the spirit which immediately concurs with this, but starts out from itself and thereby demands to know itself as united in its innermost being with the truth. (p. 14/11)

Here Hegel makes it clear that he sees a difference between grasping that certain ethical ideas and norms are part of 'public morality', or even enjoy 'mutual agreement among human beings', and the *comprehension* or *justification* of those ideas and norms. In the light of this distinction, it cannot be the case that he reduces the criteria of philosophical reflection to the widely accepted norms and meanings embedded in our institutions and practices, for it is these that need 'to be comprehended as well'. Rather, he insists that philosophical comprehension and justification must prescind from everything 'given' and instead (in an obscure phrase that will require much more elaboration) 'start out from itself'. As Hegel puts it later in the Preface, 'what matters' in philosophy 'is to recognize in the semblance of the temporal and transient the substance which is immanent and the eternal which is present' (p. 25/20). Philosophy is concerned with the present—this is its subject matter—but its concern is not merely to interpret or describe the present but to recognize its rational and 'eternal' aspect. It is this recognition of reason as 'the rose in the cross of the present' that Hegel calls 'reconciliation' (p. 26/22).

[16] In the original German, the whole passage is in fact part of one long question, but, because the question is clearly a rhetorical one, I think Nisbet's translation is faithful to Hegel's meaning.

So Hegel's claim that the task of philosophy is comprehension of the present need not commit him to a conventionalist view of practical reason. In fact, attention to what he has to say about 'comprehending' the present strongly suggests a quite different picture.[17] But what about some of the other views expressed in the Preface—Hegel's hostility towards empty moralizing about how things ought to be, his insistence on the retrospective character of philosophy, and his conviction that the 'rational is actual'? If the criteria for philosophical reflection on ethics and politics are made independent of existing institutions and practices (of everything 'given'), does this not open the door to the possibility that those institutions and practices are not rational after all and thus that the rational is not actual (because it is not in existence at all)? And would it not be conceivable that an attitude of critical, even revolutionary, moralizing would then become appropriate after all? The great strength of the conventionalist reading is that it seems able to account for Hegelian commitments on these issues.

There are, however, other ways of accounting for these commitments in Hegel's thought. In particular, Hegel seems attracted to a metaphysical thesis about the power of reason in history as well as an epistemological thesis about the possibility of reliable knowledge of rational forms of human community that have not been realized in experience.

The metaphysical thesis is perhaps best encapsulated in Hegel's remark that 'reason' is an 'infinite power' that is 'sufficiently powerful to be able to create something more than just an ideal' (*VG* 28/27). If one were to accept this thesis—Hegel claims several lines later that it is 'proven in philosophy'—then one could be confident that the rational is actual and that critical moralizing is misguided *without* assuming that actual practices and institutions provide the criteria for philosophical reflection.

It is harder to find explicit affirmations of the epistemological thesis in Hegel's writings, but, on the reading of Hegel I will develop in this study, it is a plausible (although perhaps not compelling) corollary of his view of reason. The thesis is that there is something in the nature of a rational social order that makes it difficult, or even impossible, to know what the character of that order would be unless it has been

[17] Note too that 'comprehend' is here a translation of Hegel's term *begreifen*, which, in his thought, always carries the connotation of a rational, conceptual form of grasping some truth.

instantiated somewhere in practice. As we shall see in Chapter 6 below, Hegel emphasizes that a rational social order (such as he describes in the *Philosophy of Right*) is 'effective', 'self-sufficient', and 'organic': it involves a whole system of interlocking institutions which together imbue in people dispositions that support the social order's own maintenance and reproduction. The thought behind the epistemological thesis is simply that, in the absence of any concrete empirical instantiation of some model of community, it will be extremely difficult to evaluate whether the community satisfies the 'self-sufficiency' condition needed for it to qualify as a rational social order. If Hegel does affirm an epistemological thesis of this kind, then once again his strictures against abstract moralizing, and his insistence on the retrospective character of philosophy, make sense without attributing to him conventionalist views on the foundations of practical reason.[18]

The metaphysical and epistemological theses obviously need a great deal more elaboration to be rendered even remotely plausible, but that will not be my concern here. If the theses are not defensible, then this would push Hegel's thought in a recognizably 'left-Hegelian' direction (an outcome that many of Hegel's readers would regard as welcome). Rather, the main point is that, if Hegel does affirm one or both of the theses, then his remarks in the Preface need not commit him to a conventionalist view of practical reason. If we combine this observation with an appreciation of commitments that very clearly are found in the Preface—the hostility to stopping at the merely 'given', the aspiration to find 'the eternal which is present'—then the conventionalist interpretation becomes untenable.

1.4. *The Metaphysical Reading*

In an introductory paragraph to the discussion of *Sittlichkeit* in the *Philosophy of Right* Hegel returns once more to the question of how ethical duties are justified. 'A theory of duties', he asserts,

[18] An argument of this kind is hinted at in a passage in the Preface in which Hegel criticizes Fries for reducing 'the complex inner articulation of the ethical . . . which, through determinate distinctions between the various spheres of public life and the rights they are based on, and through the strict proportions in which every pillar, arch, and buttress is held together, produces the strength of the whole from the harmony of its parts' to a mush of 'heart, friendship, and enthusiasm' (*PR*, Preface, p. 19/15–16). The idea seems to be that the moralizing pronouncements of a philosopher like Fries could not hope to be attuned to the complexly articulated, self-sustaining character of an ethical community.

unless it forms part of philosophical science, will take its material from existing relations and show its connection with one's own ideas and with commonly encountered principles and thoughts, ends, drives, feelings, etc. . . . But an immanent and consistent theory of duties can be nothing other than the development of *those relations* which are necessitated by the idea of freedom . . . (*PR* §148)

Once again it is clear that, for Hegel, the justification of ethical duties must go deeper than the 'existing relations' and 'commonly encountered principles' emphasized by conventionalist views of practical reason.[19] This time, however, he adds that 'an immanent and consistent theory of duties' must start from 'the idea of freedom'. Unlike the conventionalist interpretation just considered, the metaphysical, historicist, and self-actualization interpretations each takes seriously this suggestion that the duties of *Sittlichkeit* can be rationally warranted through an exploration of the idea of freedom. Each offers an interpretation of Hegel's idea of freedom that purports to explain why it is that Hegel thinks that the duties and virtues of modern *Sittlichkeit* provide an appropriate basis for everyday practical reasoning.

The metaphysical reading, as I shall understand it, sees a story about the self-realization of God as playing a pivotal role in accounting for this intersection of freedom and modern *Sittlichkeit* in Hegel's thought.[20] It is worth distinguishing two different ways in which God might enter the account:

1. God might be the subject, or agency, to whom the freedom enjoyed through modern *Sittlichkeit* is attributed.
2. Individual human beings might enjoy freedom through modern *Sittlichkeit* because, in that context, they are helping to further God's self-realization.

These claims need not be mutually exclusive: it is possible that *both* God *and* the individual human being enjoy freedom through modern

[19] See also *PR* §3, where Hegel comments that 'a determination of right may be shown to be entirely *grounded in* and *consistent with* the prevailing *circumstances* and *existing* legal institutions, yet it may be contrary to right and irrational in and for itself'. And *VPR17* 207: 'The object of the philosophical science of right is the higher concept of the nature of freedom, without regard to what is valid, to the representation [*Vorstellung*] of the age.'

[20] Thus I am understanding the term 'metaphysical' in a fairly restricted sense. For a broader discussion of the senses in which Hegel's philosophy is and is not 'metaphysical', see Beiser, 'Introduction: Hegel and the Problem of Metaphysics', in Beiser (ed.) *The Cambridge Companion to Hegel*.

Sittlichkeit, and that the latter enjoys freedom *because* he is furthering God's self-realization. But the two claims raise different issues and are therefore worth considering separately. Both claims can, in fact, be found in Charles Taylor's work on Hegel, which is easily the most influential and elegant statement of a metaphysical reading of Hegel's position. The discussion that follows focuses mainly on Taylor's interpretation.

(i) God as the Subject of Freedom

Taylor starts from Hegel's above-mentioned commitment to showing 'how the concrete content of duty is deduced from the very idea of freedom itself'.[21] He interprets Hegelian freedom in a very Kantian way as 'radical autonomy' and thus as requiring independence from everything 'given'—from all desires, traditions, and authority.[22] More than any of his predecessors, however, Hegel perceived the potential for emptiness lurking in this way of understanding freedom. The interpretative problem becomes one of understanding how Hegel can both affirm the Kantian view of freedom and perceive a potentially devastating objection to that view. According to Taylor, Hegel's solution is to escape the threatened vacuity of radical freedom by attributing freedom not to the human will alone but to the will of 'the cosmic spirit which posits the universe':

> Rousseau, Kant, [and] both revolutionary and liberal protagonists of radical autonomy, all defined freedom as *human* freedom, the will as *human* will. Hegel on the other hand believed himself to have shown that man reaches his basic identity in seeing himself as a vehicle of *Geist*. If the substance of the will is thought or reason, and if the will is only free when it follows nothing else but its own thought, the thought or reason in question turns out not to be that of man alone, but rather that of the cosmic spirit which posits the universe . . . everything changes if the will whose autonomy men must realize is not that of man alone but of *Geist*.[23]

Taylor draws support for this interpretation from his general account of Hegel's system but also suggests that it is the view 'Hegel was really driving at' (though 'not very perspicuously') in several specific passages in the *Philosophy of Right*.[24] At *PR* §29, for instance, Hegel explicitly rejects,

[21] Taylor, *Hegel*, 371.
[22] Ibid. 373.
[23] Ibid. (emphasis in original); see also pp. 92, 375.
[24] Ibid. 372–3.

> the view, prevalent since Rousseau, according to which the substantial basis and primary factor is supposed to be not the will as rational will which has being in and for itself or the spirit as *true* spirit, but will and spirit as the *particular* individual [besonderes *Individuum*], as the will of the single person [*des Einzelnen*], in his own distinctive capacity for choice [*in seiner eigentümlichen Willkür*]. (Cf. *PR* §258)

What Hegel is driving at in this passage, according to Taylor, is the idea that the primary factor, in thinking about ethical questions, is not the will of the individual human being but the will of '*true* spirit' or God.

Taylor's interpretative proposal can, in fact, be formulated in either a weak or a strong form. On a weak formulation, the claim is that understanding Hegel's solution to the dilemma of radical autonomy requires recognizing that *both* human beings *and* God achieve freedom through participation in *Sittlichkeit*. On the strong view, the project of philosophically warranting the institutions and practices of modern social life ultimately requires *abandoning* the standpoint of individual human beings and recognizing, *instead*, that those institutions and practices are needed for the realization of God's freedom.

There is certainly no shortage of passages, scattered liberally throughout his social philosophy, in which Hegel identifies spirit with a supra-human entity such as God and seems to accord this agent the leading role in his philosophical system (*VG* 45–9/37–43, 58–61/51–3, 69–78/60–7). For this reason, the weak formulation of Taylor's proposal is extremely plausible: it is, or should be, uncontroversial that God is *one of* the subjects, or agencies—perhaps even the most important such agency—of whom the freedom enjoyed through *Sittlichkeit* is predicated. I doubt, however, that Hegel's understanding of the intersection of freedom and *Sittlichkeit* requires *abandoning* the human for the cosmic perspective as the strong formulation would have it. For the remainder of this subsection, I want to develop three distinct objections to this view: (i) that there is another way of reading passages like *PR* §29; (ii) that it ignores the many passages in which Hegel does attribute freedom to individual human beings in *Sittlichkeit*; and (iii) that it may rest on a misunderstanding of Hegel's concept of *Geist*.

To begin with, then, let us take a closer look at the passage from *PR* §29. Commentators like Taylor read it as opposing human freedom to the freedom of some supra-human agency such as the community as a whole or 'cosmic spirit'. Another way to understand it, however, would be as contrasting the formal freedom of *Willkür*—the freedom one enjoys in being able to choose what to do[25]—with what Hegel takes to be the true freedom of rational self-determination.[26] This second reading of *PR* §29 would help to explain why Hegel places emphasis on the word *particular* rather than on *individual*: he is concerned here to reject the idea that true freedom is consistent with choosing to follow one's own particularity (one's own desires, inclinations, and so on), not to deny that freedom can be attributed to individual human beings. This alternative reading is also supported by a passage from Hegel's *Lectures on the History of Philosophy*, where he asserts that '[Rousseau's] misunderstanding of the universal will proceeds from this, that the concept of freedom must not be taken in the sense of the contingent *Willkür* of each, but in the sense of the rational will, of the will in and for itself' (*VGP* iii. 307/401). Here it is quite clear that Rousseau's mistake, in Hegel's view, is not that he misguidedly predicates freedom of individual human beings but that he stops at a conception of freedom as *Willkür* rather than going all the way to a view of freedom as rational self-determination.

More seriously for the view that Hegel abandons the human for the cosmic perspective—and this is the second objection—there are countless passages in which Hegel does attribute freedom to individual human beings, including the true freedom of rational self-determination that is realized in the state. To take just three examples, Hegel says that 'in the state the individual has, for the first time, objective freedom' (*VPR19* 209–10). He asserts that 'in duty, the individual liberates himself so as to attain substantial freedom' (*PR* §149). And he holds that 'the determinations of the will of the individual acquire an objective existence through the state, and it is only

[25] Hegel defines *Willkür* as 'wählen zu können' ('being able to choose') at *VPR19* 62 (cf. *PR* §§14–15). In general, Hegel's term *Willkür* is notoriously difficult to translate into English. Philosophers such as Kant and Fichte used it to mean the capacity, or power, to choose or decide (literally to 'elect'). By the early nineteenth century, however, it had taken on, in addition, the more pejorative meaning of 'arbitrariness' or 'caprice'. Although Hegel's usage of *Willkür* clearly has both of these meanings in mind, where I do not simply leave it as *Willkür*, I generally translate the term as the 'capacity for choice' or 'individual choice' to underscore the fact that Hegel wants to make various philosophical points against his predecessors and not just to redefine a word.

[26] See Theunissen, 'The Repressed Intersubjectivity in Hegel's *Philosophy of Right*', 4.

through the state that they attain their truth and actualization' (*PR* §261A). These and other passages[27] show that, even when discussing the true freedom of rational self-determination, Hegel attributes freedom not only to supra-individual entities but also to individual human beings. It is not clear how the suggestion that Hegel abandons the human perspective for the cosmic one can be reconciled with these kinds of texts.

Finally, it is worth noting that the inference from the fact that Hegel often attributes freedom to *Geist* to the conclusion that he is not concerned with human freedom is based on a misunderstanding of Hegel's theory of *Geist*. Although this is certainly not a misunderstanding that Taylor is guilty of, it is common enough amongst non-specialists to deserve some comment. One of the longest and most accessible discussions of *Geist* in Hegel's social philosophy can be found in the Introduction to the *Lectures on the Philosophy of History* (*VG* 54–61/47–53; cf. *VPR18* 205). There Hegel makes it clear that *Geist* can assume three quite different kinds of shapes: he refers to *Geist* when it 'assumes the shape of a human individual' (*VG* 56/48; cf. *VG* 58/50–1; *VPR19* 214), to the *Geist* of a people or nation (*Volksgeist*) (*VG* 59/51), and to the *Weltgeist* (which he closely associates with Absolute *Geist* and with God) (*VG* 60/52).[28] This account suggests that, even when Hegel does attribute freedom to *Geist*—and not explicitly to individual human beings—he may still have the freedom of human individuals in mind: for the individual human being is one shape or form that *Geist* can take. In fact, in the passage from the *Lectures on the Philosophy of History* to which I am referring, Hegel illustrates most of his propositions about the freedom of *Geist* by discussing quite explicitly the freedom of the individual human being (*VG* 54–5/47–8).

Moreover, even when Hegel is not directly referring to *Geist* as it 'assumes the shape of a human individual', his claims about *Geist* may still presuppose certain claims about human freedom. This is because of the systematic relationships and connections that Hegel sees between the different shapes that *Geist* can assume. As we shall see in Chapter 4 of this study, he holds that an individual can develop the capacities, attitudes, self-understandings, and so on that make him 'spiritual' (*geistig*) only in the context of a community of

[27] e.g. *PR* §258; *VPR18* 205; *VPR19* 226; *VG* 111/93–4.

[28] Excellent discussions of Hegel's conception of *Geist* can be found in Taylor, *Hegel*, ch. 3 and pp. 378–93, and in Hardimon, *Hegel's Social Philosophy*, 43–52.

mutually recognizing individuals. One way of putting this would be to say that it is only in a certain form of *Volksgeist* that *Geist* as individual can be developed and sustained: it is only in the context of a public culture of freedom, one in which certain ideas, practices, and self-understandings prevail, that the capacities for individual free and rational agency can be fostered and nourished. Hegel also holds that a *Volksgeist* is able to achieve a certain level of freedom only in virtue of a particular historical inheritance. A public culture of freedom does not create itself *ex nihilo* but is always, at least in part, the product of a historical process of development that draws on previous cultures and ways of living (Hegel talks of 'a progression, growth and succession from one national principle to another' (*VG* 65/56; cf. 69–73/60–3)). Hegel's thesis here, then, is that it is only in the context of a certain level of progress on the part of the *Weltgeist* that any particular *Volksgeist* can develop and sustain itself. So, *Geist* as individual can be developed and sustained only in the context of a certain form of collective *Geist*, and the collective *Geist*, in turn, is determined as it is only in virtue of being a product of the labour of history or *Weltgeist*.

The lines of dependence run in the other direction as well. The *Weltgeist* is able to progress and achieve freedom and self-understanding only through the particular *Volksgeister* in which it manifests itself: they are the indispensable vehicles of its self-realization ('The *Volksgeister* are the links [*die Glieder*] in the process whereby *Geist* arrives at free recognition of itself' (*VG* 64/55)). A *Volksgeist*, in turn, can be established and maintained only to the extent that the various ideas, values, practices, and so on that give it shape are expressed and reinforced in the everyday actions and attitudes of particular individuals.[29] It is thus only when *Geist* as individual is free that a *Volksgeist* can be free; and it is only through a free *Volksgeist* that the *Weltgeist* can become free. Hegel summarizes this relationship by noting that 'the end of the *Weltgeist* is realized in substance through the freedom of each individual' (*VG* 64/55).

The implication of these various relationships and connections between the different shapes that *Geist* can assume is that it is hardly surprising that Hegel is often unspecific about which of *Geist*'s shapes he is referring to on any particular occasion. To be talking of

[29] For discussion of the senses in which human beings are the 'vehicles' of their *Volksgeist*'s and of Absolute *Geist*'s self-realization, see Taylor, *Hegel*, 89–94, and Hardimon, *Hegel's Social Philosophy*, 49–52.

Geist in any of its three major senses is, in general, for Hegel, already to be talking about it in the other two senses. Hegel brings two of these three major senses together in his famous *Phenomenology* definition of *Geist* as 'this absolute substance which is the unity of the different independent self-consciousnesses which, in their opposition, enjoy perfect freedom and independence: "I" that is "We" and "We" that is "I"' (*Ph.G.* 145/110). Free individuals are, on the whole, the product of a public culture, or collective practice, of freedom, and such a culture is, in turn, the product of a process of historical development. Conversely, the *Weltgeist* achieves freedom and self-understanding only through particular peoples and national cultures, and these, in turn, rely on the freedom of particular individuals for their own success and flourishing.

The upshot of this is that it would be a serious mistake to think that Hegel denies the possibility of full or rational freedom to individual human beings. Even when he does attribute freedom to *Geist*, he has human freedom in mind either directly or indirectly: directly to the extent that the human individual is one shape that *Geist* can assume; indirectly to the extent that the freedom of *Geist* in its supra-individual senses can be realized only through the freedom of individual human beings.

(ii) Enjoying Freedom as a Vehicle of God's Self-Realization

One possible reason, then, for thinking that Hegel's metaphysics of 'cosmic spirit' is indispensable to his view of freedom and *Sittlichkeit* rests on the assumption that the main agent of true or rational freedom in Hegel's social philosophy is not the individual human being but cosmic spirit. Against this view, I have been arguing that, although Hegel does think that *Geist* can assume a supra-individual shape, and he may occasionally attribute freedom to *Geist* in this form, he also attributes freedom to ordinary human individuals participating in the *Sittlichkeit* of their community. To this extent, the metaphysical reading of Hegel's project fails fully to resolve the problem at hand: it does not tell us how to understand the intersection between participation in *Sittlichkeit* and individual freedom.

However, the argument that a metaphysical notion of spirit is central to Hegel's theory of freedom can take a second, more powerful, form as well—again prominent in Taylor's writings on Hegel. In many passages, Taylor's argument is not that human beings are (for

Hegel) incapable of attaining rational freedom. Rather, it is that they can do so—but only by coming to see themselves as the indispensable vehicles of cosmic spirit's, or God's, self-realization. Taylor writes, for instance, that

> human rational will finds a content not by stripping itself of all particularity in the attempt to attain a freedom and universality which can only be formal, but by discovering its links to cosmic reason, and hence coming to discern what aspects of our lives as particular beings reflect the truly concrete universal which is the Idea. What reason and freedom enjoin on man's will is to further and sustain that structure of things which so reveals itself to be the adequate expression of the Idea.[30]

In Taylor's view, freedom, for Hegel, consists in following one's true or essential purposes rather than being carried away by one's inauthentic desires and inclinations. As we saw earlier, this raises the question, which Hegel himself poses so forcefully against Kant, of what ends and purposes an agent can be said to have once he has abstracted from all of his given desires and inclinations. Taylor's argument here is that Hegel's solution involves an appeal to the doctrine of cosmic spirit and, in particular, to the idea that the 'essence' or 'basic identity' of man is to be a vehicle of cosmic spirit.[31] Since the essence of man is to be a vehicle of cosmic spirit, and human freedom consists in realizing one's essence, freedom can be said to consist in furthering and sustaining the purposes of cosmic reason (the 'idea'). There is an ineliminable metaphysical dimension to Hegel's theory of freedom, then, because it is the doctrine of cosmic spirit that provides content for freedom: it is this doctrine that allows Hegel both to endorse the Kantian view of freedom as rational self-determination and yet to perceive so clearly the potential for vacuity that is inherent in this view. Without its metaphysical dimension, Hegel's theory of freedom becomes every bit as vacuous as the Kantian view that Hegel so strongly criticizes.[32]

As Taylor himself points out, this reading of the theory leaves Hegel's position looking pretty unattractive: 'where Hegel does make a substantial claim which is not easy to grant is in his basic ontological view, that man is the vehicle of cosmic spirit, and the

[30] Taylor, *Hegel*, 373–4; see also p. 72.

[31] See ibid. 44, 92, for the claims that the 'basic identity' and 'essence' of man is to serve cosmic spirit.

[32] Some textual evidence for this interpretation can be found at *VG* 127–8/107, *VPG* 524–6/442–4, and *VPR17* 42.

corollary, that the state expresses the underlying formula of necessity by which this spirit posits the world.'[33] Here Taylor points to two distinct problems with the argument. The first is with Hegel's assumption that the essence or basic identity of a human being is to be a vehicle of cosmic spirit. This assumption might be challenged on a number of grounds. It might be objected: (*a*) that human beings have no essence or basic identity at all; (*b*) that there is no such thing as cosmic spirit, or at least nothing that remotely resembles Hegel's cosmic spirit; or (*c*) that, even if human beings do have an essence, and even if there is a cosmic spirit, the human essence has nothing to do with being a vehicle for cosmic spirit.[34]

The second problem to which Taylor draws attention relates to the claim that freedom is most fully realized through participation in the *Sittlichkeit* of one's community and, in particular, through citizenship in the state. The problem is that this claim is not really explained or justified by the view that freedom consists in realizing one's essence as a vehicle of cosmic spirit. It is unclear why we should think that it is inherent in the ends and purposes of cosmic spirit that agents should participate in the *Sittlichkeit* of their community or be good citizens of their state. Even if it is conceded that God necessarily realizes himself through a community of human agents, it does not follow (as Taylor seems to recognize in the passage quoted above) that that community must resemble the one described by Hegel in his discussion of *Sittlichkeit*: that it must contain the family, civil society, and the state; that agents must think of themselves as members rather than isolated individuals; that they must recognize certain other-regarding virtues and duties; and so on.[35] Why would God not be satisfied with the more individualistic communities described in 'Abstract Right' or 'Morality' (Parts 1 and 2 of the *Philosophy of Right*)? Why is the 'thick' sense of community that characterizes *Sittlichkeit* necessary for God's self-realization? If Taylor's interpretation is correct, then it seems that there is a serious gap in Hegel's defence of the claim that freedom is most fully achieved in this way.

[33] Taylor, *Hegel*, 387.

[34] It might also be objected that freedom has nothing to do with the realization of one's 'essence'. I discuss the senses in which Hegel's conception of freedom does and does not presuppose such a view in §2.5 (ii) below.

[35] These features of Hegel's account of *Sittlichkeit* are discussed in Chapter 6 below.

These difficulties should at least give us a strong *motive* to look for an alternative, possibly complementary, reading of Hegel's position. It is worth investigating whether Hegel's theory can be understood at another, less metaphysical level before attributing to him a view that seems so vulnerable to obvious objections. Moreover, Taylor's second criticism of Hegel might be seen as a weakness in Taylor's interpretation rather than a problem with Hegel's own position. That freedom is most fully realized through participation in the *Sittlichkeit* of a community and, in particular, in the state is one of Hegel's most important and distinctive claims. If the most adequate interpretation of a text is the one that can make best overall sense of that text as a whole and, in particular, can account for as many of the moves and transitions in the argument as possible, then it seems that an adequate interpretation of Hegel's theory of freedom should be able to explain why he thinks that freedom is realized in this particular form of social world and not some other. But, as Taylor implicitly concedes, his reading cannot do this. It remains unclear why it is integral to the plans and purposes of God (the 'idea') that human beings should belong to an ethical community and be good citizens of the state rather than participating in a more individualistic form of social life. Taylor treats this as a problem in Hegel's argument, but, if an alternative interpretation can be found that can better illuminate Hegel's position here, then this would seem to suggest that it is Taylor's interpretation that is incomplete or problematic.

A defender of the metaphysical interpretation might try to fill in this gap in the argument in one of three ways. First, it could be argued that the ways of God are essentially unknowable and transcendent (even 'mystical') and thus the objection is looking for something that simply cannot be provided: the proposition that God realizes himself through human *Sittlichkeit*, and the attendant implications for human freedom, are not fully transparent to the human intellect.[36] This view, however, seems fundamentally unHegelian: it ignores Hegel's commitment to providing his contemporaries with a *rational* reconciliation to their natural and social worlds.[37] A second approach would be to argue for the claim that God realizes himself

[36] Marx charges Hegel with 'logical, pantheistic mysticism' in *Critique of Hegel's 'Philosophy of Right'* (p. 7). Another of Hegel's famous interpreters, Kierkegaard, makes essentially the opposite charge in *Fear and Trembling*, where the argument is that Hegelian philosophy fails to leave enough room for transcendence and faith.

[37] For a good discussion of this commitment in Hegel's thought, see Plant, *Hegel*, ch. 8.

through modern *Sittlichkeit* by presenting this mode of God's self-realization as a rational response to, and resolution of, the inadequacies and insufficiencies of historically previous attempts by God to realize himself through other forms of community. Finally, a third approach might start from Hegel's assertion that 'the end of the *Weltgeist* is realized in substance through the freedom of each individual' (*VG* 64/55) and argue that God most fully realizes himself through modern *Sittlichkeit* because this is the context in which human beings most fully achieve freedom.

The interesting thing about the second and third ways of filling the gap in the metaphysical interpretation is that they point *beyond* the metaphysical story to some complementary historical and/or self-actualization story. The preceding remarks do not indicate, then, that the metaphysical interpretation is incorrect—still less that there is no metaphysical dimension to Hegel's thought. They do suggest, however, that the metaphysical interpretation is unlikely to provide the whole story. To understand fully Hegel's position on the intersection between freedom and modern *Sittlichkeit* it is necessary to turn to the historicist and/or self-actualization readings for assistance.

1.5. *The Historicist Reading*

Let us look, then, at what assistance a historicist reading has to offer. The most sophisticated recent attempt to defend such a reading can be found in a series of books and articles by Robert Pippin.[38] For Pippin, a major problem in Hegel interpretation is to understand why Hegel holds that a good, worthy, and free life involves participating in various modern social institutions and adopting and affirming the central modern social roles.[39] In the same vein as Taylor, Pippin argues that to a great extent Hegel accepts a conception of freedom as rational self-determination inherited from Rousseau, Kant, and Fichte. On this view, freedom is opposed to stopping at anything that is merely 'given' or 'positive' and is realized when the subject acts on reasons that are truly 'his own'.[40] The

[38] e.g. Pippin, *Hegel's Idealism*, *Modernism as a Philosophical Problem* and *Idealism as Modernism*.

[39] Pippin, *Idealism as Modernism*, 92.

[40] Pippin, *Modernism as a Philosophical Problem*, 64–72, and *Idealism as Modernism*, 97–104.

problem, as Pippin sees it, is to understand why, in participating in modern social institutions (in acting on what Pippin calls 'ethical reasons'), an agent is satisfying this self-determination requirement. The problem is seriously complicated by the fact that Hegel so forcefully rejects Kant's apparently similar conception of freedom as empty. Like Taylor, then, Pippin seeks to explain how Hegel can both clearly perceive the potential for vacuity threatened by the conception of freedom as rational self-determination and at the same time make such strong claims about the freedom that is achieved in the ethical life.

Hegel's solution, Pippin thinks, is to invoke a 'historical notion of rationality'.[41] According to Pippin, Hegel denies that there are any universal, transcendental standards, or 'ultimate regulative ideals', to give content to rational self-determination and instead argues for a view of rationality as embedded in the concrete practices and shared understandings of a community at a particular moment in its history:

> Hegel has proposed a conception of rationality . . . that is *essentially* social and historical, rather than rule governed, or only ideally communal, or social and historical in 'application' only. What I am doing in identifying what is rationally required for me, for my own self-determination, is appealing to what would be required for any concretely represented agent, and thereby representing *what has come to count* as essential to a historical community as indispensable to such agency (e.g. voting, choosing my own spouse) versus what is marginal or insignificant.[42]

Pippin argues that this move to a historical idea of rationality helps to explain why Hegel takes freedom to be most fully achieved in participating in modern social institutions and in affirming modern social roles:

> it means that Hegel thinks he can show that one never 'determines oneself' simply as a 'person' or agent, but always as a member of a historical ethical institution, as a family member, or participant in civil society, or citizen, and that it is only in terms of such concrete institutions that one can formulate some substantive universal end, something concretely relevant to all other such agents.[43]

[41] Pippin, *Idealism as Modernism*, 127.

[42] Ibid. 126 (emphasis in original). See also *Modernism as a Philosophical Problem*, 68–73, and 'Idealism and Agency in Kant and Hegel', 541.

[43] Pippin, *Modernism as a Philosophical Problem*, 73.

Pippin is anxious to avoid the suggestion that this account of self-determination amounts to a retreat to an uncritical form of conventionalism.[44] To say that something counts as a reason simply because 'that is the way things are done around here' not only risks lapsing into an uncritical acceptance of the status quo but, as I argued above (§1.3), plainly reintroduces the very element of 'given-ness' or 'positivity' that Hegel's theory is designed to overcome. On Pippin's reading, what gives ethical reasons their standing (what makes them *reasons*) for Hegel is not the fact that they are generally accepted but the fact that they are the product of a rational, historical process—what Pippin terms a 'collective, progressive, self-determination' of spirit.[45] It is because a community that makes certain demands on its members can be understood as part of a narrative in which it provides the solution to 'determinate insufficiencies of prior attempts at self-understanding and self-legitimation' that those demands take on the character of *reasons*.[46] Thus, for Pippin, Hegel 'does not believe that we can formulate the content of . . . a universal law except by reference to the history of ethical institutions, the history of what we have come to regard as counting as universal, as what all others would or could accept as a maxim'.[47]

I take it that Pippin is not merely claiming that history, in Hegel's view, is rational. It is clear that Hegel does hold *this* view: history, as he argues at length in his *Lectures on the Philosophy of World History*, exhibits a progressive logic involving a series of ever more successful attempts to actualize freedom and reason. It is only in the modern, 'Germanic' phase of history that 'concrete' or full Hegelian freedom (subjective + objective freedom) is realized in a stable and self-reproducing way. The claim that history is rational, however, in no way implies that reason or rationality is historical—if this is taken to mean something about the criteria and standards of rational argument, about the kinds of moves and inferences that are considered legitimate in rational deliberation, its baseline assumptions, and so forth. It is possible that Hegel holds that freedom and reason, understood in some independent, non-historical or foundationalist way, are progressively realized in ever more adequate ways as history unfolds.

[44] Pippin, *Idealism as Modernism*, 106–9.

[45] Pippin, *Modernism as a Philosophical Problem*, 69. For a similar suggestion, see Walsh, *Hegelian Ethics*, 47, 54.

[46] Pippin, *Modernism as a Philosophical Problem*, 69 (cf. p. 68).

[47] Ibid. 72.

I mention this because I suspect that some of Hegel's readers might be tempted to agree with Pippin's proposal that Hegel endorses a historical notion of rationality on the basis of textual considerations that really only support the attribution to Hegel of a rational view of history. Against this temptation, it should be acknowledged that it is possible to recognize a very significant connection between history and rationality in Hegel's thought (that is, the second of these views) and still look to a self-actualization account of why freedom is realized through modern *Sittlichkeit*. Having said this, I think it is pretty clear that Pippin does not confuse the two claims and that he wants to attribute the first view to Hegel and not just the second. How plausible, then, is Pippin's interpretation?

Before addressing this question, one final distinction is needed, this time between two ways in which the thought that reason is historical might be at work in Hegel's social philosophy. One view might be that the modern concept of freedom itself—the concept analysed and developed in the *Philosophy of Right*—is the standard or criterion that is warranted by a rational, historical narrative. Freedom so conceived has come to count for us moderns as the most important value or standard, and, if someone were to question *it*, no foundationalist or externalist response could be given: we could only give a reconstruction of the historical narrative in which this standard came to be regarded as central, a narrative in which the adoption of this standard can be viewed as a response to, and resolution of, insufficiencies and inadequacies of previous standards. I can think of very little explicit textual support for attributing this view to Hegel, but it certainly sounds very Hegelian.[48] Note, however, that, whatever the merits of this interpretative proposal might be, it does not yet help to explain the intersection between freedom and modern *Sittlichkeit* insisted upon by Hegel. The proposal historicizes the value of freedom, and thus gestures at the kinds of responses one might make to someone who is sceptical about that value, but it does not tell us why freedom so understood is most fully achieved through participation in modern *Sittlichkeit*: it does not tell us how ethical duties are to be derived from this idea of freedom. So, on this proposal, an appeal to some complementary self-actualization (or metaphysical) story turns out, once again, to be necessary.

[48] Harry Brod argues that this is Hegel's view in *Hegel's Philosophy of Politics*, ch. 2.

The other way in which the thought that reason is historical might be at work in Hegel's position—the view I think Pippin has in mind—does seek to explain this relationship between freedom and modern *Sittlichkeit*. On this view, the historicized notion of rationality works to warrant not just the concept of freedom itself but also the content of freedom—the ends, duties, and virtues that are seen as proper to, or expressive of, free and rational agency. The claim that freedom is achieved through modern *Sittlichkeit*, then, amounts to the claim that the duties and virtues of modern *Sittlichkeit* are what have come to count as good reasons for us moderns and have a certain rational, historical superiority *vis-à-vis* previous attempts to formulate good reasons.

Unlike the first view, this reading does not seem to rely on a complementary self-actualization or metaphysical account for assistance in exploring the intersection between freedom and modern *Sittlichkeit*. There are, however, several difficulties with reading Hegel's position in this way to which I want to draw attention, if only to highlight the advantages of the interpretation to be developed in this study. One difficulty is that the proposed interpretation fits only awkwardly with the structure and programmatic statements of the *Philosophy of Right* and associated lectures. A second is that the proposal does not fully eliminate the element of 'given-ness' or 'positivity' that, as Pippin himself emphasizes, Hegel is concerned to divorce from freedom. Let us look at these two points more closely.

We can begin by observing that, in the absence of further argument, there is no reason to think that Pippin's distinction between a timeless rationality of universal standards and a historical, social rationality would coincide with any distinction between ordinary, private ends of individuals (where Hegel denies they are fully free) and ones that involve participation in social institutions or affirming social roles. Indeed, it seems plausible to think that the customary morality, or *Sittlichkeit*, of our modern societies has become increasingly individualistic and privatistic, so that what now counts as a good reason for us often does not involve entering into, or sustaining, relationships with others but instead consists in 'doing our own thing'. Thus, even if Pippin is right to think that Hegel favours a purely social and historical conception of rationality, this does not explain why Hegel thinks that freedom is most fully realized in the form of ethical life described in the *Philosophy of Right*: there is a gap in the argument between the thin sense of community involved in recognizing that all reasons are ultimately social and historical in character (even the most individualistic libertarian could concede this) and the thick sense of community affirmed by Hegel that involves actively participating in, and supporting, relationships of community with others (for example, in one's family, corporation, or state).

Pippin seems to recognize this gap in the argument when he says that,

> Hegel thinks he has . . . identified what social functions have come to be essential in modernity to [self-determination] (here his most controversial claim: that modern societies require wholly new sorts of legal relations among private individuals, or 'civil society', as well as a genuinely public life, a common identification or citizenship in the state, and that these realizations of freedom are not inconsistent, but continuous, even require each other).[49]

But it is not clear where, in Pippin's view, the defence of these claims is supposed to be given or how this statement of Hegel's claims is meant to map onto the argument of the *Philosophy of Right* (or associated lectures). Presumably, the argument should have two parts to it. It should, first of all, involve a kind of cultural interpretation, which investigates our language, practices, art, and so forth, to find out what sorts of reasons and considerations have 'come to count as essential' for our historical community. Secondly, it should have a historical part to it, which demonstrates that these reasons and considerations are not *merely* 'the way things are done around here' but provide some kind of resolution to the inadequacies and insufficiencies of the past and are in this sense the product of the 'labour of spirit'. The problem for Pippin's reading is that neither sort of argument is obviously given in the *Philosophy of Right*. In particular, Hegel makes it pretty clear in the Introduction to the *Philosophy of Right* that the argument to follow will not be historical in character:

> To consider the emergence and development of determinations of right *as they appear in time is a purely historical* task. This task . . . is meritorious and praiseworthy within its own sphere, and bears no relation to the philosophical approach—unless, that is to say, development from historical grounds is confused with development from the concept, and the significance of historical explanation and justification is extended to include a justification which is *valid in and for itself* . . . Since it has now been shown that the historical

[49] Pippin, *Idealism as Modernism*, 126–7.

significance of origins, along with their historical demonstration and exposition, belongs to a different sphere from the philosophical view of the same origins and of the concept of the thing, the two approaches can to that extent remain indifferent to one another. (*PR* §3; cf. *VPR18* 205–6)[50]

But, if the historical dimension of the argument for the rationality of modern *Sittlichkeit* is not found in the *Philosophy of Right* (or associated lectures), then it is not clear where else it is to be found. Perhaps it is Pippin's view that Hegel does not actually provide such an argument anywhere but simply *lays out* the ends, duties, and virtues that he thinks qualify as rational in the appropriate sense. But this proposal would seem to conflict with Hegel's claim to be developing the duties and virtues of modern *Sittlichkeit* from the 'idea of freedom' (*PR* §148).

So one difficulty with Pippin's position as I am now construing it is that it does not seem to map onto the structure or stated ambitions of the *Philosophy of Right* in any straightforward way. At the very least, more needs to be done to connect the proposed characterization of Hegel's programme with the detailed argumentation found in his published texts and recorded lectures. The second difficulty with Pippin's reading can be stated more briefly. As we have seen, Pippin thinks that reasons 'which have come to count as essential to a historical community' have standing if and only if they can be shown to result from a rational, historical process in which they respond to previous determinations that have revealed themselves to be inadequate or insufficient. On the basis of this formulation, it might be wondered how much is contributed by the fact that the process in question is *historical*, rather than, say, a series of thought experiments, and how much is contributed by the fact that it is *rational*. The problem with emphasizing the fact that the process is historical—that its various stages and determinations actually happened—is that this seems to reintroduce an element of 'positivity' and 'given-ness' into the justification of present duties and arrangements.[51] If the fact that 'this is the way things are done around here' does not on its own count as a decisive reason for me to continue to do them that way,

[50] Hegel also insists that the order of topics discussed in the *Philosophy of Right* is not historical (*PR* §§32, A, 182A).

[51] Terry Pinkard (*Hegel's* Phenomenology, 11) makes a similar point about historical interpretations of Hegel's philosophical system, although he then goes on to emphasize the historical character of the *Phenomenology* as well as the later philosophy of right.

then why should the superiority of our practices to the way in which, say, the ancient Greeks happened to do them be any more decisive?[52]

An alternative would be to place the emphasis on the fact that the process in question is a rational one. The idea here would be to show that the set of reasons and duties that has come to count as essential to a historical community can be systematically developed from an initial situation that is itself in some sense necessary and rational. This process of development may have a rough correspondence with history (and a knowledge of history is likely to be extremely helpful in reconstructing it), but it is possible to present it 'logically', as a series of thought experiments, and it is not ultimately dependent on whether certain historical events and transformations actually occurred or not. This view, I think, is broadly accurate as a characterization of Hegel's position and is compatible with the reading to be developed in this study. Understood one way, it is a view in which a self-actualization story figures prominently in explaining the intersection between freedom and modern *Sittlichkeit* in Hegel's thought.

1.6. *The Civic Humanist Reading*

The present study will defend a variant of the self-actualization interpretation. This means that it will look for ways in which the philosophical warranting of modern *Sittlichkeit* involves the demonstration that modern institutions and practices promote, or provide the locus for, human self-actualization. For reasons to be explained below, I call the variant of this view that I shall be defending the civic humanist reading. Clearly, the details and textual basis for this reading will have to be reserved for the main body of the study, as they connect, directly or indirectly, with many of the central issues in Hegel's social philosophy. But having devoted a number of pages to suggesting that alternative interpretations are incomplete or unsatisfactory, it seems appropriate to give at least a preliminary indication of the position to be defended here.

A good place to start is with Hegel's important distinction between

[52] One way of testing the contribution made by history to the reasons-for-action we now have would be to ask whether those reasons would change if we suddenly discovered that our understanding of some historical period (e.g. the Greeks) was badly mistaken.

'subjective' and 'objective' freedom (see §2.1 below). Roughly speaking, an agent (or 'will') enjoys subjective freedom to the extent that he reflects on, and is able to find some subjective satisfaction in, his actions and relationships (his 'determinations'). He enjoys objective freedom, by contrast, to the extent that his determinations are prescribed by reason: they are the determinations to which a fully rational agent, in the circumstances, would be committed. The subjectively free agent, then, is the agent who stands back from his determinations, reflects on them critically and independently, and is able both to endorse them and to find some subjective satisfaction in them. The objectively free agent, on the other hand, is the agent who, quite independently of whether he engages in reflection, has the correct determinations—the determinations that are prescribed by reason. The fully free agent—the agent who enjoys what Hegel terms 'concrete' or 'absolute' freedom—is free in both the subjective and the objective senses. His determinations are 'his own' both in the subjective sense that they are grounded in his reflectively endorsed commitments and evaluations *and* in the objective sense that they are prescribed by reason.

Hegel claims that agents enjoy both subjective and objective freedom in modern *Sittlichkeit* and therefore attain concrete freedom in that context. As we shall see, he attributes subjective freedom to individuals in modern *Sittlichkeit* for three different reasons (see §6.4 below). One is that modern *Sittlichkeit* works in various ways to develop and maintain the capacities and attitudes associated with subjective freedom. A second reason is that modern *Sittlichkeit* respects and promotes spheres of choice for individuals where they can exercise their subjective freedom. And a third reason for attributing subjective freedom to agents in modern *Sittlichkeit* is that he thinks that modern institutions such as the family, civil society, and the state have become central to the identity and outlook of such agents. These institutions have been internalized into the subjective evaluations and commitments of modern agents in such a way that, upon reflection, they are likely both to be endorsed for the right kinds of reasons and to provide subjective satisfaction to their members.

Hegel's reasons for attributing objective freedom to agents in modern *Sittlichkeit* are more difficult to discern. On the view to be developed in this study, they can be reduced to two main propositions (see §§3.4, 6.4 below):

(1) An agent enjoys objective freedom when his determinations contribute to the realization of a community in which subjective freedom is fostered and protected.
(2) The determinations defined by modern *Sittlichkeit* contribute to the realization of a community in which subjective freedom is fostered and protected.

Combining (1) and (2) it follows that objective freedom is realized through participation in modern *Sittlichkeit*.

Proposition (1) will be developed and given a textual basis in Chapters 2 and 3 below. The central cluster of ideas underlying (1) might be set out as follows. The paradigmatic case of unfreedom, for Hegel (as for his Enlightenment predecessors), is acting on the basis of another's authority (see §2.4 below). When I act on another's authority—for instance, the authority of a priest or a spiritual adviser—then I am letting someone else's judgement determine for me what I could think through and decide for myself on the basis of my own reason. In a similar way, there is a conflict between freedom and allowing one's given desires and inclinations to count as authoritative reasons for action. To be free in my practical deliberations means not to accept any contingently 'given' authority, tradition, or desire as decisive when I could subject it to scrutiny and perhaps reject it in favour of some different consideration.

As we have already seen in considering the interpretations developed by Taylor and Pippin, this picture of freedom quickly gives rise to a suspicion of vacuity. If, in order to count as fully free, an agent cannot consider as primary any authority or tradition of the community in which he lives, or any desire or inclination that he experiences, then what kind of reason-for-action *can* he appeal to in his practical deliberations? Hegel's answer, I argue, involves the thought that even a radically reflective agent is committed to at least one end: the end of developing, expressing, and maintaining his own freedom. The act of stepping back from, and scrutinizing, all of one's given attachments, desires, and so forth presupposes a commitment to at least this end (see §3.5 below). This is part of what Hegel has in mind when he talks of 'the free will which wills the free will' (*PR* §27).

This suggestion about the content of freedom fits neatly with an intuition that I suspect many people would share: that struggling against oppressive conditions is not merely instrumental to the realization of freedom but is itself one of the prime ways of realizing or expressing one's freedom. Hegel is, of course, not terribly interested in legitimating revolutionary activity (much as he admires certain 'revolutionary' figures such as Socrates, Jesus, and Luther) but is more concerned with the kinds of freedom that agents can enjoy in reasonably well-ordered and non-oppressive societies (see §1.3 above). Still, he does not want to abandon altogether this intuition that freedom is realized through the struggle against oppressive conditions that pose a danger to it. He thinks that a whole series of activities—from obeying the law, to the deliberations of public officials, to going to war—can potentially be viewed as part of the organic process in which a free society sustains and reproduces itself through, as he puts it in one passage, 'a constant negation of all that threatens to destroy freedom' (*VG* 55/48).

This brings us to proposition (2), which is developed and furnished with textual support in Chapters 4–6 below. The argument here has two central strands. One is that the capacities and self-understandings involved in subjective freedom—the capacities for reflection, analysis, and self-discipline, the sense of oneself as a free and independent agent—can be reliably developed and sustained only in the context of certain social institutions and practices. In particular, in Hegel's view, institutions such as property and contract, that work to mediate the attraction and expression of mutual recognition, must be in place for these capacities to be fully developed and sustained.

The second strand involves the thought that a social world containing the institutions and practices that work to develop and maintain subjective freedom may not be stable and self-reproducing unless the agents who inhabit it are disposed to act in certain ways. If Hegel is right to think that such a world necessarily includes the institutions of property and contract, for instance, then agents must be disposed to accept the burdens and sacrifices involved in respecting the property of others and abiding by their contracts. Hegel's basic claim about modern *Sittlichkeit* is that it alone provides the dispositions that make possible a social world hospitable to subjective freedom. Modern *Sittlichkeit* contributes to the realization of subjective freedom, because a community containing the family, civil society, and the state is the minimum self-sufficient institutional structure in which agents can develop, maintain, and exercise the capacities and attitudes involved with subjective freedom. The underlying idea is that a social order can tolerate a high degree of individual independence and subjectivity if and only if its citizens are members of ethical institutions that imbue them with goals, values, and convictions such that, when they freely consult their own evaluations and commitments about how to act, the answers they arrive at reinforce that order rather than weakening or destabilizing it.

So, on the view being proposed here, the idea of freedom intersects with modern *Sittlichkeit* in two different ways. Modern *Sittlichkeit* realizes subjective freedom in the three different senses noted above. It realizes objective freedom because, given the way in which it works to realize subjective freedom, agents who adopt its duties and virtues are working to secure the conditions of their own freedom. Since agents enjoy both subjective and objective freedom through participation in modern *Sittlichkeit*, they are fully or 'concretely' free in that context.

For three different reasons, I want to propose 'civic humanist' as an appropriate label to describe this interpretation. The first is that the reading being proposed is clearly a 'humanist' one. As I will explain in a moment, the proposal is consistent with recognizing a significant role for God in Hegel's social philosophy, but it does not itself rest on the view that God is the agent of, or provider of content for, freedom. Instead, it seeks to explain the sense in which individual human beings achieve freedom through participation in modern *Sittlichkeit*, and it does this by exploring the conditions of human subjectivity.

A second reason for using the label 'civic humanist' to characterize Hegel's position is that it emphasizes his idea that the highest practical good for human beings involves participation in community with others and, in particular, leading the life of the good citizen. Practical freedom, for Hegel, is most fully and paradigmatically achieved through *civic* activities and dispositions. It is in adopting the ends and dispositions of a good member of one's community that one helps to advance an end to which one is committed just in virtue of being a free and reflective agent: one helps to develop and preserve the conditions of one's own freedom.

The third reason for proposing this label is that, on the interpretation being suggested, there are certain important philosophical and sociological themes that Hegel's position shares in common with thinkers in the civic humanist tradition. One common theme is the idea that a social order hospitable to freedom is a fragile accomplishment that is prone to corruption and collapse because of the individualism, indifference, and neglect of its citizens. A second is the idea that, in the light of this tendency, the success and maintenance of such an order require that certain objective and subjective conditions be in place. The objective conditions include the rule of law, the division of political authority into separate but interlocking spheres of responsibility, mechanisms to ensure the accountability of public officials, and an emphasis on public education. The subjective conditions centre on the idea that citizens must be animated by certain dispositions and virtues if the institutions of their freedom are to be guaranteed: they must be animated, to at least some degree, by what Montesquieu famously described as 'a continuous preference for the public interest over one's own'.[53] Putting all this together, we can say that, for Hegel, as for civic humanists, a free society is a fragile construction that can be sustained only if certain institutional structures are in place—structures that, among other things, ensure that citizens are not entirely devoted to their own private affairs but are sufficiently disposed to act for the good of others, including the good of the community as a whole.

To avoid misunderstanding, let me emphasize that the label 'civic humanist' is meant to suggest a *philosophical affinity* between Hegel's idea of freedom and certain themes that are often associated with the civic humanist tradition. I am not making a claim about *influences* on the development of Hegel's thought nor am I claiming that Hegel himself *belongs to* the civic humanist tradition.[54] It is clear that there are a number of themes in Hegel's thought that are *not* standardly associated with civic humanism. For instance, he quite explicitly denies that civic life is the highest good, claiming only that it is the highest *practical* good. Human beings can achieve a higher form of liberation, according to Hegel, in the *contemplative* spheres of art, religion, and philosophy (*Enz.* iii, §§553–77; *Aesthetics* 99–100; *VPR17* 189–90). Moreover, in contrast to views frequently associated with civic humanism, Hegel has a marked preference for large over small states and argues strongly that the monarchy is one of the essential elements in an institutional structure hospitable to freedom. And, perhaps most importantly, Hegel is considerably less enthusiastic about *active* political participation for ordinary citizens than many civic humanists, preferring to emphasize other ways in which the activities and dispositions of ordinary citizens are important for

[53] Montesquieu, *The Spirit of the Laws*, 36.

[54] Laurence Dickey (*Hegel*, 227–30) offers a brief but more historically minded discussion of Hegel and the civic humanist tradition.

the maintenance of a free society. I also want to avoid, if possible, taking a firm stand on complex, and much contested, historical questions concerning the essential features of the civic humanist tradition, its origins and chief proponents, its identity or otherwise with the 'republican' tradition in political thought, and so forth.[55] Even acknowledging the controversy surrounding these issues, and recognizing the ways in which Hegel departs from civic humanism, I think there is enough philosophical affinity between Hegel's idea of freedom and themes that are widely associated with the civic humanist tradition that the label is not misleading but, in fact, helps to situate Hegel's position on freedom and community in a range of philosophical possibilities.[56]

1.7. *Converging Perspectives*

Let me conclude, then, with a few remarks on the relationship between the civic humanist reading to be defended in this study and the four kinds of interpretation introduced in §1.2 above: the conventionalist, metaphysical, historicist, and self-actualization readings. The relationship with the last of these readings is the most straightforward, since, as I have suggested in a number of places, I consider the civic humanist reading to be a variant of the self-actualization view. The self-actualization view claims that Hegel seeks to give a rational warrant for existing practices and institutions (he seeks to 'reconcile' us to the present) by showing how those practices and institutions work to promote, or provide the locus for, human self-actualization. The civic humanist reading offers an explanation of why Hegel might have attributed this property to the institutions and practices of modern *Sittlichkeit*. A social world incorporating modern *Sittlichkeit* constitutes the minimum self-sufficient social structure that is able to actualize and sustain the capacities and attitudes involved in subjective freedom and facilitate the exercise and expression of these capacities and attitudes. It is thus through parti-

[55] A classic study of the civic humanist tradition in political thought is Pocock, *The Machiavellian Moment* (see especially ch. III). See also Quentin Skinner's writings on Machiavelli and the republican tradition—e.g. his contributions to Bock, Skinner, and Viroli (eds.), *Machiavelli and Republicanism*.

[56] For recent philosophical discussions of civic humanism, see e.g. Taylor, 'Cross-Purposes', 'Hegel's Ambiguous Legacy', 'Kant's Theory of Freedom', and *Sources of the Self* (p. 196); and John Rawls, *Political Liberalism*, 205–6.

cipation in modern *Sittlichkeit* that individuals are able to realize subjective, objective, and, hence, concrete freedom.

The civic humanist reading shares in common with the conventionalist view the idea that the *everyday* practical reasoning of agents has as its content the duties and virtues of modern *Sittlichkeit*. In most practical contexts, it is appropriate for agents to decide what to do on the basis of the duties and virtues embedded in the family, civil society, and the state, together with their own subjective desires and ambitions. It differs from the conventionalist reading, however, on the question of whether it is possible, in Hegel's view, to adopt a standpoint of philosophical reflection that abstracts from the duties and virtues embedded in existing institutions and practices and looks for a rational warrant for those institutions and practices themselves. The conventionalist reading insists that there is no such external standpoint for Hegel, whereas the civic humanist view being proposed here argues that Hegel's ambition is to reconcile us to modern institutions and practices by demonstrating how they work to develop and maintain human freedom. Thus, in contrast to the conventionalist view, the civic humanist view points to a way of prioritizing the duties and virtues embedded in different institutions and practices (and thus helps to explain Hegel's insistence that the state take priority over the family and civil society) and it provides some reassurance, or 'reconciliation', for those who are struck by the apparent conservative implications of Hegel's views on *Sittlichkeit* and practical reason.

The civic humanist reading shares with the metaphysical view the idea that Hegel is committed to giving a rational warrant for existing institutions and practices through philosophical reflection. But the two views understand this process of warranting in quite different ways: whereas the metaphysical reading sees God as playing a pivotal role in the warranting narrative, the civic humanist view confines itself to claims about human subjectivity and its conditions. Having marked this difference, however, it is open to the advocate of the civic humanist reading to recognize a very significant metaphysical dimension in Hegel's social philosophy. It is consistent with the civic humanist interpretation to say, for instance, that God achieves freedom through modern *Sittlichkeit* because the freedom of the individual depends on modern *Sittlichkeit* and 'the end of the *Weltgeist* is realized in substance through the freedom of each individual' (*VG* 64/55). Following on from this point, the civic humanist view can also allow that the individual committed to the duties and virtues of modern *Sittlichkeit* can think of his ends and dispositions as rational, not just in the sense that they contribute to the realization of a community that makes his own freedom possible, but also in the sense that they contribute to the realization of a community through which God expresses and realizes himself. Finally, the civic humanist reading is compatible with the suggestion that modern *Sittlichkeit* enables the flourishing of certain contemplative modes of relating to God: it enables the freedoms enjoyed in the spheres of art, religion, and philosophy (*VG* 113/95, 124–5/104–5).

Most complex of all, perhaps, is the relationship between the civic humanist and historicist readings. The two readings share the view that it is possible to step outside existing institutions and practices in order to provide them with some rational warrant that can reconcile us to them. However, whereas the civic humanist interpretation locates this reconciliation in a claim about human freedom and the institutional conditions of its full actualization, the historicist reading (on at least one construal) emphasizes the ways in which modern institutions and practices are meant to resolve various problems and insufficiencies of historically earlier forms of community. Having said this, the civic humanist reading is in no way obliged to ignore historical themes that obviously are present in Hegel's thought, nor is it incompatible with one quite plausible way of reading a historicist story into Hegel's position. It need not deny the obvious truth that, for Hegel, history is rational and it is plainly consistent with Hegel's view that objective and subjective freedom appear at different historical stages and are jointly realized only in the modern European, or 'Germanic', world. Finally, the civic humanist reading is also compatible with the thought that the Hegelian view of freedom itself can ultimately be warranted only by reference to a historical narrative that draws out the ways in which freedom so conceived responds to and resolves the tensions in earlier attempts to formulate a foundational value. The civic humanist interpretation does not suggest a justification of freedom itself but only seeks to explain why Hegel posits an intersection between freedom as he understands it and participation in modern *Sittlichkeit*.

2
Freedom as Rational Self-Determination

2.1. *Introduction*

According to one of Hegel's most important formulations, the free agent is one who 'limits himself, but in this other is with himself' (*daß es in seiner Beschränkung, in diesem Anderen bei sich selbst sei*) (*PR* §7A). Citing Goethe's dictum that 'Whoever aspires to great things must be able to limit himself' (*PR* §13A), Hegel denies that an agent is free when he refuses to commit himself to any particular activity or relationship with others (to any 'determination'). Moreover, even when he does commit himself to some determination, it does not necessarily follow that he is free. For this to be the case, Hegel insists, the agent must be 'bei sich selbst' in the determination he chooses, a phrase that can be translated as 'with himself', 'self-sufficient', 'self-aware', 'independent', or even 'at home'.[1] Freedom, he sometimes says, is 'Beisichselbstsein' (*VG* 55/48).

The broadest question that can be asked about Hegel's conception of freedom, accordingly, is what this condition of 'being with oneself' amounts to. Under what circumstances am I self-sufficient, self-aware, independent, and at home, even while committing myself to some particular action or relationship in the world around me?

Hegel's most general answer to this question is that an agent is 'with himself' in some determination if and only if two conditions are satisfied: a *subjective* condition and an *objective* condition (*VPG* 529/447). Hegel's usual way of putting this is to assert that 'absolute' or 'concrete' freedom—the kind of freedom that one enjoys in 'being with oneself in an other'—consists in the unity of two one-sided forms of freedom: 'subjective' freedom and 'objective' (or occasionally 'substantial') freedom (*PR* §§144–7, 258; *VPG* 134–8/104–7,

[1] Hegel often directly characterizes freedom as *Selbständigkeit* (self-sufficiency), *Unabhängigkeit* (independence), *Selbstbewußtsein* (self-consciousness), and as being *zu Hause* (at home). For good discussions of the phrase *bei sich selbst* and its relationship to these other terms, see Wood, *Hegel's Ethical Thought*, 45–6, and Hardimon, *Hegel's Social Philosophy*, 114.

540/456; *VPR18* 219). An agent is 'with himself' in some particular determination if and only if he is both subjectively and objectively free with respect to that determination.

Hegel tends to emphasize two different ideas in explaining what he means by subjective freedom (he mentions both ideas, plus a third, at *PR* §25). In some passages, he connects subjective freedom with 'particularity' and the occurrence of subjective satisfaction in the pursuit of one's determination: 'The fact that this moment of the *particularity* of the agent is contained and implemented in the action constitutes *subjective freedom* in its more concrete determination, i.e. the *right* of the *subject* to find its *satisfaction* in the action' (*PR* §121). In other places, he attributes subjective freedom to the agent who reflects on his determinations rather than blindly acting on authority or trust, or unquestioningly following the conventions and traditions of his community: subjective freedom, he says, consists in 'the reflection of the individual in his own conscience' (*VPG* 135/105; cf. 308–11/252–4, 402/333; *PR* §§26A, 185; *Enz.* i, §81A; *Enz.* iii, §503).

Hegel is often not very specific about the precise character of the 'reflection' involved in subjective freedom, although, as we shall see, this turns out to be quite important to understanding his conception of freedom. The fact that he sometimes associates subjective freedom with the satisfaction one enjoys in performing an action suggests that the reflection in question may at times be as simple as stepping back from one's determinations and asking whether they can be endorsed on the basis of one's contingently given desires and inclinations. This suggestion finds further confirmation in Hegel's view that subjective freedom has an important role to play in decisions about marriage and occupation, since these are areas, he thinks, in which the individual's particular desires and inclinations ought to exert some influence (*PR* §§124, 162, 185, 206). In some passages, however, Hegel employs phrases such as 'infinite subjectivity' (*PR* §§104, 131A, 187; *LPR* iii. 340), 'subjectivity as infinite form' (*PR* §144), 'subjectivity as infinite relation to itself' (*VPG* 393/325), and the 'infinite greed of subjectivity' (*PR* §26A). Here he seems to have in mind a condition of *complete* reflective awareness with respect to one's determinations and the reasons underlying them, an awareness that does not stop at anything 'given'. He characterizes this more radical form of subjectivity as 'a unity excluding all others' (*VPG* 393/325), an 'antithesis within the subject itself' that is 'intensified to its universal, i.e. its most abstract extreme' (*LPR* iii. 310), and an independence from 'every type of restriction whatsoever' (*LPR* iii. 109).

Objective or substantial freedom can be attributed to an agent if and only if the agent's determinations accord with reason, something that Hegel associates with the virtuous performance of the tasks and functions of a good citizen of the state: 'substantial freedom', he says, 'is the reason which is implicit in the will [*die an sich seiende Vernunft des Willens*], and which develops itself in the state' (*VPG* 135/104; cf. *PR* §§ 26A, 257–8). Whether or not a determination accords with reason, on Hegel's view, seems to have two aspects (see §2.3 below). It depends on whether the content of the determination accords with reason (for example, paying taxes, voting, etc.) and on whether the disposition that motivates the agent to pursue the determination accords with reason (for example, patriotism, love, etc.).

Putting this all together, then, Hegel holds that an agent is 'with himself' in some action or relationship, and therefore is fully free, if and only if: (1) the agent has both reflected on the determination in question and found some subjective satisfaction in performing it; and (2) the content of the determination, and the disposition that motivates the agent to pursue the determination, are both prescribed by reason. Another way of expressing Hegel's view would be to say that an agent is free if and only if his determinations are 'his own' both in the subjective sense that they are grounded in his reflectively endorsed desires and evaluations *and* in the objective sense that they are grounded in his own true, rational, or essential goals and purposes.

Obviously a striking feature of this view of freedom is its claim that freedom has what might be termed a 'particular content'. On the account that has just been sketched, one side of concrete freedom is objective freedom and this requires that the agent commit himself to certain determinate activities, relationships, and dispositions—ones that are in some sense deemed to be rational. Hegel's claim, in effect, is that one is really 'self-determining', or 'deciding for oneself', only when one picks certain particular options. When other options are selected, someone or something else is the determining agency.

As I suggested in Chapter 1, the claim that freedom has 'particular content' is crucial to Hegel's project of warranting the duties and virtues of *Sittlichkeit* by showing that they are required by the 'idea of freedom'. We can be confident that the duties and virtues of *Sittlichkeit* represent the content of everyday practical reasoning in part because those determinations represent the particular content of freedom. It is thus of considerable importance for Hegel's project to explore whether the claim that freedom has 'particular content' is philosophically defensible.

One possible objection is that this way of understanding freedom has little or nothing to do with our everyday or 'common-sense' understanding of the concept. According to this line of argument, freedom, as it is ordinarily understood, is not tied to any specific actions, relationships, or dispositions but is open-ended: its content is not restricted or predetermined by anything but the agent's own empirically given ideas and purposes. Hegel's view might turn out to be philosophically coherent—so the objection goes—but it is not an exposition of *our* conception of freedom so much as an attempt to redefine the term. A second objection is that the view that freedom has 'particular content' seems to presuppose an untenable conception of human beings as split into two selves. It suggests a picture of the agent as divided into a true, rational self, whose unhindered expression represents full liberation, and a recalcitrant 'empirical' self, which needs only to be swept aside.

These two objections to the claim that freedom has 'particular content' point to a third apparent problem, which highlights the ideological danger implicit in understanding freedom this way. The suggestion that, in choosing certain options, an agent is not really 'deciding for himself' leads inevitably, it is argued, to the perverse and illiberal view that it is possible to force someone to be free. Once freedom is associated with a particular content, and the 'true' self is divorced from the 'empirical' self, then the concept of freedom may no longer be deployable against the oppressive exercise of state power but may instead offer a means of legitimating authoritarian rule. A final objection worth mentioning to the view that freedom has 'particular content' is that it seems difficult to reconcile with our practice of attributing responsibility to evil-doers. If the 'particular content' in question includes the duties and virtues of *Sittlichkeit*, and evil involves a violation of these duties and virtues, then how can we consider evil-doers free and therefore responsible for their actions?

For reasons that should become apparent, I will call Hegel's conception of freedom 'freedom as rational self-determination'. The aim of the present chapter is to develop an interpretation of freedom as rational self-determination. I shall be especially concerned to clarify why Hegel thinks that commitment to certain determinate actions, relationships, and dispositions is an indispensable component of true or full freedom, why this is not simply a gross confusion, or even perversion, of our ordinary notion of freedom, and how Hegel might be defended from objections such as those mentioned above. My interpretation of freedom as rational self-determination involves two central claims. The first is that there is an important sense, for Hegel, in which freedom involves abstracting from one's contingently given desires and inclinations and acting on the basis of thought and reason alone. The second is that an agent guided by 'thought and reason alone' will have amongst his determinations the 'particular content' that Hegel associates with objective freedom. The present chapter will focus on articulating and defending the first of these claims, leaving a consideration of the second claim for Chapter 3.

If the interpretation I am proposing is correct, then it would be fair to say that there is a strong Kantian element in Hegel's conception of freedom. Like the position I will be attributing to Hegel, the Kantian view posits a fundamental opposition between an agent's capacities for freedom and reason, on the one hand, and his or her empirically given wants, desires, and inclinations, on the other. For Kant, I am free only if my will enjoys 'independence of all empirical conditions', an independence that precludes all reliance on a 'desired object', 'impulse', or 'inclination'.[2] To have no possible basis for one's activity other than the promptings of one's empirically given determinations, for Kant, is to be in a condition of heteronomy. Autonomy is a property of the will only in so far as the will is able to abstract completely from all of its given determinations and find a basis for action in the ends and duties to which it is committed just in virtue of its freedom and rationality.[3] According to Kant, to be able to regulate one's conduct in this entirely self-determined, rational way is to be subject to one fundamental principle—the moral law. A free will and a will subject to the moral law are thus one and the same thing.[4]

[2] Kant, *Critique of Practical Reason*, 29, 33–4. All references to this work are to the page numbers of the edition issued by the Royal Prussian Academy in Berlin, which are included in most standard editions. *Kritik der praktischen Vernunft* is in vol. v.

[3] Kant, *Groundwork of the Metaphysics of Morals*, 440, 446–7. All references to this work are to the page numbers of the edition issued by the Royal Prussian Academy in Berlin, which are included in most standard editions of that work. *Grundlegung zur Metaphysik der Sitten* is in vol. iv.

[4] Ibid. 447.

I suspect that for some readers a 'Kantian' reading of Hegel's conception of freedom will not seem terribly controversial. According to a fairly traditional view, Hegel agrees with philosophers such as Kant and Fichte about the relationship between freedom, reason, and desire and departs from the Kant–Fichte framework mainly in his insistence on a different account of the *content* of reason: where Kant, for instance, looks to a formal principle, such as the Categorical Imperative, to determine what reason demands, Hegel seeks to develop a richer, more concrete account of the ends and duties prescribed by reason, one that appeals to the 'ethical life' or 'customary morality' (*Sittlichkeit*) of the community.[5] As we shall see, however, several recent commentators have argued that Hegel has much sharper and more pervasive disagreements with the Kant–Fichte conception of freedom than this traditional view suggests and have concluded that Hegel's conception of freedom takes a considerably more accommodating stance towards the agent's contingently given desires and inclinations than is usually thought.

The view defended in this chapter is that, although this recent scholarship forces us to be careful in articulating the precise ways in which Hegel agrees and disagrees with what he takes to be the Kantian position, it should not lead us to abandon altogether an understanding of Hegel's position as having a significant Kantian dimension. For those who are convinced by the 'Kantian' reading right from the start, I hope that the chapter will none the less offer a precise formulation of freedom as rational self-determination, clarify the intuitive basis of Hegel's position, and show how it might be defended from some of the standard objections.

2.2. *Three Models of Freedom*

To understand Hegel's position *vis-à-vis* the Kantian one, the best place to start is probably the Introduction to the *Philosophy of Right* (and the corresponding lectures). This represents Hegel's most sustained and philosophically sophisticated discussion of the concept of freedom and its relationships with reason, desire, choice, and so on. The text is difficult and obscure in places, but certain central themes stand out and can help us to situate Hegel's view.

[5] See Schacht, 'Hegel on Freedom', 297–303; Taylor, *Hegel*, 76, 82, 368–75; Inwood, *Hegel*, 477–83.

The Remark to §21 sets the issue up quite succinctly. 'It is only as thinking intelligence', Hegel writes, 'that the will is truly itself and free.' 'Thinking intelligence', he adds, involves a process of 'superseding' (*Aufheben*) one's desires and inclinations and 'raising [*Erheben*] them to universality' (*PR* §21). The exegetical problem that must be addressed for the time being concerns what exactly this process of 'superseding' and 'raising to universality' amounts to.[6] To what extent, and in what ways, does Hegel follow Kant on the relationship between freedom, reason, and desire, and where does he differ? As almost every Hegel commentator points out, the term *Aufheben* and its cognates are central to Hegel's logic and usually refer to a process of both cancelling (*hinwegräumen, negieren*) *and* preserving (*aufbewahren*) (*Enz.* i, §96A). Applied to §21, this would suggest that the agent's desires and inclinations are somehow preserved in the process of thought and not just cancelled.[7] We still need to know, however, in what ways an agent's desires are preserved and in what ways they are cancelled when he is free in pursuing some particular determination.

To shed some light on this issue, it is useful to step back for a moment and notice something about the structure of Hegel's discussion in the Introduction to the *Philosophy of Right*. In particular, we can observe that in two separate passages Hegel quite carefully distinguishes between three different conceptions or models of the will that he has been considering (*PR* §§15, 21). He calls the first 'the will as determined solely by natural drives' or 'the natural will' (at *PR* §21, 'the will, as drive and desire'); the second the 'reflective will'; and the third the will that is 'free in and for itself' or which 'has being in and for itself'. For ease of reference, these can be referred to simply as *natural freedom*, *reflective freedom*, and *rational freedom* respectively. An examination of what Hegel has to say about each of these conceptions shows that there is at least some sense in which he is committed to an essentially Kantian view of freedom, reason, and desire.

[6] This issue is obviously just one instantiation of a more general interpretative problem arising in the context of Hegel's logic: the problem of what it is for some representation (*Vorstellung*) or desire given by experience to be *aufgehoben* by the process of thought. The general question is addressed by Rosen in *Hegel's Dialectic and its Criticism*, 63–70. Many of the texts cited by Rosen in favour of what he terms a 'generative' reading of Hegel's dialectic help to reinforce the case I make in the text for a 'Kantian' interpretation of Hegel's position on the relationship between freedom and desire.

[7] Cf. Pippin, *Idealism as Modernism*, 101, and Pinkard, *Hegel's* Phenomenology, 273 n. 4.

An agent enjoys natural freedom when his actions and determinations are grounded in his drives, desires, and inclinations. They are *his* desires, as Hegel points out, and to this extent he is *self*-determining in following them (*PR* §11; *VPR19* 62; *VPR18* 216). The defect in this conception, in Hegel's view, is that it stops at something given from outside: it stops at drives, desires, and so forth, whose content is determined not by the agent but by nature (construed broadly to include the agent's social environment (*PR* §195, A)). In this deeper sense, it is not a model of self-determination at all but of determination by something alien. With the natural will, Hegel says, 'I am still not free. For the content is still not posited as mine, but is something given, as a determination of nature' (*VPR18* 216).

This argument leads Hegel to a consideration of reflective freedom. An agent enjoys reflective freedom if and only if he not only follows his own desires and inclinations but has also engaged in reflection and deliberation about which desire or inclination to follow (*PR* §15). Hegel intends this model to embrace a broad spectrum of different cases, from the agent who simply chooses which of his desires to follow (*PR* §§14–15) to the agent who reflects and deliberates about how to integrate his different desires and inclinations into a complete life of happiness (*PR* §20, A). Hegel clearly feels the intuitive pull of reflective freedom, associating it with Kantian *Willkür* and suggesting that it is 'the commonest idea [*Vorstellung*] we have of freedom' (*PR* §15; cf. *VPR19* 64). He is especially drawn towards the happiness model: 'In happiness, thought already has some power over the natural force of the drives, for it is not content with the instantaneous, but requires a whole of happiness' (*PR* §20A).

But in a deeper sense he holds that the reflectively free agent is not fully self-determining, because the material of his reflection and deliberation, the menu from which he chooses, is given by nature: 'If we stop our enquiry at the power of choice [*Willkür*], at the human being's ability to will this or that, this does indeed constitute his freedom; but if we bear firmly in mind that the content of what he wills is a given one, it follows that he is determined by it and is in this very respect no longer free' (*PR* §15A). Despite his preference for happiness over other forms of reflective freedom, Hegel explicitly includes the will oriented around happiness in this judgement: 'Happiness thus contradicts freedom; happiness has as its content drives and determinations of nature and as such they are opposed to universality in the form of freedom . . . With happiness I find myself in a circle of dependency, in a situation of subjugation to change, a change which comes from outside. The principle of happiness is therefore in contradiction with the higher principle of freedom' (*VPR* iv. 138).

The third model, rational freedom, identifies freedom with thought and rationality: it involves the process of 'superseding' one's desires and inclinations and 'raising them to universality' that was referred to earlier (*PR* §21). The fact that Hegel *contrasts* rational freedom with reflective freedom sheds light on what must be involved in this process of 'superseding' and 'raising to universality'. This process must require something more than integrating one's choices into a rational harmony with one's other choices, desires, goals, and so on, for this is, roughly speaking, what Hegel means by happiness. It must, in some sense, involve a more *complete* abstraction from one's actual desires, inclinations, and so on, for not to do so would be to stop at something 'given' from 'outside' and this is precisely the ground on which Hegel rejects reflective freedom as a model of self-determination.

Hegel's distinction between reflective and rational freedom, and his clear preference for the latter, thus strongly suggest that he endorses some version of the Kantian view that an agent is fully free only if his determinations can be completely grounded in his own thought and reason and not at all in his contingently given desires or inclinations. It is not enough that an agent be able to ground his determinations in some degree of reflection and deliberation if in the end this involves stopping at his given desires and inclinations: by rejecting reflective freedom Hegel expressly rules this out. Freedom, for Hegel, requires a grounding in reason that goes *all the way down*: it is opposed to any process of determining one's ends that stops at contingently given desires and inclinations, even one that involves a degree of reflection and deliberation.

So attention to Hegel's distinction between three models of self-determination and a careful reading of what he has to say about each shows that there is an important sense in which he does endorse the idea of an opposition in free agency between reason and an agent's given wants, desires and inclinations. For Hegel, I am free in my determinations only if my determinations have their source in my 'thinking intelligence', and this means that they must not be grounded in any merely 'given' desire or inclination.

This picture finds confirmation in the many other passages in Hegel's writings and lectures that associate freedom with a struggle between reason and desire. Consider, for example, the following characterization of *Bildung* (the process of education and socialization in which one becomes free (see Chapter 4 below)) as consisting in a process of 'eliminating' (*wegarbeiten*) and 'hard work against' (*die harte Arbeit gegen*) one's immersion in needs and desires:

[Reason's] end is rather to work to eliminate *natural simplicity*, whether as passive selflessness or as barbarism of knowledge and volition—i.e. to eliminate the *immediacy* and *individuality* in which spirit is immersed, so that this externality may take on the rationality *of which it is capable*, namely the *form of universality or of the understanding*. Only in this way is the spirit *at home* and *with itself* in this *externality* as such . . . Within the subject . . . liberation is the *hard work* of opposing mere subjectivity of conduct, of opposing the immediacy of desire as well as the subjective vanity of feeling and the arbitrariness of caprice. (*PR* §187; cf. *VPR19* 63)

The same idea of an opposition between reason and desire is expressed even more bluntly in a number of passages in Hegel's *Lectures on the Philosophy of History*. He says, for instance, that,

Sensation [*Empfindung*], sensuality [*Sinnlichkeit*] and the drives are also ways of realizing the inner, but in the individual they are temporary, for they are the changing content of the will. That which is just and ethical, however, belongs to the essential, universal will, which has being in itself, and in order to know what right demands one must abstract from inclination, drive and desire, as from the particular; one must know what the *will* is *in itself*. (*VPG* 524/442)

And he frequently claims that there is an opposition between freedom, reason, and spirit, on the one hand, and 'nature', on the other, a term he often uses as shorthand for an agent's empirically given needs, desires, inclinations, and so forth. For example, he asserts that 'Man realizes his spiritual essence only when he overcomes his nature [*überwindet seine Natürlichkeit*]' (*VPG* 453/377), and he talks of spirit 'liberating' itself from the natural (216/174), making a 'break' with the natural (403/333), and 'negating' the natural (*tilgen*) (386/319). In his 1817–18 lectures on *Rechtsphilosophie* he claims that, whereas freedom is the 'foundation' (*die Grundlage*), nature is 'something dependent' (*ein Unselbständiges*) (*VPR17* 38; cf. *VPR18* 211). And in his 1824–5 lectures, he asserts that, 'Freedom does not allow itself to be mixed with nature, but wants to be alone and only recognizes nature as something that is entitled by it' (*VPR* iv. 80).

All of these passages have a strongly Kantian flavour to them: they suggest that there is an important sense for Hegel, as for Kant, in which one's freedom and reason are radically opposed to one's contingently given desires and inclinations and require something more than integrating one's desires and choices into a coherent whole.

2.3. *Hegel's Conception of Freedom: A Formulation*

There is compelling textual evidence, then, that Hegel does accept some version of the Kantian opposition between an agent's freedom and reason, on the one hand, and his contingently given wants, desires, and inclinations, on the other. But how can we square this with the interpretation of *Aufheben* suggested earlier and with the prominent anti-Kantian themes that can also be found in his writings and lectures? In one of Hegel's early theological essays, for instance, he argues that the divided Kantian self simply internalizes the bondage to positivity characteristic of most established religions, replacing obedience to external religious authority with obedience to an inner command of duty that remains alien to the agent's experience (*ETW* 211). In his mature philosophical work, Hegel goes on to develop a clear statement of the objection that the Kantian view of freedom and morality is incompatible with our understanding of action. Against a morality of 'duty for duty's sake', he argues that impulses, inclinations, and subjective interests are an indispensable condition of there being any action at all:

> An action is a purpose of the subject, and it is his activity too which executes this purpose: unless the subject were in this way [even] in the most unselfish action, i.e. unless he had an interest in it, there would be no action at all.—The drives and passions are on the one hand contrasted with the empty reverie of a natural happiness, where needs are supposed to find their satisfaction without the subject doing anything to produce a conformity between immediate existence and his own inner determinations. They are on the other hand contrasted with the morality of duty for duty's sake. But drive and passion signify nothing but the liveliness [*Lebendigkeit*] of the subject and they are needed if he is really to be himself in his purpose and its execution. (*Enz.* iii, §475; cf. *VGP* iii. 304–5/400; *VG* 81–2/70)

Hegel also thinks that the Kantian view of freedom underestimates the ethical significance of various emotions and feelings.[8] One aim of

[8] For a good discussion of this point, see Wildt, *Autonomie und Anerkennung*, 15–19 and part I (especially sections 3–5). For the argument that Kant can go much further than is generally supposed by Hegelians in accommodating these kinds of

the doctrine of *Sittlichkeit* is to integrate dispositions such as love, honour in one's estate, and patriotism into a theory of freedom and into ethics more generally. Finally, Hegel's name is widely associated with the empty formalism objection. As we shall consider in detail in Chapter 3, he charges that Kant is not successful at explaining how the autonomous agent, abstracted completely from all of his empirically given determinations, would have any determinate reasons or principles of action left at all (*PR* §§133–5).

Considerations like these have convinced some commentators that there is a much more fundamental and comprehensive disagreement between the Hegelian and Kantian ways of understanding freedom than my observations above would suggest. Allen Wood sums this view up as follows:

> Fichte identifies the self with reason, so freedom is acting from one's own reason rather than according to the authority of someone else. Following Kant, he identifies the self more properly with *pure* reason, so mere nature is also other, including one's empirical desires and natural inclinations. To be absolutely self-active is to act solely from duty or respect for the moral law given by pure reason. British idealist ethics (especially Bradley and Bosanquet) carried on the Fichtean tradition, identifying freedom with the triumph of the active or rational self over the supine, empirical, or irrational self. Because the British idealists are supposed to be 'Hegelians', Hegel's name has sometimes been associated with such views in English-speaking philosophy. In fact, Hegel rejects this entire conception of autonomy along with the conception of self and other on which it rests.[9]

For Wood, Hegel's notion of rational self-determination treats an agent's empirically given needs and desires as constituent elements of the self that is actualized through rational self-determination. To be rationally self-determining in the Hegelian sense, an agent must strive to integrate his choices into a rational harmony with his other choices, his desires, and other aspects of his situation.[10]

This last proposal sounds a lot like Hegel's notion of happiness and to this extent, as we saw in the previous section, it is quite explicitly rejected by Hegel as a characterization of freedom. Having said this, it still seems important to try to reconcile the obviously anti-Kantian themes in Hegel's writings and lectures with the claim, being defended here, that there is an important Kantian dimension to

considerations, see Ameriks, 'The Hegelian Critique of Kantian Morality', and Pippin, *Idealism as Modernism*, 111–24.

[9] Wood, *Hegel's Ethical Thought*, 44.

[10] Ibid. 49, 70.

Hegel's own conception of freedom. What is needed is a more refined formulation of Hegel's conception of freedom than I have so far offered rather than the wholesale suppression of the Kantian strands in his position. We need to interpret Hegelian freedom in a way that *both* acknowledges the opposition he sees in the free will between reason and desire *and* is consistent with the significant disagreements he took himself to have with Kant.

In formulating such an interpretation it is helpful to return to Hegel's distinction between 'objective' and 'subjective' freedom as the two dimensions of full or 'concrete' freedom. An agent enjoys objective freedom, we saw earlier, if and only if his determinations are prescribed by reason and, more specifically, if and only if they have a rational content and are pursued from a motive or disposition that is appropriate, or reasonable, under the circumstances. Let us begin by asking whether this notion of objective freedom can be understood in the Kantian sense outlined above without conflicting with Hegel's objections to the Kantian position.

On the Kantian interpretation, we can say that an agent's determinations have a rational content if and only if the pursuit of those determinations by the agent *could be* fully justified by appeal to reasons that are independent of the agent's contingently given desires and inclinations. This interpretation of objective freedom, it should be clear, involves an opposition between reason and desire, since the criterion of rationality it invokes abstracts from the agent's contingently given desires and inclinations. But it does not raise the problems of motivating or explaining action that Hegel associates with the Kantian position, nor does it conflict with the idea that certain ethical feelings and dispositions have special value, since it does not say anything at all about the agent's *actual* desires, motives, intentions, and so forth, nor about the character of his actual deliberations or practical reasoning. We need not examine the agent's motives or intentions, or the character of his practical reasoning, to reach a judgement about the rationality of the content of his determination. We just need to decide whether the agent is pursuing an action or relationship that reason prescribes or not—an action or relationship that he has reason to pursue independently of what his desires and inclinations happen to be.[11]

[11] The Kantian equivalent would be acting *in conformity* with duty. See Kant, *Groundwork*, 398.

Hegel does, however, impose some requirements on the kinds of desires and motives from which one can act in different circumstances, and, as I suggested earlier, this is probably best seen as part of his notion of objective freedom. An important doctrine expounded by Hegel is that there are particular dispositions (*Gesinnungen*), feelings, and motivations that it is appropriate for an agent to have in particular situations. 'It is required not only that we know God, right, and the like, that we have consciousness of and are convinced about them', he says, 'but also that these things should be in our feeling, in our hearts. This is a just requirement; it signifies that these interests ought to be essentially our own—that we, as subjects, are supposed to have identified ourselves with such content' (*LPR* i. 391; cf. *LPR* i. 274). Within the context of the family, for instance, it is appropriate to perform one's duties with a 'consciousness of [marriage] as a substantive end' and a sense of 'love, trust and the sharing of the whole of individual existence' (*PR* §163). The member of an estate and corporation should have dispositions such as rectitude, honour, loyalty, and fellow-feeling (*PR* §§207, 253, 255) and the citizen should be motivated by patriotism (*PR* §268) and civic virtue (*PR* §273).

Hegel's characterization of what makes these dispositions appropriate or reasonable again invites a Kantian interpretation. It is appropriate to have a certain feeling in a particular situation, he says, if the 'source' (*Quelle*) (*Enz.* iii, §471) of that feeling—that which 'justifies' (*rechtfertigen*) the feeling (*Enz.* iii, §400; cf. *LPR* i. 272, 393–5)—is not itself some feeling or inclination but thought and reason:

> It is silly [*töricht*] to regard the intellect as redundant [given the necessity of] feeling, heart and will or even as harmful to them. The truth, and, what is the same thing, the actual rationality of the heart and will, can only reside in the universality of the intellect and not in the individuality of feeling as such. When the feelings are of the right kind, it is because of their determinacy, that is, their content, and this is only the case when the content is universal, that is, when it has its source in thinking spirit. (*Enz.* iii, §471; cf. *LPR* i. 273–6, 392–6)

An agent who reflected on whether it is a good thing, in certain contexts, to be motivated by dispositions such as love, fellow feeling, and patriotism could find reasons for so being that did not appeal to his contingently given desires and inclinations but only to purely rational considerations. When it is rational for an agent to have some particular motive or disposition (for example, patriotism) in this way, then Hegel calls that motive a *virtue*: 'We call it virtue when the passions (inclinations) are so related to reason that they do what reason commands' (*VGP* ii. 223/204).

Once again, however, the Kantian opposition between reason and desire that is central to Hegel's account of what makes a feeling or disposition appropriate in a particular situation does not conflict with the objections Hegel makes to the position he associates with Kant. Hegel clearly rejects the idea, which he attributes to Kant, that an action can be motivated by reason or duty alone rather than by some inclination or desire of the agent. As we saw earlier, Hegel thinks that the doctrine of 'duty for duty's sake' not only makes it difficult to understand how there could be any action at all but also seems to underestimate the ethical significance of certain feelings, emotions, and dispositions. But the Kantian account of what makes a desire or disposition reasonable or appropriate does not conflict with these commitments. Hegel's point is not that the objectively free agent is motivated by reason but that he is motivated by a desire or disposition that it is reasonable or appropriate for him to have in the circumstances. This point is consistent with appealing to a 'criterion' (*Kriterium*) (*Enz.* iii, §400) of appropriateness or rationality that abstracts from the agent's contingently given desires and inclinations and looks only to pure thought and reason.

So Hegel's notion of objective freedom helps us to see how he can both posit a sharp opposition between reason and desire in the free will and still make certain strong objections to Kant's apparently similar position. A conception of reason that abstracts from all desire is the criterion for determining whether an agent enjoys objective freedom, because it is the criterion for deciding whether the content of an agent's determination, and the desire or determination that motivates him to pursue that determination, is prescribed by reason or not. And nothing in this idea commits one to thinking that a free agent is motivated *by* reason or to undervaluing the significance of certain feelings and dispositions.

Things become a little more complicated when we turn to subjective freedom. Subjective freedom, as we know, is attributable to an agent who reflects on the determination he is pursuing and finds some subjective satisfaction in pursuing it. The complications arise in trying to specify the exact character of the reflection involved here and in trying to relate it to Hegel's claims about reason and desire. As should become clear, there is no real danger of a conflict between

Hegel's notion of subjective freedom and his objections to Kant. But it will be useful to set out Hegel's notion of subjective freedom as precisely as possible in order to move to a summary statement of freedom as rational self-determination.

Some of Hegel's commitments seem to suggest that the actual reflection and deliberation necessary for freedom are fairly minimal. As we have seen, freedom in Hegel's view is most fully actualized by participating in the 'ethical life' or 'customary morality' (*Sittlichkeit*) of one's community, and this, it is sometimes argued, means that freedom is compatible with unthinkingly or habitually adopting the customs and mores of one's social environment.[12] Although there is some textual evidence to support this interpretation, the preponderance of evidence suggests that Hegel would not accept it and would instead claim that freedom involves a significant degree of rational reflective awareness.[13] In the Preface to the second edition of the *Science of Logic*, for instance, he writes that,

> The broad distinction between the instinctive act and the intelligent and free act is that the latter is performed with an awareness of what is being done; when the content of the interest in which one is absorbed is drawn out of its immediate unity with oneself and becomes an independent object of one's thinking, then it is that spirit begins to be free, whereas when thinking is an instinctive activity, spirit is enmeshed in the bonds of its categories and is broken up into an infinitely varied material. (*SL* 37)

In the *Lectures on the Philosophy of World History* he asserts that 'no truly ethical existence is possible until individuals have become fully conscious of their ends' (*VG* 91/77). And throughout his discussion of *Sittlichkeit* in the *Philosophy of Right* he emphasizes again and again how 'the good' and 'the universal' (the duties and virtues of *Sittlichkeit*) are present in the agent's self-consciousness and self-awareness (e.g. *PR* §§ 142, 146–7, 152, 257–8, 260, 268). He says, for instance, that 'the ethical character knows that the end which moves it is the universal which, though itself unmoved, has developed through its determinations into actual rationality, and it recognizes that its own dignity and the whole continued existence of its particu-

[12] See e.g. Tugendhat, *Self-Consciousness and Self-Determination*, 315–16.

[13] Good discussions of this point that I have drawn upon can be found in Wood, *Hegel's Ethical Thought*, 217–18; Hardimon, *Hegel's Social Philosophy*, 32–6; and Siep, 'The *Aufhebung* of Morality in Ethical Life'. See also Schacht, 'Hegel on Freedom', 299–300, who emphasizes that Hegelian freedom consists in '*self-conscious* rational self-determination' (emphasis added).

lar ends are based upon and actualized within this universal' (*PR* §152; cf. *VG* 91/77).

The importance that Hegel attaches to achieving a rational reflective awareness with respect to one's determinations is perhaps most apparent in the distinction he draws between the 'immediate' or 'natural' *Sittlichkeit* (which he associates with the ancient Greeks) and modern *Sittlichkeit*.[14] In both cases, individuals are assumed to have the 'right' ends (for example, serving their state) and the 'right' motives and dispositions (for example, patriotism). The difference between the cases hinges on the degree of reflection and self-conscious awareness that individuals have with respect to their actions and motives. Whereas, according to Hegel, the Greeks stood in an essentially unthinking and unreflective relation to the customs and mores of their community, modern Europeans refuse to recognize any demand or obligation as valid that they do not perceive as rational (*Enz.* iii, §503). 'While customs and mores [*Sitte und Gewohnheit*] are', for the Greeks, 'the form in which the right is willed and done, that form is a stable one, and has not yet admitted into it the enemy of immediacy—reflection and subjectivity of will' (*VPG* 308/252). 'Of the Greeks in the first and genuine shape of their freedom, we may assert, that they had no conscience; the habit [*Gewohnheit*] of living for their fatherland without further reflection was the principle dominant among them' (*VPG* 309/253). Although Hegel often refers nostalgically to the harmony and integrity of Greek life, there is little uncertainty about which of the two forms of *Sittlichkeit* he takes to be the freer: the Greek spirit, he says, 'is not yet absolutely free and not yet completed *out* of itself, not yet stimulated by itself' (*VPG* 293/238). It is only with the advent of Christianity—with its principle of 'infinite subjectivity'—that 'absolute' or 'concrete' freedom becomes fully possible (*PR* §185, A).

It is tempting to think that Hegel excludes actual reasoning and deliberation from freedom and *Sittlichkeit* because there is an important sense in which he does think of reflection as a kind of illness, manifesting the 'self-will' (*Eigenwilligkeit*) (*PR* §152; *VPR18* 248–9) and 'vanity' (*Eitelkeit*) (*PR* §139; *VPR17* 91) of the individual. But he is quite careful to point out that his objection here is not to reflection

[14] Hegel also associates 'immediate *Sittlichkeit*' with the mode of living of those belonging to the 'substantial estate (*Stand*)', in which 'reflection and the will of the individual play a lesser role' and the disposition is 'based on the family relationship and on trust' (*PR* §203).

and conscience as such but to the suggestion (which he associates with philosophers such as Fries) that the criterion for determining what is good or right consists in whatever principles and convictions the individual happens to find, upon reflection, in his conscience (*PR* §§152, 137–40; *VPR19* 124). It is the subjectivist view that something is good or right just because I have deliberated about it and am convinced that it is good or right that Hegel equates with 'self-will' and 'vanity', and not reflection or deliberation more generally.[15] There is an 'ambiguity associated with conscience', Hegel thinks, which 'consists in the fact that conscience is assumed in advance to signify the identity of subjective knowledge and volition with the true good, and is thus declared and acknowledged to be sacrosanct, while it also claims, as the purely subjective reflection of self-consciousness into itself, the authority [*Berechtigung*] which belongs only to that identity itself by virtue of its rational content which is valid in and for itself' (*PR* §137). The state, he says, cannot recognize conscience as authoritative concerning what the true good consists in 'any more than science can grant any validity to subjective *opinion*, *assertion*, and the *appeal* to subjective opinion' (*PR* §137). Nevertheless, conscience—as 'the unity of subjective knowledge and that which has being in and for itself'—is 'a sanctuary which it would be *sacrilege* to violate' (*PR* §137). For Hegel, then, reflection, deliberation, and conscience are always in danger of turning into the 'self-will' and 'vanity' of a private, self-validating reason, but, so long as they recognize an objective rationality in ethics, they remain indispensable components of freedom.

So freedom, for Hegel, does involve a significant form of actual reflective awareness with respect to one's determinations. But does it require that the actual reflection and deliberation of a free agent go 'all the way down'? Does it require, in other words, that the agent reflects and deliberates to the point where he actually perceives and understands that his determinations have a justification that is independent of his contingently given desires and inclinations? Or, to put this in language introduced earlier, does it require that the agent enjoy 'infinite subjectivity' with respect to the determination (a complete or full rational awareness with respect to the determination, one which stops at nothing 'given') or is it enough that he enjoy ordi-

[15] See Siep, 'The *Aufhebung* of Morality in Ethical Life', 153: 'What [Hegel] rejects is simply the veneration for the decisions of conscience as being beyond criticism'. See also Pippin, *Idealism as Modernism*, 108–9.

nary subjective freedom with respect to his determination (where he reflects on the determination and sees that it is continuous with his particularity)?

It seems to me that Hegel wavers on this point. (A good example of the ambiguity in his position is the curiously worded *PR* §147.) There is, I think, a genuine tension in his conception of freedom between the emphasis on thought and philosophical reflection (which he always associates with freedom), on the one hand, and the desire to attribute freedom to ordinary agents living out the customary morality of their social institutions in an only partially reflective way, on the other.[16] Most of Hegel's explicit statements on the issue, however, somewhat surprisingly lean towards a full reflective awareness requirement. In a text quoted above, for instance, in which he suggests that 'the ethical character knows that the end which moves it is the universal' (*PR* §152; cf. *VG* 91/77, 111/93), the implication seems to be that the fully free agent in *Sittlichkeit* does achieve a full reflective awareness concerning the basis of his determinations and is not *just* reflectively attracted to his determinations on the basis of his particularity. And, when Hegel characterizes the concrete freedom achieved through citizenship in a rational state, he again insists that that freedom involves a rational perception and understanding that one's activity as a citizen has its basis in a 'universal' or 'substantial' interest (*PR* §§ 260, 268).

So let us now try to bring together some of these different observations and specify what the conditions are under which Hegel takes an agent to be rationally self-determining and free. By doing so, it should become clear just how Hegel can insist on an important opposition between reason and desire in the free will without running foul of his own objections to the position he associates with Kant. From what we have seen, Hegel seems to hold that the following conditions must be satisfied for some subject *S* to be rationally self-determining in pursuing some end *E* from a desire *D*:

(1) *E* must be prescribed by reason: there must be reasons for *S* to have *E* as his end that are independent of *S*'s contingently given desires and inclinations.
(2) *D* must be the desire that it is appropriate for *S* to have in the situation: there must be reasons to think it is appropriate for *S*

[16] For texts in which Hegel seems to play down the role of reflection in *Sittlichkeit*, see e.g. *Enz.* iii, §514 and *VPR17* 90–1.

to be motivated by *D* that are independent of *S*'s contingently given desires and inclinations.

(3) *S* must perceive and understand the rationality of pursuing *E* from *D*: he must be aware of the reasons for having *E* as his end and *D* as his motivation that are independent of his contingently given desires and inclinations.

Consider, for instance, the case of a husband who performs one of the duties of his position out of love for his family. Barring unusual circumstances, Hegel would, I think, hold that conditions (1) and (2) are satisfied in this case: the man would be performing an action prescribed by reason with the desire that it is appropriate for him to have in the situation. Whether or not he can be judged fully free would then rest on condition (3). If he performs his duties unreflectively, or with only a limited awareness of the rationality of what he is doing, then Hegel would rule that he is not fully free. But if, in addition to performing the right action with the right disposition, he has an awareness of the rationality of his activity—an awareness that does not appeal to any contingently given desire—then Hegel would judge that he is rationally self-determining and free.

Note that, although this account of rational self-determination does assert an important opposition between freedom and reason, on the one hand, and an agent's given set of desires and inclinations, on the other, it does not conflict with Hegel's rejection of the idea that an agent can be moved to action by reason. In the example just mentioned, for instance, there is no claim that the man is motivated by reason rather than his contingently given desires and inclinations: to the contrary, he is motivated by love. But this does not mean that Hegel is retreating to a very weak conception of rational self-determination requiring only that the agent pursue the ends prescribed by reason. Freedom as rational self-determination also requires that the agent have an appropriate or reasonable motive and that he have an awareness of the rationality of his determination: an awareness that he has a reason to act as he does, with the desire that he has, that is independent of his given desires and inclinations. Nor does Hegel's notion of rational self-determination conflict with his thesis that certain feelings and dispositions have ethical significance. Far from undervaluing such feelings and dispositions, or requiring agents to struggle against them, Hegel's idea of rational freedom positively requires agents to have them in certain situations. In some contexts, enjoying freedom as rational self-determination means acting from a particular disposition such as love or patriotism that is reasonable or appropriate in the circumstances.

The problem with attributing a thoroughly anti-Kantian position to Hegel on the basis of his criticisms of Kant is that such a line of argument fails adequately to distinguish between the motivational conditions of freedom (where Hegel does take what he thinks is an anti-Kantian position) and the question of what the 'criterion' or 'justifying' consideration is in assessing the rationality of an action or motive and in deliberating and reasoning about what to do or believe. With respect to the latter question, Hegel clearly does endorse the Kantian view that rational self-determination requires an independence of one's contingently given desires and inclinations and an appeal only to one's own thought and reason.

2.4. *Freedom, Authority, and Desire*

My main objective so far has been to formulate the conditions under which Hegel is willing to grant that an agent is 'with himself', and therefore free, in engaging in some particular action or relationship. The upshot of the discussion is that freedom, for Hegel, entails a complex set of conditions involving both subjective and objective requirements. The agent's activity must be grounded in a process of justification that does not *stop* at his given desires and inclinations (even if it is *necessary* that he find satisfaction in his activity) but seeks a basis in pure reason alone, where this is taken to mean that his determinations need to be (*a*) prescribed by reason, (*b*) done from a motivation prescribed by reason, and (*c*) performed with a consciousness of their reasonableness.

In the remainder of this chapter I want to explore why Hegel thinks that this is a correct understanding of freedom and to argue that his account is more plausible than it might look. This task will have two main parts. In the present section the focus will be on showing how Hegel's conception of freedom as rational self-determination is connected with an everyday intuition we have about freedom: the idea that freedom and authority are opposed to one another. I begin by investigating and analysing Hegel's views on the relationship between freedom and authority and then proceed to argue that agreeing with Hegel about this relationship commits one to accepting at least a central part of his much more ambitious idea of freedom as rational self-determination. In the final section of the chapter, I then consider how Hegel's position fares against some of the standard objections mentioned at the start of the chapter.

As we saw earlier, Hegel rejects both the 'natural-will' and 'reflective-will' conceptions of free agency and instead insists that the agent must be able reflectively to affirm his determinations 'all the way down': there must *be* a reason for him to act as he does that is independent of his contingently given desires and inclinations and he must be *aware* of this reason. Even setting aside the standard objections mentioned at the start of the chapter, this view is controversial for at least two different reasons. First, the natural and reflective will conceptions are attractive because they seem so obviously different from the case of the agent who is coerced or who slavishly follows the authority of another: the desire he follows is *his own*—it is a mental state that he and only he experiences—and so it seems sensible to think that he is *self*-determining when his action satisfies it. Secondly, Hegel's view is in at least partial conflict with a tradition of thinking about freedom, often associated with nineteenth-century romanticism, that identifies freedom with spontaneity and sees reflection as a mark of unfreedom. The paradigmatic example of the free individual, on this view, is the person who spurns the confining traditions and customary modes of reasoning of his society and listens to nothing but the promptings of his own heart instead, his own desires and inclinations.[17]

Hegel argues that this natural or romantic conception of freedom is not a true conception of *self*-determination, since it allows the will to be determined by something 'given' and 'external' (see §2.2 above). Although it is true that the naturally free agent follows his own drives and desires, *what* drives and desires he has is determined by outside factors. Hegel makes much the same point against reflective freedom: the reflectively free agent deliberates about which of his drives and desires to follow but remains unfree to the extent that his menu of possibilities is 'given' from 'outside'. On their own, these do not seem like very persuasive arguments: it might be responded that *every* human decision is made in the context of an externally given situation, so that the presence of external or given factors as such cannot be sufficient for declaring somebody to be unfree. Since it is

[17] See Benn, *A Theory of Freedom*, 174.

impossible to imagine a human situation in which the goals, values, and ambitions of individuals are not affected by outside factors or in which their framework of choice is not externally determined, the mere presence of outside or given factors cannot be a decisive consideration against either the natural or reflective views of freedom.[18]

A revealing passage from the Preface to the *Philosophy of Right* suggests, however, that Hegel may have a more nuanced conception of stopping at something 'given' than this objection to his arguments implies. He argues that,

> what [the truth] needs is to be *comprehended* as well so that the content which is already rational in itself may also gain a rational form and thereby appear justified to free thinking. For such thinking does not stop at what is *given*, whether the latter is supported by the external positive authority [*Autorität*] of the state or of mutual agreement among human beings, or by the authority [*Autorität*] of inner feeling and the heart and by the testimony of the spirit which immediately concurs with this, but starts out from itself and thereby demands to know itself as united in its innermost being with the truth. (*PR* Preface, p. 14/11)

In this passage at least, to 'stop at what is given' is not equated with the presence of external influencing or constraining factors as such but with taking something on authority, whether it be the authority of the state, of public opinion, or of the agent's own feelings and passions.[19] If this is indicative of Hegel's more general view, then it suggests that he views acting on desire rather than reason as a mark of incomplete freedom not simply in virtue of the external origin of one's desires but because acting on desire is in some way analogous to, or even a case of, acting on authority.

A review of some of Hegel's remarks about the relationship between freedom and authority suggests that this is indeed his general view. A striking and curiously neglected feature of Hegel's theory of freedom is his thesis that there is a basic opposition between freedom and authority.[20] A general formulation of this thesis can be found, for instance, in his 1822–3 lectures:

[18] See Dworkin, *The Theory and Practice of Autonomy*, 36, 38, and Benn, *A Theory of Freedom*, 179.

[19] Except where otherwise indicated, 'authority' is a translation of Hegel's *Autorität*.

[20] Inwood is one of the few commentators to appreciate the importance attached by Hegel to the opposition between freedom and authority; see his *Hegel*, 469–70, 479.

Finally, we may also describe as objective the will which is completely immersed in its object, such as the will of the child, which is founded on trust and lacks subjective freedom, and the will of the slave, which does not yet know itself as free and is consequently a will with no will of its own. In this sense, every will whose actions are guided by an alien authority and which has not yet completed its infinite return into itself is objective. (*PR* §26A)

Hegel also claims that the distinguishing feature of the modern, European understanding of freedom is its incompatibility with any kind of subjection to authority:

This *subjective* or *moral* freedom is what, in the European sense, is especially called freedom. As capable of the right to this freedom, man must possess a personal knowledge of the distinction between good and evil in general: ethical and religious principles shall not merely lay their claims on him as external laws and precepts of authority to be obeyed, but have their assent, recognition, or even justification [*Begründung*] in his heart, disposition, conscience, intelligence, etc. (*Enz.* iii, §503)[21]

But the anti-authoritarian theme is perhaps most consistently emphasized in Hegel's discussion of the medieval Church and of the differences between the Protestant and Catholic religions. In his *Lectures on the Philosophy of History* Hegel argues that the medieval Church attempted to set itself up as an authority over the realm of religious belief and experience, instructing its followers about what to believe, how to interpret the scriptures, and what outward actions to take in order to secure salvation (*VPG* 453–60/377–83). Instead of each Christian exploring his own relation with God, using his own conscience and reason, spirituality is reduced to what Hegel terms 'the slavery of authority' (*VPG* 493/413), in which obeying the commands of the Church and performing the required outward acts and rituals are seen as the road to salvation. 'The Church took the place of *conscience* and treated individuals like children' and so 'through the perversion of the principle of freedom, absolute unfreedom became the law' (*VPG* 455–6/378–9). 'In this way the relationship of absolute unfreedom is imported into the principle of freedom itself' (*VPG* 457/379).

It was only with Luther and the Reformation, Hegel continues, that a true Christian freedom could be actualized (*VPG*

[21] Other passages in which Hegel affirms an opposition between freedom and authority include: *VPR18* 205, 259; *Enz.* i, §31A; *Enz.* iii, §392A; *VGP* iii. 329/423, 367/469.

492–502/412–22). Luther repudiated the authority of the Church and set up in its place the Bible, as interpreted by each individual, and the 'testimony of the human spirit' (*VPG* 497/417): 'This is a vast change of principle: the whole tradition, and the edifice of the Church, become problematic and the principle of the authority of the Church is overthrown' (*VPG* 497–8/418). Luther challenged the doctrine that a person could obtain salvation by slavishly obeying the instructions and prescriptions of the Church and instead held that true spirituality is essentially a matter of the individual's inner faith and understanding. The actualization of Christian freedom requires that each individual work through questions of religious belief and practice for himself—not, of course, because the truths of the Christian religion are ultimately subjective, but because 'each has to accomplish the work of reconciliation on his own self' (*VPG* 496/416). 'With this', Hegel concludes,

> is unfurled the new, the last standard around which the peoples rally—the banner of *free spirit*, which is with itself and, indeed, is in the truth and only this way is with itself. This is the banner under which we serve, and which we bear. Time, since [the Reformation] has had, and has now, no other work to do than the imbuing of the world with this principle . . . This is the essential content of the Reformation: man is destined [*bestimmt*] through himself to be free. (*VPG* 496–7/416–17)

That certain peoples (such as the Spanish and the Italians) have not yet undergone such a Reformation, and are content to have their concerns settled for them by the Church, could only be a sign that 'their inner life is not their own' and that their actions are not 'self-possessed' (*selbsteigenes*) (*VPG* 501–2/420–1).[22]

It is clear from these passages that Hegel does see an important tension between freedom and authority: by following authority rather than consulting one's own conscience and convictions one may end up with the 'right' ends (attending mass, giving to the poor, and so on), but one cannot be said to be free or self-determining. This may strike some readers as a surprising conclusion, since Hegel is widely thought to have wanted to reconcile individual freedom with the authority of the state.[23] There are indeed texts in which Hegel

[22] The influence on the young Hegel of an anti-authoritarian ideal of Protestant civil piety is an important theme in Dickey, *Hegel: Religion, Economics and the Politics of Spirit, 1770–1807*.

[23] For the claim that Hegel seeks to reconcile freedom and authority, see e.g. Krieger, *The German Idea of Freedom*, 125–6, 130, 132, and Benhabib, 'Obligation, Contract and Exchange', 175–6.

claims that the individual realizes freedom in obeying the state or the commands of ethics more generally. However, he is usually quite careful to distinguish the different forms that this obedience might take: '[the] laws can take the shape [*die Gestalt*] of something given by God, or something having divine authority or the authority of the state, or they can take the shape of something [grounded in] the insight of reason, where one recognizes [*erkennt*] that they are posited through the concept of freedom' (*VPR* iv. 398; cf. *VPR17* 37). Obedience is reconcilable with freedom only when it is grounded in rational insight, not in authority:

> A *third* moment of ethics [*Sittlichkeit*] is that *obedience* be directed towards the ethical and rational, as an obedience to laws which I recognize as just, not a blind and unconditional obedience which does not know what it is doing, and whose course of action is a mere groping about without clear consciousness or intelligence. It was exactly this latter kind of obedience that passed [before the Reformation] for the most pleasing to God, one which sets the obedience of slavery, imposed by the arbitrary will of the church, above the true obedience of freedom. (*VPG* 457–8/380; see also *VPG* 503–4/423; *PR* §270, pp. 425–8/299–301; *VPR* iv. 82–3; *LPR* iii. 252–3)

Hegel's view seems to be that I am free in obeying a law only if: (*a*) that law is just or rational, and (*b*) I recognize it as just or rational. If this is the case, then Hegel seeks to reconcile freedom with the authority of the state only in a very weak sense. He thinks that I can be free in obeying an authority but only if, in so doing, I have an awareness of the rationality of what I am being asked to do and in this sense am acting not *on* authority but on the basis of my own insight and reason.

It also seems clear from the passages we have been examining that Hegel believes that his idea of a conflict between freedom and authority can be generalized to help explain and guide other judgements about freedom and unfreedom. For instance, in the passage I quoted from the Preface to the *Philosophy of Right* (p. 14/11), he refers, slightly oddly, to the *authority* of one's feelings and emotions, suggesting that he sees an important parallel between acting on the authority of the Church or state, say, and acting on one's own unexamined desires and inclinations. He also holds, as we just saw, that the Reformation occupies a place in history of fundamental importance in that it decisively introduced the principle of free spirit. Since the Reformation, Hegel asserts, history has consisted in little more than the elaboration and application of that principle to new domains and areas of life (*VPG* 496/416). In addition, he says that 'What Luther inaugurated as faith in feeling and in the testimony of the spirit is the same thing that the spirit, at a more mature stage of its development, endeavours to grasp in the *concept* so as to free itself in the present and thus find itself therein' (*PR*, Preface, p. 27/22). These comments suggest that Hegel regards the Reformation opposition between freedom and authority as central to an understanding of the modern conception of freedom that he espouses.

Hegel's claim, then, would seem to be that the reasons for thinking that there is an opposition between freedom and authority also turn out to be reasons for thinking that there is an opposition between freedom and appeals to one's contingently given desires and inclinations. Just as taking something on authority is a case of stopping at something 'given' from 'outside', so is grounding one's determinations in one's desires and inclinations, and thus both are equally cases of unfreedom. Hegel's suggestion is an intriguing one, in so far as the intuition that there is a basic opposition between freedom and authority is one that many people will find plausible. If Hegel really can show that his full conception of freedom arises naturally from this common-sense intuition, then this would suggest that it is on much firmer ground than is standardly supposed.[24]

But is there really the kind of parallel between acting on authority and following one's own desires and inclinations that Hegel claims? What bothers Hegel about the person who subjects himself to authority is his contentment to have his concerns settled for him by another and thus his failure to consult his own inner convictions and conscience, his own thought and reason, in deciding what to do or believe: 'when power and authority are granted to others to determine and prescribe what actions I should perform . . . or how I should interpret the dictates of conscience, religious truth, etc.' then this constitutes 'the alienation of intelligent rationality, of morality, ethical life, and religion' (*PR* §66). The person who subjects himself to authority lacks full freedom, in Hegel's eyes, because he relies on

[24] My assumption is that the intuition is an attractive one not that it could not be challenged philosophically. Whether or not autonomy and authority are opposed is a matter of some controversy amongst contemporary philosophers. For the view that they are, see e.g. Wolff, *In Defense of Anarchism*, 12–15, 72; Scanlon, 'A Theory of Freedom of Expression', 215–16; Benn, *A Theory of Freedom*, 175–83; and Feinberg, 'Autonomy', 36. For criticisms of this view, see Dworkin, *The Theory and Practice of Autonomy*, 21–9; Raz, 'Introduction' to *Authority*, 3–12, and 'Government by Consent', 341–4, 349; and Miller, *Anarchism*, 26–9.

somebody or something else for direction where he could try to think through the question of what to do for himself; he lacks the 'obstinacy' of the person who refuses to accept anything that has not been justified in his own thought (*PR*, Preface, p. 27/22). Hegel's point can be illustrated by considering the case of an agent who, faced with some practical dilemma, relies on his priest or spiritual adviser, rather than his own conscience, for instruction and guidance (this is Hegel's example at *PR* §66A). It seems natural to think of this man as not fully engaged in shaping and directing his own life and to this extent as not fully free or autonomous. The basic problem appears to lie not in the presence of external constraints and influences as such, nor (in any straightforward sense) in the causal origins of his actions, but in the character of his practical deliberations and reasoning. He lacks full freedom because he relies on somebody or something else for direction where he could try to think through the question of what to do or believe for himself. He takes the instructions of the priest to be sufficient justification of his action even though he could question and scrutinize those instructions and act on his own judgement of the balance of reasons instead.

Now consider a different case, one that introduces the second more controversial element in Hegel's conception of freedom, the opposition between freedom and desire. This is the case of the agent who relies on his own unexamined desires and inclinations to make some important decision. Hegel's suggestion, as we saw, is that the reasons for thinking that the agent in the first case lacks full freedom are also reasons for thinking that this second agent is incompletely free. In both cases, the process of deliberation and justification with which the agents approach their decisions to act are essentially the same.

Two parallel features of the cases suggest that Hegel's argument should be taken seriously. First, in each case, the agent allows the determination of some external agency or mechanism to be a sufficient reason or justification for his action. In the first case, the agent passively allows the instruction of the authority to stand as a justification of his final decision to act; in the second case, he passively allows the social and natural processes that determine what desires he experiences to count as a sufficient guide to what he should do. Secondly, in both cases, the agent *could* subject the problem of what to do to his own thought and reason. In the first, he could ask questions such as 'Are the instructions of the authority reasonable?' or

'Are there other relevant considerations besides the view expressed by the authority?' In the second, he could reflect on whether it is a good thing that he act on his desire and whether there are other relevant considerations besides the fact of experiencing his desire.

If we think that the agent who subjects himself to authority is incompletely free in virtue of letting an external agency determine for him what he could attempt to think through for himself, then we must reach the same conclusion about the agent who makes some important decision by consulting only his own desires and inclinations. He too is letting external mechanisms and processes determine for him what he could attempt to think through for himself. That is to say, if the one agent is incompletely free in virtue of not being sufficiently ambitious in his practical deliberation and justification, then we seem driven to the same conclusion about the other agent.

The problem with the romantic or natural conception of freedom is that it misleadingly opposes acting on one's own desires and inclinations to conforming with the customs, mores, and expectations of one's social environment. The opposition is misleading because, although it is true that only I experience my desires as motivating, it is also the case that *what* desires I have is conditioned by my social environment and its expectations as well as by my biological make-up. The claim that the authority and desire cases are alike is in effect the claim that an uncritical acceptance of the promptings of one's social and natural environment is no more a mark of freedom than is an uncritical obedience of authority.

Similar considerations would apply against the reflective conception of freedom. Consider, for instance, the case of someone whose reflections about what to do or believe consist solely in an attempt to balance and put into harmony the received wisdom and assumptions of her community and her own needs and desires. Even though she is engaging in some degree of reflection and self-evaluation, we cannot if we endorse Hegel's analysis of the freedom–authority relationship think of her as a completely 'free thinker' or as leading a fully autonomous life. She is simply accepting a framework for reflection, bounded by the content of her needs and desires and the customs and mores of her community, that narrowly constrains the kind of determination she could reach—a framework that she could deliberate about and possibly reject. In the authority case, the agent is unfree in virtue of simply accepting something external that she could think through for herself. But the same thing is true in this more complex case of the partially reflective agent who acts on the basis of an interpretation of her society's customs and conventions and of her own basic needs and desires: she is accepting an externally determined 'agenda' or framework for decision-making that could itself be critically examined.

The upshot of this argument is that one central part of Hegel's conception of freedom is on much firmer ground than is commonly thought. Our common-sense idea of autonomy involves the idea of 'deciding for oneself' rather than letting outside forces and agencies decide on one's behalf. The agent who puts himself under an authority, it seems right to say, fails to live up to this ideal because he passively allows somebody else's ideas and purposes to direct his life for him. To be fully free or autonomous, one must not rely on any kind of external authority in one's practical deliberations but do one's best to make up one's own mind on the basis of one's own ideas and purposes. It can be concluded from this that something like ordinary 'subjective freedom', in Hegel's sense of this term, is at least one of the conditions of true freedom. It is necessary for freedom that the agent engage in some degree of reflection and deliberation and that this reflection and deliberation make reference to his own desires and evaluations and not just to the authority of others.

More controversially, if the argument I have been elaborating is correct, then it seems that what Hegel calls 'infinite subjectivity' is also a condition of true or full freedom. It is necessary for freedom or autonomy that an agent consult his own desires and inclinations in deciding what to do, but, if this is *all* the reflection the agent engages in, then he is not fully deciding for himself but is letting whatever social and natural processes determine his desires and inclinations decide for him. Only the agent whose determinations can be reflectively justified all the way down can truly be said to be deciding for himself.

Does this argument take us all the way to Hegel's conception of freedom as rational self-determination? Not yet. It still needs to be shown that an agent who engages in radical reflection—who abstracts from all of his contingently given desires, inclinations, and so forth—has some reasons-for-action remaining that can give practical guidance and, in fact, point to the kinds of determinate actions, relationships, and dispositions that Hegel associates with objective freedom. In Hegel's language, it still needs to be shown that 'infinite subjectivity' dialectically 'passes over' into objectivity (*PR* §26), into an objective set of principles of action that agents can find themselves committed to just in virtue of their freedom and rationality. Trying to make sense of this crucial step in Hegel's account of freedom will be the challenge taken up in the next chapter. For now, however, we have seen enough of Hegel's conception of freedom as rational self-determination to consider in more detail the four standard objections introduced at the beginning of the chapter.

2.5. *The Standard Objections*

(i) Hegelian Freedom and Ordinary Freedom

The first and most basic objection that needs to be considered is the argument that rational self-determination has little or nothing to do with our everyday understanding of freedom.[25] Writers like Berlin and Oppenheim assume that the everyday conception of freedom can be identified with the enjoyment of as wide an area of choice and opportunity as possible: freedom, on this view, is not tied to any particular duties or codes of conduct but is essentially open-ended and indeterminate.[26] They further argue that the temptation to equate freedom with rational self-determination arises because of a tendency to confuse freedom with other values and goals such as self-realization and morality.[27] This *is* a confusion, it is claimed, because it seems perfectly possible to imagine cases of people who are self-realized but unfree (for example, the slave whose capacity for precision craftsmanship is fully developed), free but immoral, and so on.

A first point to make about this argument is that Hegel would not necessarily regard it as an *objection* to his account of freedom. Hegel is fond of boasting of the discrepancy between his conception of freedom and the everyday conception, which he thinks equates freedom with 'being able to do as one pleases' (*PR* §15; *VPR19* 64). Still, it

[25] In *Self-Consciousness and Self-Determination* Tugendhat asserts that 'Hegel initially grasped the word *freedom* roughly as it is ordinarily understood. But he subsequently introduced a change in its meaning; and the consequence of this change was that the word stands for exactly the opposite meaning' (p. 317). He also claims that Hegel's identification of freedom with necessity represents 'a perversity that is certainly no longer merely conceptual but also moral' (p. 316).

[26] See Berlin, *Four Essays on Liberty*, pp. lii, 162, and Oppenheim, *Dimensions of Freedom*, 169.

[27] Berlin, *Four Essays on Liberty*, p. lvi, and Oppenheim, *Dimensions of Freedom*, 154–5, 167–9.

would be problematic for Hegel's project if his notion of freedom had as little to do with the common-sense idea of freedom as some of his critics suggest. One of Hegel's aims is to reconcile modern Europeans to the central institutions and practices of their social world (*PR*, Preface, p. 27/22).[28] This project involves giving people reason to feel 'at home' in their social institutions and practices rather than 'alienated' and unfulfilled, by showing those institutions and practices to be necessary for the full actualization of their freedom. If this approach to the problem of reconciliation is to be compelling, then Hegel needs to be working with a view of freedom that has at least some connection with the idea of freedom that we know and value.

One of the strengths of the interpretation that I have been developing is that it can show what this connection might be. Although it is true that Hegel does not espouse the 'negative' concept of liberty that has such a central place in the common-sense understanding of freedom, I have argued that a core part of his conception of freedom as rational self-determination can nevertheless be understood as an extension and generalization of an everyday intuition we have about freedom—the intuition that there is a basic opposition between free or autonomous agency and subjection to authority. The reasons for thinking that autonomy and authority are opposed also turn out to be reasons for favouring one of the central elements of Hegel's conception of freedom as rational self-determination. Understanding Hegel's conception of freedom in this way also makes it clear that the conception does not rest on any confusion of freedom with other values and goals. Whereas we instinctively feel that the man who consults his priest rather than his own conscience and reason is not fully free or autonomous, we may not think that he is acting immorally, or is lacking in self-realization. To the extent that Hegel's view of freedom as rational self-determination is an extension of his analysis of the relationship between freedom and authority, it does not rest on any illicit identification of freedom with self-realization or morality.

It might, however, be argued that Hegel's idea of freedom conflicts with our ordinary ideas and intuitions in a slightly different way. Hegelian freedom, as we have seen, requires that agents achieve a radical form of reflective awareness with respect to their determinations, one that does not stop at any given authority, or any desire or

[28] See Hardimon, *Hegel's Social Philosophy*, esp. ch. 3.

inclination that they might have, but only at their own thought and reason. And this seems to imply that Hegelian freedom is much more demanding than we would normally take freedom to be. In order to qualify as fully free, it would appear, an agent must go through a process of philosophical reflection every time he makes an important decision. And surely this would be expecting much more than our common-sense understanding of freedom would have it: if freedom requires this much use of one's practical reason, then hardly anybody, if anybody at all, could ever have been said to be free.

I suggested earlier that there is a tension in Hegel's account of freedom between an emphasis on thought and philosophical reflection, on the one hand, and a desire to attribute freedom to ordinary agents living out the customary morality of their social institutions in an only partially reflective way, on the other. For the most part, however, Hegel does seem serious about requiring that a 'concretely' free agent achieve a full degree of reflective awareness concerning his determinations. He would probably concede that this is a stronger condition than our ordinary understanding of freedom would require, although he might once again insist that it is continuous with an everyday intuition we have about freedom and authority. It would be a mistake, though, to construe the condition in too extreme a form. Hegel is saying not that the free agent must be a philosopher but only that he must at least be aware that his determinations serve 'universal' or 'substantial' interests that are separate from his 'particularity'. This would be true, for instance, of the citizen who decides to vote on the grounds that voting is a way of contributing to the maintenance of a free society and not just because it seems an enjoyable thing to do. Agents need to be philosophically reflective to be fully free on Hegel's account, but they do not need to be philosophers. Hegel seems to expect that members of the 'universal estate' (public officials), and perhaps ordinary citizens in some contexts (*PR* §268), would be able to attain freedom in this sense.

(ii) An Untenable Doctrine of the Self

Another standard objection to the view of freedom as rational self-determination argues that it presupposes an untenable conception of the self. This argument is eloquently developed by Isaiah Berlin in his essay 'Two Concepts of Liberty'. Parodying what he takes to be the 'positive' concept of freedom, he asks:

Have not men had the experience of liberating themselves from spiritual slavery, or slavery to nature, and do they not in the course of it become aware, on the one hand, of a self which dominates, and, on the other, of something in them which is brought to heel? This dominant self is then variously identified with reason, with my 'higher nature', with the self which calculates and aims at what will satisfy it in the long run, with my 'real', or 'ideal', or 'autonomous' self, or with my self 'at its best'; which is then contrasted with irrational impulse, uncontrolled desires, my 'lower' nature, the pursuit of immediate pleasures, my 'empirical' or 'heteronomous' self, swept by every gust of desire and passion, needing to be rigidly disciplined if it is ever to rise to the full height of its 'real' nature.[29]

Berlin and others identify at least three different problems with this theory of the split-level self. One is that it is not confirmed by human experience: Berlin calls the real self an 'occult entity' that is 'belied by all that [we] overtly feel and do and say' and of which 'the poor empirical self in space and time may know nothing or little'.[30] Another is that the identification of the 'true' self with rationality is simply a matter of prejudice:

The view that my rationality is 'really me' while my desires are not is, I think, pure prejudice. I may, when rational, prefer my rational 'higher self' to my 'lower self' thought of as those desires which sometimes tempt me from my rationally thought out plans. But I do not see any reason to take the lower self to be any less me than the higher self. If anything, my 'merely empirical desires' seem a more constant feature of my character over time than either my powers of rational deliberation or the interests, purposes, and plans which emerge from such deliberation.[31]

A third problem with the split-level-self doctrine is its perverse tendency to identify the 'true' or rational self with agencies such as the state that are literally outside the individual and then to conclude that self-determination occurs when these agencies command and the individual obeys.[32]

Some of Hegel's statements do support the claim that he draws a distinction between an empirical self and a true, rational, or essential self. For instance, he contrasts the arbitrariness and capriciousness of the agent who surrenders to his own desires and inclinations with the 'liberation' that is won by the rational agent who 'attains his

[29] Berlin, *Four Essays on Liberty*, 132.

[30] Ibid. 133.

[31] Crocker, *Positive Liberty*, 42.

[32] Berlin, *Four Essays on Liberty*, 132, 134; at p. 150 Berlin attributes this inflation of the real self to Hegel.

essential being' (*PR* §149A); he says that, 'since the determinations of ethics constitute the concept of freedom, they are the substantiality or universal essence of individuals' (*PR* §145A); and he suggests that the state is the 'essence' of individual self-consciousness in explaining why the individual achieves substantial freedom in the state (*PR* §257). The argument of this chapter, however, suggests that to take this distinction to be central to Hegel's view would involve a subtle but important distortion of his understanding of freedom. The key point for Hegel is not *which* self, or what *part* of the self, rules, or commands but what kind of 'criterion' or 'justifying' consideration *the* self can appeal to in its practical deliberations and reflection (*Enz.* iii, §400; cf. *LPR* i. 272, 393–5).[33] Hegel's claim, as we have seen, is that an important condition of having full freedom is that an agent be able to appeal only to reasons that are logically independent of his contingently given desires and inclinations. This claim, it should be clear, does not rest on any metaphysical assumptions about the nature of the self.

Once again the point is illustrated by Hegel's idea that there is an opposition between freedom and authority. The problem with the man who consults his priest rather than his own conscience and reason is with the character of his practical reasoning and, in particular, with the sorts of reasons he appeals to in justifying his action. We might choose to say that he is unfree because the wrong 'part' of his self is in command, but this would only be a metaphorical (and, I think, misleading) way of saying (roughly) that he takes the priest's instruction to be sufficient where he could subject the situation to his own thought and reason.

This is not to deny that there is something deeply controversial about Hegel's position. The assumption that there are reasons-for-action that are logically independent of one's contingently given desires and inclinations is one that many philosophers since Hobbes and Hume have not accepted. Much of the next chapter will be devoted to exploring and evaluating Hegel's position on this issue. The important point for now, however, is that nothing in Hegel's defence of rational self-determination commits him to bizarre and untenable assumptions about the self.

[33] Allison makes a similar point about Kant's conception of freedom in 'Kant on Freedom: A Reply', 452–3. Hill ('The Kantian Conception of Autonomy', 102–4) also emphasizes the importance, for Kant, of the character of an agent's practical deliberations in determining his autonomy.

(iii) The 'Forced-to-be-Free' Objection

A third objection is that thinking of freedom as rational self-determination commits one to the perverse and illiberal view that it is possible to force someone to be free. The argument here is that, if being free consists in following the dictates of reason, and it is granted that some people are more successful at discerning and enforcing these dictates than others, then this seems to open up the possibility that the rational people can force, coerce, or manipulate the irrational into pursuing the right ends and thereby make them free. But this, it is maintained, is perverse, since by its very nature freedom is opposed to force, coercion, manipulation, and so on.[34]

This objection might seem highly damaging to Hegel, since he notoriously holds that individuals achieve full freedom only through membership of the state—an institution that is often associated with the use of force and coercion.[35] In its present form, however, the objection can easily be deflected by recalling that freedom, for Hegel, is not simply a matter of performing the right actions (those prescribed by reason) but also of having the right motivation as well as an understanding of the rationality of one's activity. It is possible to force someone to go through the right motions, but it is self-defeating to force or coerce or manipulate a person into having the right motivation or understanding.[36] The importance for Hegel of this inner acceptance of one's action can, as we have seen, be traced back to his admiration for the Reformation idea that spiritual freedom involves not just a set of rituals and performances but, crucially, an inner reconciliation with God.

However, the objection can be reformulated in a more damaging way. It might be granted that forcing someone to be free is strictly speaking impossible on Hegel's view but objected, nevertheless, that Hegel's conception of freedom has the counter-intuitive implication that certain applications of force or coercion will not be registered as *diminishing* an agent's freedom. John Christman explains this possibility as follows: 'On the view that only rational, fully informed selves are autonomous, it follows that the most fierce and uncom-

[34] See Berlin, *Four Essays on Liberty*, 132–8; Oppenheim, *Dimensions of Freedom*, 169; and Cranston, *Freedom: A New Analysis*, 21. Both Oppenheim and Cranston mention Hegel by name.

[35] But see my discussion of Hegel's conception of the state in §6.2 below.

[36] See Wood, *Hegel's Ethical Thought*, 41.

promising interferences with a person's value judgements, desire formation, or thought patterns are not interferences at all if those values, desires, or thoughts are irrational ones.'[37] Say, for example, that one of the duties prescribed by reason is to vote. It is granted that freedom requires not only that one fulfil this duty but also that it be done with the right motive (patriotism, civic virtue) and with an awareness of the rationality of what one is doing. Nevertheless, the state might be tempted to coerce people into voting, not on the grounds that this would by itself be liberating people, but in the hopes that people would eventually come to see the rationality of their activity and acquire the right sorts of motivations. The objection is that this case of coercion does not even register as a diminution of freedom on Hegel's account, since people are only being prevented from doing something they have no real reason to be doing (they are in Hegel's language only being restrained from their own 'indeterminate subjectivity' (*PR* §149), 'dependence on mere natural drives' (*PR* §149), and 'self-will' (*PR* §152)).

Although there is a stoicist streak in Hegel's thought that denies that the free will is the kind of thing that *can* be coerced (*PR* §91), Hegel's usual response to this sort of objection would be to remind his critic once again that, on his view, freedom has both an objective and a subjective dimension: being free involves both pursuing the ends that are prescribed by one's reason *and* a kind of inner acceptance of one's ends—an understanding of, and identification with, them as one's own. It is true *ex hypothesi* that the sort of coercion being contemplated does not diminish the extent to which one is pursuing the ends prescribed by reason, but it *does* diminish the degree to which one is acting on ends that one has endorsed as worth pursuing. The state's attempt to coerce me may make me freer in one sense—it may orient me towards the right ends—but, crucially, in another sense, it makes me less free, since it means that I am no longer pursuing the ends to which *I* attach value and significance. That is to say, the application of force or coercion by the state might conceivably enhance my objective freedom, but it would almost invariably diminish my subjective freedom. As Hegel puts it in his 1818–19 lectures, 'If I am being coerced [*gezwungen*], then I do not have myself in this activity; it is not [my] subjective will' (*VPR18* 218). Strictly speaking, then, virtually any application of force or

37 Christman, 'Introduction' to *The Inner Citadel*, 12. See also Berlin, *Four Essays on Liberty*, 133 n., 153.

coercion *is* likely to be registered by Hegel's conception of freedom, even when it restrains the agent from his own 'self-will', for it will diminish the extent to which he is acting on his own (most preferred) desires and evaluations whatever they may be. It is worth noting in this context that Hegel attaches relatively little value to mere objective freedom, associating it with the will of a slave and attributing it even to history's first civilization (the Chinese) (*PR* §26A; *VPG* 135–6/105). By contrast he identifies subjective freedom with Christianity and calls it 'the pivotal and focal point in the difference between *antiquity* and the *modern* age' (*PR* §124).

(iv) Freedom and Responsibility

A fourth objection is one that is often levelled against Kant (most famously by Sidgwick),[38] but which might just as easily be made against Hegel. This is the objection that it is difficult to reconcile an understanding of freedom as rational self-determination with our practice of attributing responsibility to evil-doers. Hegel holds that:

(1) To be fully free one must perform the ends and duties prescribed by reason.
(2) The evil-doer has as his principle his 'own particularity' rather than 'the universal in and for itself'—i.e. he does not perform the ends and duties prescribed by reason (*PR* §139).
(3) Responsibility can only be attributed to free agents (*PR* §139, A; *VG* 106–7/90–91).
(4) The evil-doer is responsible for his actions (*PR* §139A).

The obvious problem is that on the face of it these four propositions are not mutually consistent: they imply that, on the one hand, an agent must be free to be held responsible and that, on the other, the evil-doer is both unfree and responsible.

The example of the man who subjects himself to authority helps to show why this objection fails, however, for it helps to bring out the idea that there are different kinds and degrees of freedom that an agent can enjoy at any given moment. For instance, the man who consults his priest may well have freely chosen to do so.[39] To this extent we can hold him responsible for acting as he does, even when the priest instructs him to commit an evil action. This attribution of

[38] Sidgwick, *The Methods of Ethics*, appendix, pp. 511–16.
[39] See Dworkin, *The Theory and Practice of Autonomy*, 28.

responsibility is compatible with holding (as I think we do) that in a different sense the man is not a fully free or autonomous agent because he is acting on the priest's judgement rather than thinking his practical dilemma through for himself. The same argument applies *mutatis mutandis* for the man who lets himself be determined by his desires and inclinations (that is, we can hold him responsible so long as he *let himself* be determined by his desire and was not, in some strong sense, compelled to act).

The problem with the objection, in other words, is that the freedom required by proposition (3) is not the full freedom described in (1). The freedom required by (3) is the freedom to choose—in particular, to choose between good and evil (*PR* §139A); it is what Hegel sometimes refers to as the 'formal' freedom of *Willkür* (*PR* §15).[40] This freedom is a necessary but not a sufficient condition of full freedom (that is, the freedom referred to in (1)). Full freedom places, in addition, a restriction on *what* one can choose: it requires that one not 'let oneself' be determined by an external authority or desire, that one not abdicate one's power to think the problem through for oneself. There is no conflict then between freedom as rational self-determination and the practice of holding evil-doers responsible for their actions: it is not rational self-determination that is required for responsibility but the more basic freedom of *Willkür*.[41]

[40] In a handwritten note to *PR* §139 Hegel refers to the freedom that underlies responsibility as the freedom of *Willkür*. See p. 263 of the German edition.

[41] See Tugendhat, *Self-Consciousness and Self-Determination*, 312. For discussion of Kant's similar solution to the problem, see Silber, 'The Ethical Significance of Kant's *Religion*'.

3

The Reciprocity Thesis in Kant and Hegel

3.1. *The Reciprocity Thesis*

Following Henry Allison's terminology in his book *Kant's Theory of Freedom*, I shall take the *reciprocity thesis* to be the thesis that morality and freedom are reciprocal concepts.[1] To be free, the reciprocity thesis claims, is to stand in a certain relationship to the demands of morality; to stand in the appropriate relationship to the demands of morality is to be free.

Despite quite different understandings of the domains of ethics and morality, Kant and Hegel both affirm versions of the reciprocity thesis. For Kant, the thesis is that freedom and subjection to the moral law are reciprocal conditions. As he puts it at the beginning of chapter III of the *Groundwork of the Metaphysics of Morals*: 'a free will and a will under moral laws are one and the same. Consequently if freedom of the will is presupposed, morality, together with its principle, follows by mere analysis of the concept of freedom.'[2] This assumption of reciprocity is an explicit premiss in the subsequent argument that, since a rational agent must take himself to be free, he must consider himself subject to the moral law. And it reappears again in the *Critique of Practical Reason*'s reversal of this argument, which claims that, since a rational agent has a sense of himself as subject to the moral law (the so-called fact of reason), he therefore has a consciousness of his freedom.[3] Something like the reciprocity thesis also underlies much of the argument of chapters I and II of the *Groundwork* as well as the opening arguments of the second *Critique*: for in these texts Kant frequently moves directly from the proposi-

[1] Allison, *Kant's Theory of Freedom*, ch. 11.

[2] Kant, *Groundwork*, 447. All references to this work are to the page numbers of the edition issued by the Royal Prussian Academy in Berlin, which are included in most standard editions. *Grundlegung zur Metaphysik der Sitten* is in vol. iv.

[3] Kant, *Critique of Practical Reason*, 29–30, 42–50. All references to this work are to the page numbers of the edition issued by the Royal Prussian Academy in Berlin, which are included in most standard editions. *Kritik der praktischen Vernunft* is in vol. v.

tion that the will is determined independently of all of its desires and inclinations (it is free) to the conclusion that it must be subject to the moral law.[4]

For Hegel, the requirements of duty and morality are not expressed by a moral law, or Categorical Imperative, but are to be found in *Sittlichkeit*: in the customary ends and obligations of the major institutions of the modern community—including the family, civil society, and the state. This does not stop Hegel, however, from joining Kant in explicitly affirming a version of the reciprocity thesis. Commenting on Kant, for instance, Hegel asserts that 'In doing my duty, I am with myself and free. The merit and exalted viewpoint of Kant's moral philosophy are that it has emphasized this significance of duty' (*PR* §133A). As we saw in Chapter 1, Hegel also claims that 'an immanent and consistent theory of duties can be nothing other than the development of *those* relations which are necessitated by the idea of freedom . . .' (*PR* §148). And he says that 'In duty, the individual liberates himself so as to attain substantial freedom' (*PR* §149). For Hegel, then, the reciprocity thesis is the thesis that freedom—and, in particular, 'objective' or 'substantial' freedom—and actually 'doing my duty' are reciprocal conditions.[5] This thesis, we know from Chapter 1, is an important part of his argument for thinking that the duties and virtues of modern *Sittlichkeit* offer an appropriate basis for everyday practical reasoning.

For both Kant and Hegel, the case for the reciprocity thesis has two main steps. The first is to establish a particular conception of freedom as rational self-determination. As we saw in Chapter 2, on this view, an agent is free if and only if his determination is not grounded in any of his contingently given desires and inclinations but only in his own thought and reason. The second step involves a defence of the claim that an agent who is fully guided by his own thought and reason is necessarily an agent who is standing in the appropriate relationship with ethical requirements. At first glance, it must be conceded, neither step looks very promising. The first seems to assert an impossibly extreme conception of freedom, which not only clashes with our common-sense understanding of free or

[4] e.g. Kant, *Groundwork*, 400–2.

[5] An important difference between the Kantian and Hegelian formulations of the thesis, then, is that the former identifies freedom with the *capacity* to follow ethical requirements whereas the latter identifies it with actually *exercising* this capacity. See Allison, *Kant's Theory of Freedom*, 94–9; Hill, 'Kant's Argument for the Rationality of Moral Conduct', 11–12; and Wood, *Hegel's Ethical Thought*, 39.

autonomous agency but also seems to lead to a number of irresolvable problems and paradoxes. The second seems to involve an attempt to derive ethical requirements from the mere concept of rationality—a project that most philosophers today have concluded is doomed to failure.

In Chapter 2 I sought to formulate Hegel's conception of freedom as rational self-determination and to show that that conception can be seen as grounded in a common-sense intuition we have about freedom and defended against certain standard objections. In this chapter I want to focus on the second step in the argument for the reciprocity thesis in Kant and Hegel respectively: the move from rational self-determination to ethical requirements. I shall try to give a sense of just how difficult this move is by taking a fairly close look at how the argument unfolds in Kant's practical philosophy: even as defended by recent commentators such as Henry Allison and Christine Korsgaard, I will maintain, Kant's argument cannot be judged a success. I will then offer an interpretation of the step from rational self-determination to ethical requirements as it can be reconstructed from Hegel's writings and lectures. We shall see that this argument, although incomplete in certain respects, contains at least some of the resources needed for a successful defence of the reciprocity thesis.

3.2. *The Empty Formalism Objection*

Throughout Chapter 2, I bracketed a major objection to the view that freedom consists in rational self-determination. This is the objection that rational self-determination is essentially vacuous: the conditions that an agent must satisfy in order to qualify as rationally self-determining are such that there never has been, and never could be, a free agent. This objection is directed against Kant by Hegel himself at §§133–5 of the *Philosophy of Right*. According to Hegel, Kant goes so far in divorcing the 'particular' from the 'universal' aspects of the will, and has such an abstract account of the latter, that nothing remains to generate the determinations and duties that are to give content to freedom: 'all that is left for duty itself, in so far as it is the essential or universal element in the moral self-consciousness as it is related within itself to itself alone, is abstract universality, whose determination is *identity without content* or the abstractly *pos-*

itive, i.e. the indeterminate' (*PR* §135). Or, as Hegel puts it in his *Lectures on the History of Philosophy*, freedom, on the Kantian view, turns out to be 'empty' because it is nothing more than 'the negative of everything else' (*das Negative alles anderen*) (*VGP* iii. 367/460).

This objection, which can be termed the *'empty formalism' objection* (*PR* §135), should be distinguished from a somewhat different objection that is woven together with it by Hegel in the Remark to §135. The second objection is directed at what Hegel terms 'Kant's further form', by which he means Kant's Categorical Imperative test for determining what particular ends and duties give content to an agent's freedom. Hegel argues that this procedure for giving content to morality and freedom is essentially indiscriminate (*PR* §135, A; *VGP* iii. 367–9/460–1; *Ph.G.* 316–23/252–62; *NL* 75–80). Kant's test requires that agents act only on maxims that they could at the same time will to be universal law. The core of Hegel's argument is the claim that *every* maxim is capable of passing this test and thus that every action counts as morally permissible and expressive of the agent's freedom. Kant's account of freedom is indiscriminate in the sense that it cannot distinguish free and moral actions from unfree and immoral ones.

Although there is a long tradition of endorsing this objection to Kant's Categorical Imperative test, most recent commentators agree that it is mistaken.[6] There is a natural interpretation of Kant's test according to which it clearly can generate contradictions and rule some maxims out without at the same time rejecting every maxim. If Kant's test is seen as looking for contradictions between (1) willing the purpose contained in the maxim and (2) willing that the maxim be universalized, then it clearly does have particular content and is not indiscriminate.[7] Contrary to what Hegel claims, in Kant's famous deposit example, for instance, there *would* be a contradiction,

[6] For sympathetic discussions of Hegel's objection, see Walsh, *Hegelian Ethics*, ch. 4; Taylor, *Hegel*, 371; and Smith, *Hegel's Critique of Liberalism*, 73–5. For recent attempts to defend Kant against the charge that the moral law is empty, see Korsgaard, 'Kant's Formula of Universal Law'; O'Neill, *Acting on Principle*, ch. 5; Wildt, *Autonomie und Anerkennung*, 84–96; and Wood, *Hegel's Ethical Thought*, 155–61. My discussion most closely follows Korsgaard.

[7] This is how Korsgaard interprets Kant's test in 'Kant's Formula of Universal Law'. Even if Korsgaard's interpretation of how *Kant* understood the Categorical Imperative test is incorrect, it remains the case that there is a non-vacuous *Kantian* understanding of the test. This is damaging to Hegel's critique, which is aimed at a whole approach to ethics (which he terms *Moralität* as opposed to *Sittlichkeit*) and not merely at Kant's own position.

because the agent would, in effect, be willing both that he increase his property (the purpose contained in the maxim) and that the means through which he intends to do this—the institution of deposit-leaving—not be present (the implication of universalizing the maxim); he would be willing both the end and the abolition of the proposed means.

The first, 'empty formalism' objection is, however, potentially much more damaging, and it is this objection and the possible responses to it that I want to explore in this chapter. The problem, as Christine Korsgaard has pointed out, takes the form of a regress and relates, in Kant's case, to the *derivation* of the Categorical Imperative rather than to its content.[8] We can imagine asking an agent why he acted as he did and his answering with an appeal to some desire or authority. We then ask him why he takes that desire or authority to be a reason-for-action and he responds by citing some further desire or authority. And so on. Eventually, the agent may simply put a stop to this chain of reason giving by insisting that some desire or authority constitutes his bedrock reason-for-action. If he does this, however, then he would not be fully free in Kant's and Hegel's sense because he would simply be accepting an external instruction that he could subject to his own thought and reason. On the other hand, if he does not put a stop to his deliberations in this way, then it seems that his chain of reasoning must extend *ad infinitum*. Either way, it seems that there never has been nor could be a rationally self-determining agent. Charles Taylor summarizes this argument effectively when he says:

> The dilemma of radical freedom can be restated succinctly as follows: if freedom is to renounce all heteronomy, any determination of the will by particular desires, traditional principle or external authority, then freedom seems incompatible with any rational action whatsoever. For there do not seem to be any grounds of action left, which are not wholly vacuous, that is which would actually rule some actions in and others out, and which are not also heteronomous.[9]

Hegel recognizes the challenge that this objection poses to his own view in an interesting passage from his 1824–25 lectures:

[8] Korsgaard, 'Morality as Freedom', 28; see also Wood, *Hegel's Ethical Thought*, 161–7; Pippin, 'Idealism and Agency in Kant and Hegel', 539; and Taylor, *Hegel*, 373, 559–62.

[9] Taylor, *Hegel*, 373.

> These are the two moments which belong to the will as such. The first is the negation of all that is particular, the second the negation of all indeterminacy; the first is the transition to indeterminacy, the second the transition to particularity; the first [is] to free myself from all determination, the second [is] to posit all determination. Every man will find these two determinations in his self-consciousness: this is freedom. Man appears now as a being full of contradictions; he is contradiction itself and only through this [contradiction] comes to consciousness. It is the power of spirit which can endure this contradiction within itself; no other natural being can exist with it. Spirit, however, is not merely the existence of this contradiction, but is just as much its resolution, and this is the concept of the will. (*VPR* iv. 118)

Here Hegel acknowledges that the will's 'negation of all that is particular'—the requirement that it refuse to recognize as a decisive reason-for-action any particular instruction from authority or desire that it might experience—is in conflict with the idea that the will has particular content, thus generating a 'contradiction' in human freedom. The more that abstraction and independence are emphasized as conditions of freedom, the more it seems that there never has been and never could be a free agent.[10]

It is precisely this objection that both Kant and Hegel must address in their arguments for the reciprocity thesis. They must show that an agent who is independent of all authority and of all his contingently given desires and inclinations does nevertheless have at least one reason-for-action and that is to follow certain ethical standards. Or, to express this in language introduced in Chapter 2, they must show that the will that has achieved 'infinite subjectivity', or independence of everything 'given', is still committed to, or 'passes over to', some set of objective, ethically oriented ends and principles.

3.3. *Kant's Argument for the Reciprocity Thesis*

Kant's most explicit statements of the reciprocity thesis can be found in the opening paragraphs of chapter III of the *Groundwork*[11] and in §5 and §6 of the Analytic in the *Critique of Practical Reason*.[12] Although the terminology is somewhat different in each version,

[10] As Allen Wood (*Hegel's Ethical Thought*, 163) has suggested, *Enz.* i, §54 also seems to manifest an awareness of this contradiction; see also *VGP* iii. 367–8/459–60.

[11] Kant, *Groundwork*, 446–7.

[12] Kant, *Critique of Practical Reason*, 28–9.

and, as Henry Allison has pointed out, the assumption of transcendental freedom is more explicit in the second *Critique* than in the *Groundwork*,[13] the basic argument in each text, I think, is more or less the same. Although this argument might be set out in a number of different ways, I have sought to reduce it down to three essential steps, focusing on Kant's proposition that the free will is necessarily subject to the Categorical Imperative.

(1) The first step is the assumption that a rational agent can and must have one or other of two sorts of reasons-for-action as the 'determining ground' of his action. His determining ground can and must consist either in (i) some given desire or inclination of his that will be satisfied by the action, or in (ii) the 'legislative form' of his 'maxim'—that is, its capacity to be universalized, or to be willed at the same time as a universal law for all rational agents. Kant identifies the first sort of determining ground with the 'material' or 'matter' of the agent's maxim or practical law and the second with the 'form' of that maxim or law.

(2) The second step appeals to a conclusion that we reached in the previous chapter in the context of exploring Hegel's conception of freedom as rational self-determination. To the extent that the agent is free or autonomous, it is not sufficient for him to appeal to some given desire or inclination as his reason-for-action any more than it is for him to appeal to some external authority; his determining ground must be something different.

(3) And the third step simply draws out the logical implication of the first two. To put it in Kant's own words: 'Therefore, the legislative form, in so far as it is contained in the maxim, is the only thing which can constitute a determining ground of the [free] will.'[14] In other words, a free will is a will that is subject to the demands of the Categorical Imperative.

Since the conclusion does seem to follow from the two premisses, and I have argued that something like (2) can be defended in terms of everyday ideas that we have about freedom, the weight of the argument must now fall onto (1). Is Kant justified in asserting that a rational agent must have as his 'determining ground' one or other of the

[13] Allison, *Kant's Theory of Freedom*, ch. 11; 'On a Presumed Gap in the Derivation of the Categorical Imperative', 10.

[14] Kant, *Critique of Practical Reason*, 29.

two sorts of reasons-for-action mentioned in (1)? I shall argue that he is not and that the argument therefore fails. In particular, I shall argue that there are two ways a Kantian might try to defend (1). On the first, (1) does not offer an exhaustive catalogue of the different kinds of reasons-for-action that an agent might appeal to in justifying his action. On the second, there is no defensible distinction between the two sorts of reasons mentioned in (1). Either way, the argument—which works by elimination—does not go through.[15]

The standard Kantian case for (1) is I think the following.[16] There are reasons-for-action that appeal to one's desires and inclinations and there are those that do not. Since what distinguishes one rational agent from another is the desires and inclinations they each have, reasons-for-action that are not grounded in desires and inclinations must be reasons that apply to any rational agent as such and in this sense have the property of universality. There are thus two sorts of reasons: those that appeal to desires and inclinations; and those that have the property of universality. But this is all that (1) says: for it says that there are two sorts of reasons-for-action that might serve as the determining ground of a rational agent—those that appeal to the agent's given desires and inclinations and those that appeal to the universalizability of the agent's maxim. Therefore, (1) is correct.

The problem with this argument is that it runs together two importantly different senses of universality or universalizability.[17] On one sense of the term, an agent's reason-for-action is universalizable, or has the property of universality, if and only if it is a reason for every rational agent as such. In a second sense, an agent's reason-for-action is universalizable, or has the property of universality, if and

[15] Obviously, this is just one possible line of criticism that might be pursued here. A second would be to argue that (1) is incoherent because it supposes that there are what Bernard Williams has called 'external reasons'—that is, reasons that an agent might have independently of his given desires, inclinations, commitments, projects, and so on (what Williams calls his 'motivational set'). Williams argues against the proposition that there are 'external' reasons on the grounds (*a*) that for something to qualify as an agent's reason it must be able to figure in an explanation of that agent's actions, and (*b*) that an external reason cannot figure in such an explanation (see Williams, 'Internal and External Reasons'). For criticisms of Williams's position, see Benn, *A Theory of Freedom*, ch. 2, and Korsgaard, 'Scepticism about Practical Reason'. As far as I can see, nothing in the argument of this chapter assumes either that there are or that there are not external reasons.

[16] See Kant, *Critique of Practical Reason*, 27, and *Groundwork*, 402.

[17] Here I follow Wood, *Hegel's Ethical Thought*, 161–7. See also Allison, *Kant's Theory of Freedom*, ch. 11, and 'On a Presumed Gap', 3–5; Hill, 'Kant's Argument for the Rationality of Moral Conduct', 19; and Bittner, *What Reason Demands*, 85 n. 187.

only if the agent could at the same time will that every relevantly situated rational agent act on that reason. These two senses of universality are clearly not equivalent. I am acting universally in the first sense when I can acknowledge that other similarly situated agents have reason to perform the same action as I do. By contrast, universality in the second sense requires not only that I be able to acknowledge that other agents have the same reason as I do but also that I be able to will that those others actually do what they have reason to do.

Allen Wood, who originated this line of objection, illustrates the distinction between the two senses of universality by imagining someone who acts on a Principle of Rational Egoism.[18] Such a person could conceivably acknowledge that every rational agent has reason to follow this principle and at the same time be thankful that other rational agents are too cowardly, or uptight, to do what they have reason to do. He could not *will* that others act from the Principle of Rational Egoism (because this might well conflict with his own pursuit of advantage), but he could acknowledge that they would be acting reasonably if they did.

The Kantian argument I outlined for (1) starts by assuming universality in the first weaker sense. The plausibility of this rests on the thought that an agent who does not have as his determining ground some desire or inclination (something that is particular to him) must then have as his determining ground some reason-for-action that applies to any rational agent as such. But the conclusion of the argument was then expressed in terms of universality in the second sense—that the determining ground of an agent's action must either be desire based or refer to the legislative form of the agent's maxim, to its capacity to be willed at the same time as a universal law for all rational agents. Since the two senses of universality are not equivalent, a gap in the argument for (1) clearly remains. As it stands, there seems to be no reason to think that the catalogue of possible reasons given in (1) is an exhaustive one; as the example of the rational egoist is meant to suggest, there could be non-desire-based reasons other than the legislative form of one's maxim.

Henry Allison has attempted to defend Kant against this kind of objection by arguing that it ignores Kant's explicit assumption of transcendental freedom: the freedom that consists in complete 'inde-

[18] Wood, *Hegel's Ethical Thought*, 164–5.

pendence from everything empirical and hence from nature generally'.[19] When transcendental freedom is plugged into the gap, he argues, it becomes clear that a Principle of Rational Egoism, say, could not in fact serve as a determining ground of the will. The reason for this is that principles such as the Principle of Rational Egoism covertly assume a 'material' determining ground of the will. 'Such a policy is deemed reasonable in the first place', according to Allison, 'only because of certain presupposed ends, which derive whatever justification they might possess from the agent's desires. Consequently, these desires and not the intrinsic reasonableness or lawfulness of the policy function as the "determining ground of the will".'[20]

In the previous chapter we explored the argument which claims that an agent who justifies his action to himself merely by appealing to some given desire lacks full freedom. Freedom requires that he stand back from his desire and reflect on whether it is a good thing that he act on it or not—that he advance a reason or justification on its behalf. Moreover, it is not enough that he justify his desire simply by appealing to some other desire of his, because then, as we saw in §3.2, the same question just arises again. Allison seems to be making the same point about the agent who attempts to justify acting on some desire by appealing to the Principle of Rational Egoism: to be free, he is claiming, the agent would have to be able to advance some reason or justification for following *that* principle. And what else could this be but some desire or inclination—reopening the whole problem once again? The objection to the Kantian defence of (1) fails, then, because principles that purport to be universal in the first sense but not in the second are not in fact universal at all: they covertly rest on some desire or inclination. Thus, if an agent's reason-for-action does not appeal to some desire or inclination, then it must appeal to the legislative form of his maxim—which is essentially what (1) says.

I think that Allison is right to insist that Kantian autonomy should require that the Principle of Rational Egoism itself be justified but wrong to think that he has thereby rescued (1) or Kant's attempt to show reciprocity between freedom and subjection to the Categorical Imperative more generally. The problem with Allison's argument is

[19] Allison, *Kant's Theory of Freedom*, 207; the quote is from Kant, *Critique of Practical Reason*, 97.

[20] Allison, 'On a Presumed Gap', 12.

this: if full autonomy requires that an agent rationally reflect on a principle such as the Principle of Rational Egoism, then, in the absence of some further argument or distinction, it surely also requires that the agent stand back and look for a justification for following the Categorical Imperative. Allison may be right to say that the Principle of Rational Egoism could only be 'deemed reasonable in the first place . . . because of certain presupposed ends', but would this not also be the case with the Categorical Imperative? Why would an agent recognize *this* principle as authoritative? Allison clearly thinks that the Categorical Imperative, unlike other possible principles, is *intrinsically* reasonable[21]—the agent need ask for no further justification—but this begs the question. Why could the Principle of Rational Egoism not be deemed intrinsically reasonable—thus protecting it from the justification requirement as well?

In effect, I am arguing that on Allison's defence of (1) the distinction between the two sorts of reasons-for-action mentioned in (1) collapses altogether. There are no longer any reasons that can be deemed to have the property of universality, because all reasons turn out to rest covertly on desires and inclinations. And, with the collapse of the distinction in (1), the overall argument clearly falls apart, since it proceeds by attempting to eliminate alternatives.

I suspect that at the back of Allison's mind may be two assumptions that are more explicitly made by Christine Korsgaard in her own discussion of Kant's reciprocity thesis.[22] The first is that a 'spontaneous' or transcendentally free agent—an agent who is independent of all authority and of all his contingently given desires and inclinations—has as a highest order reason or 'incentive' the preservation and promotion of his spontaneity, his independence of all empirical conditions. The second is that someone who had this incentive would reject, upon deliberation, every principle of action except the principle of acting on only those maxims that could at the same time be willed as universal law.

I will return to the first assumption later in the chapter when I look at Hegel's argument for the reciprocity thesis, so for now let me focus on the second assumption. It is important to note for a start that the second assumption is by no means obviously true, since it claims that an agent committed to the essentially *self-regarding* end of preserving and promoting his own spontaneity would necessarily reject the

[21] Allison, 'On a Presumed Gap', 12.
[22] Korsgaard, 'Morality as Freedom', 29–31.

Principle of Rational Egoism (which is also self-regarding) but endorse the *other-regarding* Categorical Imperative principle. So what argument does Korsgaard offer for this claim?

The only argument I can find is the rather disappointing one that 'The moral law does not impose a constraint on the will; it merely says what it has to do in order to be an autonomous will at all. It has to choose a law.'[23] This argument is unpersuasive because it trades on an ambiguity in the idea that the will must 'choose a law' that exactly mirrors the ambiguity in the term 'universality' that I explored earlier. Korsgaard may be right to say that the will must 'choose a law' if, by this, she means that it must always act on some reason or other, or even on some reason that applies to any rational agent as such. But, as I argued earlier, this is by no means equivalent to 'choosing a law' in the sense of acting on a reason (or maxim) that one could at the same time will that all other rational beings act on as well. It is not at all obvious why a will must 'choose a law' in this second sense 'in order to be an autonomous will at all'. Indeed, this is precisely what needs to be shown by Kant and his defenders. Thus, on Korsgaard's reconstruction, the gap in Kant's argument identified earlier reappears. We still need to know why a free agent would necessarily act not just on a maxim that any rational agent as such would follow, but also on a maxim that he could at the same time *will* that all other rational agents follow.

I conclude that Kant's argument for the reciprocity thesis cannot be judged a success. The argument, as I set it out at the beginning of this section, is a valid one, but its key premiss, premiss (1), is never adequately justified. Either premiss (1) does not offer an exhaustive catalogue of the different sorts of reasons-for-action that an agent might have, or the distinction it proposes seems to collapse. Whichever is the case, Kant's argument that morality and freedom are reciprocal concepts is, in the end, unsuccessful.

3.4. *Towards a Resolution: The Concrete Universal*

The preceding discussion not only vindicates a version of Hegel's 'empty formalism' objection but also gives a sense of just how difficult it will be for anyone to defend the reciprocity thesis. It is no

[23] Ibid. 30.

wonder that Hegel considers freedom a 'contradiction': once the will has negated all of its 'particular' commitments, it is not clear how there could be *any* reasons left to determine it to action. But Hegel is equally adamant that the contradiction *can* be resolved and he gives various suggestions about how this might be done. In one text he says that spirit is the solution (*VPR* iv. 118), in others that God provides the solution (*LPR* iii. 109), and in others that the 'concrete universal' provides the solution (*PR* §§7, 24). He also suggests that the agent who has abstracted from all of his particular desires and inclinations still has one end or purpose left: his own freedom (e.g. at *PR* §21).

There is no general consensus amongst Hegel commentators about what these different suggestions add up to, nor about how they might fit together into a coherent theory. We looked at some of the more influential views of Hegel's position in Chapter 1, including Charles Taylor's suggestion that the contradiction is resolved through a theory of cosmic spirit and Robert Pippin's interpretation emphasizing Hegel's 'historical notion of rationality'. I argued that, on their own, neither of these solutions to the problem of generating content for Hegelian freedom is fully satisfactory. It is now time to begin setting out an alternative account of Hegel's solution. To this end, I want to see what mileage we can get out of taking seriously Hegel's suggestions that the 'concrete universal' is crucial to his solution and that the free will somehow wills its own freedom.

Hegel distinguishes a concrete universal from the ordinary universals we use in our everyday understanding and reasoning (*PR* §24). The latter kind of universal, he thinks, merely picks out a property or element that a series of particulars share in common and therefore depends on the content of the particulars for its own content. Like an ordinary universal, a concrete universal has particular content, but, unlike this relationship of mere 'communality', it is not dependent on its particulars for its content but, rather, somehow generates them out of itself. The free will is an example of such a concrete, or self-particularizing, universal in that it need not appeal to its desires or inclinations to get particular content but generates determinate ends on its own (*PR* §24).

Hegel makes no serious attempt in the Introduction to the *Philosophy of Right* to elaborate his doctrine of the concrete universal but instead simply cites his treatment of the issue in his logic. Much of that account is impossibly dense and seems to do little more than reiterate the claims about concrete universality already referred to and link them up with other ideas and bits of jargon that Hegel introduces in the logic. Rather than attempt to reconstruct the doctrine as a whole, I want instead simply to draw attention to one interesting, and relatively accessible, claim that Hegel makes about the idea of a concrete universal, which seems highly pertinent to his understanding of freedom.

The claim is that a concrete universal can be understood in terms of Hegel's closely connected accounts of teleological and organic relationships. Teleology is discussed by Hegel in one of the concluding sections of his logic. A basic task of the discussion is to analyse the teleological relationship from three distinct perspectives: the first, 'subjective end', examines how an end or purpose can be viewed as 'an urge and a striving' that is purely subjective and opposed to the external world; the second, 'means', concerns the way in which the subjective end is mediated by objective reality; and the third, 'realized end', focuses on the transformed objective sphere that is achieved through the deployment of the various means (see *SL* 734–54; *Enz.* i, §§204–12). Hegel's interesting claim, from our point of view, is that the idea of a concrete, or self-particularizing, universal can be understood in terms of this teleological, or ends–means, relationship. 'End', he asserts, 'is the concrete universal, which possesses in its own self the moment of particularity and externality and is therefore active and the urge to repel itself from itself' (*SL* 739).

Some of Hegel's remarks about the concepts of organism and purposiveness in Kant's third *Critique* suggest a similar characterization of a concrete universal:

> [Kant] ascribes to the reflective power of judgement the principle of an intuitive understanding. That is to say, whereas the particular [*das Besondere*] had up to now appeared, so far as the universal of abstract identity was concerned, contingent and incapable of being deduced from it, it is now determined by the universal itself—as can be seen in the products of art and of organic nature. The outstanding feature of the *Critique of Judgement* is that, in it, Kant has expressed a representation [*Vorstellung*], even the thought, of the Idea. The representation of an intuitive understanding, of inner purposiveness [*innerer Zweckmäßigkeit*], and so forth, is thought of as a universal which is at the same time concrete. In these representations alone, then, the Kantian philosophy shows itself to be speculative. (*Enz.* i, §55)

Here it is implied that the idea of a concrete universal finds application in the products of organic nature, in particular, and in anything guided by 'inner purposiveness' more generally. The same theme is reinforced two paragraphs later where Hegel once again brings together the 'living products of nature' (*lebendigen Naturprodukte*), the teleological relationship, and the idea of a 'determining universal' (*bestimmende Allgemeine*): 'The principle which the reflective power of judgement applies to the *living products of nature* is determined to be the *end*, the active *concept* [*Begriff*], or the universal at once determining and determinate in itself' (*Enz.* i, §57).

Now, whatever else Hegel might mean by a concrete, 'determining', or self-particularizing universal, there is a relatively clear sense in which a purposively, or organically, understood entity can be thought of as generating its own particular content. An end, as Hegel observes in his discussion of teleology, points to certain specific means, which are instrumental to its realization. Likewise, an organism is an entity that adapts itself to ensure the realization of its goal of self-preservation. The 'content' of an organism—its parts or 'members'—consists in the means or conditions of its own survival: 'In the living thing [*im Lebendigen*] . . . the end is the immanent determination and activity of the matter, and every member is in its turn a means as well as an end' (*Enz.* i, §57; cf. *VGP* i. 382–4/332–3).

If a universal is viewed as in some way purposive or organic, then there is a straightforward sense in which it can be said to be self-particularizing and self-determining. A universal, so understood, generates a particular content in the sense that it points to a determinate set of particulars that must be deployed if its purpose is to be achieved. These particulars can be called its own, and thus self-generated, because they were already contained in the purpose of the initial, abstract determination: they are the conditions of the possible realization of that purpose. Despite the fact that certain particulars have been deployed, nothing is present at the end that was not there in the beginning.

I noted earlier that the free will, for Hegel, is an example of a concrete universal. It is worth mentioning that he also directly associates freedom with both teleology and the concept of an organism. He writes, for instance, that, 'Teleology possesses in general the higher principle, the concept in its existence, which is in and for itself the infinite and absolute—a principle of freedom that in the utter certainty of its self-determination is absolutely liberated from the external determining of mechanism' (*SL* 737; see also *SL* 747). And, in the *Lectures on the Philosophy of History*, he attributes an 'organic' structure to the free and rational will: 'The rational will alone is the universal principle which determines and develops itself independently and unfolds its successive moments as organic members' (*VG* 144/121; cf. *PR* §278 and *VGP* i. 382–4/332–3).[24]

These various remarks on concrete universals, teleology, and organicism, which have typically been ignored in discussions of Hegel's theory of freedom, suggest that a very simple and familiar idea about the content of self-determination may be at work in Hegel's thought. For all the jargon of the Introduction to the *Philosophy of Right*, he seems, at least in part, to have in mind the simple idea that a will is self-determining when and because its determinations contribute to the realization of its purpose. In some sense, at least, the generation of the content of freedom simply involves the application of Kant's famous dictum that 'he who wills the end, wills (so far as reason has decisive influence on his action) also the means which are indispensably necessary and in his power'.[25]

3.5. *The Recursive Structure of Freedom*

On their own these observations about Hegel's notion of a 'concrete universal' are not particularly helpful for generating content for the free will. Ends–means rationality generates particular commitments only where there are given ends, but this is exactly what seems to be missing in a will that has 'negated', or abstracted from, everything particular. To complete the argument Hegel would still need to show that there is some 'universal' purpose to which the free will as such is necessarily committed even when it has withdrawn from all desires, inclinations, and instructions of authority. If he can identify such a purpose, then the more particular content of freedom would (according to the interpretation of the 'concrete universal' sketched above) consist of the determinations that contribute to its realization. In order to bring an end to the regress that afflicts the conception of freedom as rational self-determination, the purpose in question must be a reason that the agent can appeal to in his practical deliberations but that is exempt from the justification requirement and so need not

[24] The organicism theme is most prominent in Hegel's account of the state, which is, of course, what he takes to be the locus of full, rational freedom. See *PR* §§267–9.

[25] Westphal also suggests that Hegel's 'argument rests on an unspoken principle much like Kant's principle of rational willing: Whoever rationally wills an end is rationally committed to willing the necessary means or conditions for achieving that end' (Westphal, 'The Basic Context and Structure of Hegel's *Philosophy of Right*', 247).

itself be subject to further deliberation. Kant, we saw, proposes the Categorical Imperative as such a foundational principle, but this proposal, I have argued, is hard to defend.

Hegel, on the other hand, puts forward what I think must be the only possible reason that can fit the bill. He maintains that, even when the will abstracts from all its contingently given desires and inclinations, and attempts to justify its action in terms of its own thought and reason alone, it remains committed to one important end: the end of promoting and sustaining its own independence and freedom. Although, as I suggested earlier, this idea is implicitly attributed to Kant by Korsgaard, it is much more explicitly assumed by Hegel.[26] For example, in the published text of the *Philosophy of Right* Hegel asserts that 'When the will has universality, or itself as infinite form, as its content, object, and end, it is free not only *in itself* but also *for itself*—it is the Idea in its truth' (*PR* §21). In his 1817–18 lectures, he claims that 'The will is *free*, however, in so far as it makes itself its object and content, and thus wills itself, that is, in so far as it wills to be free' (*VPR17* 39). And in his 1822–3 lectures, he says that 'The will in its truth is such that what it wills, i.e. its content, is identical with the will itself, so that freedom is willed by freedom' (*PR* §21A).

But why should this purpose—the aim of maintaining one's own freedom and independence—but not, say, Kant's Categorical Imperative be exempt from the justification requirement? Why does an appeal to this principle bring a halt to the regress? After all, an agent could come to question the end of freedom itself, and so, when he does not, we might think that he is simply accepting some externally given determination that he could subject to further scrutiny and examination. A serious weakness in Hegel's defence of the reciprocity thesis, and in his account of freedom more generally, is that he never explicitly addresses this question.

None the less, the end of promoting and sustaining one's own freedom and independence does seem different from other externally given determinations—and to this extent Hegel looks to be on the right track. The reason for this is that the commitment to promoting and sustaining one's own freedom and independence already seems to be presupposed by one of the constituting features of freedom: 'subjective freedom' (and especially 'infinite subjectivity'). To come

[26] Hegel himself joins Korsgaard in attributing the idea to Kant: see *VPG* 524–5/442–3; *VGP* iii. 366–7/458–9.

to the point where one is reflectively independent of one's given desires and inclinations requires a certain set of attitudes, goals, and capacities. It demands, for instance, a capacity and willingness to distance oneself from one's immediate desires and inclinations and to subject them to critical examination. It depends on the imagination to conceive of oneself living a different kind of life: an awareness of oneself as having options and alternatives. And it requires the self-discipline to tear oneself away from one's desires and inclinations in order to pursue one's true or authentic goals. Unless the agent has this set of attitudes, goals, and capacities, he could never engage in the kind of radical reflection and abstraction that sets up the regress problem in the first place. He would never ask the difficult questions about *who* he is, and what his *true* purposes are, that raise the problem of generating content for freedom.

So 'subjective freedom' and 'infinite subjectivity' are constituting parts of freedom and they seem to presuppose a commitment to the end of sustaining and promoting one's own independence and freedom. In this sense, it is possible to say that the end of sustaining and promoting one's independence and freedom is partly constitutive of free agency: one could not be a free agent, on Hegel's account, without being committed to this end. Looked at one way, the commitment to one's own freedom is just like other desires and inclinations one might experience: it will have animating force, it will be 'given' from 'outside', and so on. Nevertheless, if the above argument is correct, this 'desire for freedom' (*VPR* iv. 79) occupies a peculiar place in the structure of a free agent's practical reasoning: unlike his other desires, an agent can look upon this desire not as a limitation on his free agency, and thus as something that should be cleared away, but as the very basis of that agency.[27]

[27] It seems to me that Taylor is making a similar point in the following passage (*Hegel*, 93):

'Surely there must be some goal which is taken as the starting point, even if everything that is done is determined by strict reasoning from this basic aim. For otherwise how can reasoning by itself come to any conclusion as to what action to take? But then is this basic goal not simply given? The answer is, in a sense, yes. But not in a sense which need negate the radical freedom of *Geist*. For *Geist* can be thought to have as its basic aim simply that spirit, or rational subjectivity, be; and the rest can be thought to follow of necessity . . . But then the only input into this skein of rational necessity would be the goal, let rational subjectivity be. Once this "decision" is taken, the rest flows of itself. But it cannot be thought of as a limitation on the freedom of *Geist* that this "decision" is preformed. That subjectivity should be is not a limit on its freedom, but the very basis of it; and that it should be rational, i.e., expressed in conceptual consciousness, is thought by Hegel to belong to the very essence of subjectivity.'

If this conclusion is combined with the earlier argument about how the notion of a 'concrete universal' helps to generate content for freedom, then we arrive at the claim that the particular content of Hegelian freedom is given by the conditions for achieving freedom. A free or autonomous agent does not take any of his contingently given desires or inclinations, or any instruction from an external authority, as a sufficient reason-for-action but endeavours to determine his own activity by employing his own thought and reason alone. A decisive reason-for-action for such an agent, Hegel is claiming, involves an appeal to the end of developing and maintaining his own freedom. On the interpretation of the 'concrete universal' proposed earlier, this means that the particular content of freedom is given by the various determinations that are conditions of the realization of the end of developing and maintaining one's own freedom and independence.

Is this formulation circular? At first glance, it might seem so, since it is reasonable to suppose that the conditions of *x* can be identified only once we have some idea of the character or content of *x*. If this is right, then it is clearly not permissible to turn around and define the content of *x* in terms of the conditions of *x*. Although Hegel's formulation seems to violate this simple principle, there is in fact a way around the circularity objection open to Hegel. It involves once again recalling that freedom, on his account, has both a subjective and an objective dimension. The freedom whose 'particular content' Hegel is seeking to specify is 'objective freedom'. The conditions of freedom that generate this content on the interpretation I am proposing are the conditions of subjectivity: they are the various conditions of the development and maintenance of the attitudes, capacities, and self-understandings associated with being an independent, reflective, self-conscious agent.

Freedom, on this view, is not circular but *recursive*:[28] the determinations that give content to freedom turn out to be the ones that agents must pursue if they are to be in a position to deliberate about and pursue the ends and determinations that give content to freedom.[29] That freedom has such a recursive structure is suggested by Hegel in an important passage in the *Lectures on the Philosophy of History*:

[28] I am indebted to Michael Rosen for suggesting this term to me.

[29] Like 'the True' in Hegel's *Phenomenology*, then, freedom is the 'process of its own becoming' (*Ph.G.* 23/10; see also *PR* §23).

When the spirit strives towards its centre, it strives to perfect its own freedom; and this striving is fundamental to its nature. To say that spirit exists would at first seem to imply that it is a completed entity. On the contrary, it is by nature active, and activity is its essence; it is its own product, and is therefore its own beginning and its own end. Its freedom does not consist in static being, but in a constant negation of all that threatens to destroy [*aufheben*] freedom. (*VG* 55/48)

Here Hegel affirms that the process of 'striving' for freedom is fundamental to the nature of spirit. There is no 'static being' of freedom; only the dynamic process of establishing freedom and maintaining freedom, the process of negating all that threatens to destroy freedom. Freedom, on this view, consists in the perpetual struggle for liberation.[30]

3.6. *Completing the Argument*

Hegel's general strategy for defending the reciprocity thesis, then, will involve an attempt to show that in performing one's ethical duties one is somehow helping to establish and maintain one's own freedom; one is engaged in the 'constant negation of all that threatens to destroy freedom' (*VG* 55/48). Freedom consists in rational self-determination and this means engaging in actions that one can fully endorse on a rational basis. Freedom and ethics are reciprocally linked, because in acting ethically an individual is contributing to the realization of an end that is partially constitutive of his status as a free agent—the preservation and promotion of his own freedom. As

[30] Taylor comes close to recognizing this in the conclusion to *Hegel* (pp. 561–2). He claims that the only kind of situation that can give content to the radical view of freedom espoused by Kant and Hegel is one of struggling for liberation. The problem he argues is that, once liberation is achieved, nothing is left to generate further content for freedom: 'But liberation is understood as a process which *results* in freedom. On this view, there is no situation such that the response it calls for would *be* free action at its fullest extent as against just clearing the way to such action. Full freedom would be situationless. And by the same token, empty. Complete freedom would be a void in which nothing would be worth doing, nothing would deserve to count for anything.' Taylor concludes that Hegel sought to 'overcome this emptiness' by 'showing man to be the vehicle of cosmic reason, which generated its articulations out of itself'. If my interpretation of Hegel is correct, however, then there is, for Hegel, no 'result' or content of freedom independent of the struggle for liberation. Freedom consists in nothing other than a perpetual struggle to establish and maintain itself. It is only when the free will 'wills itself' in this way that it is engaging in an activity that it can reflectively endorse 'all the way down'.

I indicated earlier, however, this claim about ethics is by no means self-evident, as it seems to involve a jump from a self-regarding consideration (establishing and maintaining one's own freedom and independence) to an other-regarding one (a concern for the freedom and welfare of other members of the community). Why should acting ethically be considered a contribution to the development and maintenance of one's own freedom? Interestingly Hegel does have an account to offer here, and, although I want to postpone any detailed exploration of it until subsequent chapters, it is worthwhile just setting out some of its main steps now in order to give an indication of how the argument might be completed. Three steps are important:[31]

(a) The first is that Hegel assumes that the capacities, goals, and attitudes of a free agent—his commitment, for instance, to engaging in the kind of reflection and deliberation that is required by the conception of freedom as rational self-determination—are not a natural property of all adult human beings but are acquired only as a result of a process of education and socialization that he sometimes terms *Bildung*.

(b) Secondly, central to this *Bildung* process is the idea of recognition: Hegel holds that to become and remain a free agent one must enjoy the recognition of other agents. Moreover, famously, this is not a recognition that can be workably coerced out of others; it must be mutual. A necessary condition of developing and sustaining one's free agency, then, is that one be part of a community of mutually recognizing free agents.

(c) Finally, Hegel argues that a community of mutually recognizing free agents can itself be established and maintained only if agents are committed to the ethical requirements defined by certain institutions—the family, civil society, and the state. This is in part because recognition must be mediated by certain specific social customs and practices but also because a community of mutual recognition is likely to be a fragile construction that can be secured only if its members are sufficiently motivated by a concern for one another.

In summary, then, Hegel's case for the reciprocity thesis might be set out as follows. A free agent who abstracts from all given author-

[31] Points (*a*) and (*b*) are developed further in §§4.2 and 4.3 below. Point (*c*) is developed further in §§4.4 and 6.3.

ity or desire still has one reason-for-action: he has reason to establish and maintain his own freedom and independence. A failure to abstract from this end does not detract from the agent's freedom, since a commitment to this end is the very basis of engaging in the kind of practical reasoning that is constitutive of free agency. This foundational reason-for-action can then be developed into more specific reasons and ends by investigating what kinds of ends and arrangements are required if individuals are to become and remain free agents. The argument for the reciprocity thesis is completed with a defence of the claim that one crucial condition of becoming and remaining free is that agents must, in general, be committed to the ethical requirements of their community. By acting ethically, an agent is contributing to the development and maintenance of his own subjectivity and thus *is* objectively free.

4
Hegel and Social Contract Theory

4.1. *Introduction*

One of Hegel's central aims is to provide his contemporaries with reasons to feel reconciled with the main institutions and practices of their social world. Hegel hopes to develop an account of the rationale of institutions such as the family, civil society, and the state, and of practices such as punishment, attributing responsibility, and showing concern for the welfare of others, that can convince his fellow Europeans to affirm and accept these pervasive features of their social life rather than feeling alienated and unfulfilled. His main strategy in pursuit of this aim is to demonstrate that the major institutions and practices of modern European societies are all instantiations of what he calls 'right' (*Recht*), a term he defines to mean 'any existence in general which is the *existence* of the *free will*' (*PR* §29). Thus, Hegel's intention is to reconcile his contemporaries to their social world by showing that it is 'the realm of actualized freedom' (*PR* §4). He thinks he can establish that, if his fellow Europeans think deeply enough about what it is to be free, and about what the implications of this freedom are for the way in which the social world should be arranged, then they will come to see that their social world is a 'home': far from being something alien, it represents the essential condition and locus of the full realization of their freedom.

In taking freedom to be the fundamental principle of his project of reconciliation,[1] Hegel acknowledges an important debt to Rousseau, Kant, and Fichte. 'It was the achievement of Rousseau to put forward the *will* as the principle of the state,' he writes, 'a principle which has *thought* not only as its form . . . but also as its content, and which is in fact *thinking* itself' (*PR* §258). 'It is a great advance', he adds in discussing Kant's practical philosophy, 'when the principle is established that freedom is the last hinge on which man turns, a highest possible pinnacle, which does not allow itself to be impressed by

[1] The phrase 'project of reconciliation' is from Hardimon, *Hegel's Social Philosophy*.

anything, so that man allows no authority, or anything else, to be valid if it goes against his freedom' (*VGP* iii. 367/459).[2] But, although Hegel agrees that freedom constitutes the fundamental axiom of moral and political argument, he strongly rejects the contractarian account of social and political legitimacy that Rousseau and his followers take to be an implication of that axiom: 'Marriage cannot . . . be subsumed under the concept of contract . . . The nature of the *state* has just as little to do with the relationship of contract, whether it is assumed that the state is a contract of all with all, or a contract of all with the sovereign and the government' (*PR* §75). This attitude to his predecessors provokes a number of questions that I want to explore in this chapter. How can Hegel both accept the starting point of social contract theory (the commitment to freedom) and reject what social contract theorists take to be an obvious implication of that starting point (the contractarian account of legitimacy)? And what alternative account of social and political legitimacy does Hegel think he can draw from the principle of freedom?

In a remark in his 1822–3 lectures, Hegel distinguishes between two possible approaches to political philosophy, one of which is clearly identifiable with contractarianism, the other with his own view:

> there are always only two possible viewpoints in the ethical realm: either one starts from substantiality, or one proceeds atomistically and moves upward from the basis of individuality [*Einzelheit*]. This latter viewpoint excludes spirit, because it leads only to an aggregation, whereas spirit is not something individual [*Einzelnes*] but the unity of the individual [*Einzelnen*] and the universal. (*PR* §156A)[3]

The problem I want to address is this: how can Hegel start from an apparently individualist premiss shared with contractarians—that freedom is the basis of right—and then end up deploying what might be termed a 'communitarian' style of argument—one that focuses on

[2] Hegel also acknowledges his debt to Rousseau, Kant, and Fichte at *VGP* iii. 306–8/400–2, 413/503.

[3] Earlier in the same passage Hegel says that 'The spirit has actuality, and the individuals [*die Individuen*] are its accidents.' Both *Individuum* and *Einzelne* can be translated as 'individual'. In contexts like this, Hegel seems to use *Einzelne* to refer to the atomized individual and *Individuum* to refer to the individual as he is constituted by society (see also *PR* §258). This is a good illustration of one the central tenets of the present chapter: that Hegel is not concerned to ignore or devalue the free individual as such, only to discredit atomistic modes of understanding individuality that ignore the ways in which the community works to constitute individuals as free and rational. I am grateful to Hans-Jakob Wilhelm for drawing my attention to Hegel's distinction between *das Individuum* and *der Einzelne*.

the 'substantiality' of the ethical realm and on determinations of 'spirit'? The problem, it seems to me, is not just of antiquarian interest. Individualists often talk as though communitarian political theorists are caught in a dilemma: either there is nothing really that distinctive about their approach (for all the fine words about community); or their approach does manage to be distinctive but only in a sinister way that threatens individual freedom. It will be interesting to see whether Hegel's alternative to the individualism espoused by social contract theorists is able to escape this dilemma: whether it can succeed at being genuinely 'communitarian' in its approach without abandoning its concern for the freedom of individual human beings.

The standard picture of Hegel's relationship with the social contract tradition emphasizes two points. The first is that, for all his praise of Rousseau and other contractarians, Hegel's starting premiss is really quite different from the one that these theorists have in mind. This is because what Hegel means by freedom is quite radically different from what a contractarian would understand by the term. Whereas an open-ended, individualistic conception of freedom lends itself to a social contract theory of political legitimacy, Hegel's more rationalist, less individualist, conception naturally leads to an account of spirit. The dispute between Hegel and social contract theorists, then, is ultimately a disagreement about how best to interpret the concept of freedom.[4]

A second point that is commonly made in discussions of Hegel and social contract theory allows that Hegel's theory does manage to retain a very weak link between individual freedom and political legitimacy. But he does this, it is argued, only by insisting that, even if the state is not established by the voluntary decisions and actions of individuals, one characteristic of a good state is that it is subjectively assented to and affirmed by its members. This way Hegel does not entirely cancel, but also manages to preserve, a role for the individual will in political legitimacy. As Patrick Riley puts it, for instance, 'In the absence of will in any active sense in Hegel's theory of the state—not only contract theory but also most elections, participation, opinion, and conscience conventionally defined are denigrated—what is left is will as recognition, above all as acceptance of the rationality of the universal.'[5]

[4] See e.g. Riley, *Will and Political Legitimacy*, 167, 173, 182, 191–3, and Taylor, *Hegel*, 365–76.

[5] Riley, *Will and Political Legitimacy*, 192; see also pp. 192–4, 199.

There is certainly some measure of truth in this standard picture, particularly as far as the first point is concerned. It is not difficult to locate passages in Hegel's writings and lectures in which he suggests that his main disagreement with contractarians concerns how best to interpret the concept of freedom. One aim of this chapter, however, is to show that Hegel's critique of social contract theory is considerably deeper than this and should be taken seriously by anyone starting from contractarian premisses. If we conclude that divergent interpretations of the concept of freedom are all that divide Hegel and social contract theory, then we are likely to underestimate the force of his criticisms of that theory and understand only incompletely the precise character of his alternative.

The second element in the standard picture also has a grain of truth in it, in so far as Hegel does build into his conception of the state an element of subjective affirmation or patriotism (see §6.2 below). If the argument of this chapter is correct, however, it would be a mistake to suppose that this moment of subjective freedom that is secured by the state constitutes the sense in which Hegel claims to be grounding his theory of political legitimacy in freedom or the will. A major theme of the chapter will be the importance that Hegel attaches to the ways in which the major institutions of the modern community work to develop and sustain individual free agency. This function of *constituting* free individuals risks being ignored by contractarians, who typically view community (in particular the state) in more instrumental terms. Hegel's alternative strategy of starting from the substantiality of the ethical order is, in effect, an attempt to determine what a community must be like if it is to be successful in fulfilling its function of developing and sustaining free agency.

In the previous chapter we examined Hegel's approach to generating 'particular content' for objective freedom. It was argued that a determination is prescribed by reason, in Hegel's view, and thus gives content to objective freedom when it helps to foster and maintain the conditions of the agent's own subjectivity. When a determination satisfies this requirement, an agent can look upon it, not as a limitation on his free agency, but as consonant with a commitment that is a constituting feature of that agency. At the end of the chapter I very briefly indicated how attributing this recursive view of freedom to Hegel can help to explain why he thinks that objective freedom is realized through commitment to the duties and virtues of modern *Sittlichkeit*. By committing himself to these duties and virtues, I suggested, the agent is willing his own freedom because these duties and virtues contribute to the realization of a structure that fosters and stabilizes freedom. The argument of the present chapter will help to corroborate and fill out the last part of this reading of Hegel's position. If the interpretation to follow is correct, then one of the central ways in which Hegel is seeking to present the institutions and practices of the modern social world is as forming a structure that works to develop and sustain the capacities, attitudes, and self-understandings that make up free agency.

4.2. *Hegel's Critique of Social Contract Theory*

Hegel shows some awareness of the diversity within the social contract tradition that he criticizes. In the *Philosophy of Right*, for instance, he invokes the distinction between the view that the state is a contract of all with all and the view that it is founded on a contract of all with the sovereign (*PR* §75).[6] He also distinguishes between the contractarianism of 'earlier times', which he associates with the aristocratic reactionaries of his own day (who view political rights and duties as the 'immediate private property of individuals' to be bartered with the state)[7] and the social contract theories of 'more recent times' (*PR* §75). Hegel does not, at §75, mention any particular social contract theorists by name but seems to assume either that his criticisms would apply to a range of different formulations of social contract theory or that his intended audience would be familiar with the theories he discusses and would know from the context which particular claims, by which particular thinkers, he was attacking.

At *PR* §258 Hegel singles out Rousseau and Fichte for criticism, and it seems likely that their versions of social contract theory are foremost in his mind. It is less clear whether he would include Kant's theory of the social contract amongst the targets of his criticisms. As will become apparent from the discussion to follow, Hegel's main

[6] For a good discussion of this distinction, see Gough, *The Social Contract*, 2–3.

[7] This variant of contractarianism is discussed most extensively by Hegel in his 1822–3 and 1824–5 lectures (*VPR* iii. 265–72 and *VPR* iv. 251–4 respectively). See Losurdo, *Hegel et les libéraux*, ch. 3, for a good treatment of Hegel's account. As Losurdo points out, those who take Hegel's anti-contractarianism to be a mark of his conservatism tend to overlook the fact that Hegel directs his criticisms at radical democrats such as Rousseau *and* reactionary German conservatives who had taken up the rhetoric of contractarianism in defence of their feudal privileges.

criticism of social contract theory does not really work against Kant's 'hypothetical' formulation of the theory. Unlike Rousseau and Fichte, Kant agrees with Hegel's contention that we have a duty to belong to a rational state whether we have consented to such an arrangement or not.[8]

The central claim of social contract theory, as Hegel interprets it, is that the state is 'based on', or 'grounded in', the individual (or 'principle of the individual will').[9] The following, for instance, is a fairly typical characterization of social contract theory for Hegel: 'According to Rousseau, self-sufficient individuals, as atoms, constitute the foundation of the state' (*VPR19* 82). More specifically, he takes social contract theorists to be grounding the state in the *Willkür* (choice, discretion) of the individual as this is expressed in the decision to give or withhold consent to a social contract. This characterization of social contract theory remains extremely vague, however, to the extent that it fails to specify what aspects of the relationship between individual and state are said to be grounded in individual consent. A survey of passages in which Hegel discusses social contract theory reveals at least three different ways in which he further specifies what precisely is being grounded in individual consent:

(1) whether or not a 'state' ('union within the state', 'government', 'people') is to be 'established' ('founded', 'brought into existence');
(2) whether or not the individual has a duty to become and remain a member of the state (or simply 'to be in the state');
(3) whether or not 'the sovereign and the state' are to be regarded as having (certain) rights.

Noticeably absent from these formulations is any explicit recognition of the claim—central to much social contract theory—that consent determines:

(4) whether or not the individual has a duty (or obligation) to obey the law (and perhaps to support the state in other ways).

[8] See Kant, 'Metaphysical First Principles of the Doctrine of Right', in *The Metaphysics of Morals*, §42; and *Political Writings*, 79.

[9] Hegel's main discussions of social contract theory can be found at: *PR* §§75, A, 258; *VPR17* 58; *VPR18* 267–8; *VPR19* 82, 212–13; *VPR* iii. 265–72; *VPR* iv. 251–4; *VG* 116–18/98–9, 145–6/122; and *VGP* ii. 107–8/92–3, 226/208. My characterization of Hegel's interpretation of social contract theory in this paragraph and the next draws on these sources.

It is reasonable to suppose, however, that Hegel does intend formulations (1)–(3) to imply (4). For one thing, the idea of a duty of membership referred to in (2) is itself vague and needs further filling out (as does the idea of a state 'existing' referred to in (1)). It could mean something fairly minimal, like a duty to reside on a territory in which an effective state is up and running, or it could, more demandingly, involve having a duty (or obligation) to obey the state (and perhaps to support it in other ways). The second, stronger interpretation is supported by Hegel's discussion of membership in Part III of the *Philosophy of Right* (and the corresponding lectures), where the notion of membership in ethical institutions (including the state) is strongly associated with having certain duties to those institutions (§§148, 149, 155, 261). The latter include 'the duty to submit to the court's authority' (§221) and duties to perform certain 'services and tasks . . . on behalf of the state' (§261), including military service if the state's independence is at risk (§§324–6). Formulation (3) is also frustratingly vague in so far as it fails to specify what kinds of rights the state is said to acquire through the consent of individuals. The most obvious right that Hegel may have in mind, however, is the right to make authoritative rules and decisions—a right that is traditionally thought to correlate with the individual subject's duty to obey. If this is what Hegel means—and he clearly does accord such a right to the state—then he does indeed recognize something like formulation (4) in his account of social contract theory, and we should read him as offering a critique of it.

Hegel's most general objection to social contract theory is that it misapplies the norms and principles of the bourgeois sphere of civil society to the normative theory of the state. 'The intrusion of this relationship [of contract], and of relationships concerning private property in general, into political relationships has created the greatest confusion in the normative theory of the state [*Staatsrecht*] and in actuality' (*PR* §75). 'To apply the contract relationship here is a complete distortion' (*VPR* iii. 266). As these passages suggest, there is, for Hegel, an important distinction between the spheres of *Privatrecht* and *Staatsrecht*: the norms and values that it is appropriate to appeal to in one sphere are not those of the other (cf. *VPR* iii. 269). Social contract theory ignores this distinction by treating the questions of membership, authority, and obligation as though they were essentially problems of bargaining and exchange.[10]

[10] Some eighteenth-century German contractarians really do go quite far in using the language of commercial transactions to describe the normative foundations of the

On its own, however, this objection is not very persuasive unless Hegel can tell us why it is inappropriate to treat *Staatsrecht* as continuous with *Privatrecht*. A social contract theorist might argue that there is nothing wrong with applying the norms and principles that prevail in civil society to the political sphere: an ideal of consensual exchange is essential to both, it might be contended, because this ideal is grounded in the principle of freedom itself.

In opposition to this view, Hegel argues that, because social contract theory insists on respecting individual choice (*Willkür*) and consent, it ends up treating membership, authority, and obligation as though they were optional (*PR* §75, A, §258; *VPR17* 58). Individuals may choose to enter into the state, or they may not; they may legislate some set of institutions for the state, or they may not; they may recognize the authority of the state and assume certain obligations, or they may not. Against this implication of social contract theory, Hegel cites Aristotle's dictum that 'a man who could live alone would either be an animal or a god' (*VPR19* 210; cf. *VGP* ii. 227/208) and asserts that 'it is the rational destiny [*Bestimmung*] of human beings to live within a state, and even if no state is yet present, reason requires that one be established' (*PR* §75A). 'It is false', he adds, 'to say that the *Willkür* of everyone is capable of founding a state: on the contrary, it is absolutely necessary for each individual to live within the state' (*PR* §75A). 'It is not optional [*ein Belieben*] for men, whether they enter into a state or not, but rather it is their absolute duty to do so' (*VPR19* 210; cf. *VPR18* 232). Hegel's argument, then, is that, since contracts are the product of individual choice or *Willkür* (they are entered into at the discretion of the contracting parties), they provide too capricious (*zufällig*) and unreliable a foundation on which to build the authority of the rational state. Or, to return to the earlier formulation, his claim is that it is inappropriate to apply the norms and principles of contractual relationships to the political sphere, since, unlike a commercial transaction, there is nothing optional or discretionary about being a member of a rational state: some political arrangements are reasonable and legitimate, and therefore owed allegiance, whether they are agreed to or not.

Against an argument of this form defenders of social contract theory might respond in one of two ways. They might argue that Hegel seriously underestimates the degree to which contractarians

state. According to Gough (*The Social Contract*, 175) Justus Möser, for instance, compares civil society to a joint-stock company in which each citizen is a shareholder.

already place rational constraints on what individuals can and cannot freely agree to. To take one prominent example, John Locke never equates the freedom he attributes to individuals in the state of nature with the kind of wildly arbitrary and contingent choice that Hegel seems to have in mind but is always careful to insist that it is a rational freedom, bounded by the laws of nature, that they are assumed to possess.[11] Rousseau has a similar idea in mind when he asserts that 'to say that a man gives himself [to slavery] freely, is to say what is absurd and inconceivable; such an act is null and illegitimate, from the mere fact that he who does it is out of his mind'.[12] And Fichte makes it plain that the character of institutions like the state is not to be left up to the discretion of individuals but derived from the law of right.[13] While Hegel's objection may be valid against certain extreme and implausible voluntarist strands in the contractarian tradition, this suggests that it may not be so forceful against the more subtly constructed theories of thinkers such as Locke, Rousseau, and Fichte.

This rejoinder does not help against Hegel's objection, however. It is true that Hegel generally paints an excessively voluntarist picture of contractarianism, which fails to acknowledge any rationalist dimension in contractarian thought. But social contract theorists such as Locke, Rousseau, and Fichte never go so far as to connect the freedom they attribute to individuals in the state of nature with any positive requirement to join and remain in a rational state, nor do they say that individuals have a duty to obey and support such a state independently of whether they have given their consent. On the contrary, one of their most distinctive theses is that authority and political obligation are grounded in the freely given consent of individuals: the decision to join and remain in any particular state is ultimately a matter for individual choice and discretion and nobody has any duties *vis-à-vis* a state until and unless he has given his consent.

Consider, for instance, Fichte's account of the relationship between consent, on the one hand, and political membership and obligation, on the other.[14] A central argument of the *Grundlage des Naturrechts* is that a certain form of community, ultimately includ-

[11] Locke, *Two Treatises of Government*, 288–9, 301–2.
[12] Rousseau, *The Social Contract*, 186.
[13] Fichte, *Grundlage des Naturrechts*, 14.
[14] See also Locke, *Two Treatises of Government*, 348–9, and Rousseau, *The Social Contract*, 190, 193, 277.

ing property and the state, is needed to constitute agents as free individuals. As Frederick Neuhouser points out, it is reasonable to suppose that, on this view, 'it no longer seems to be a matter of arbitrary choice whether or not we enter such a political order'.[15] However, as Neuhouser recognizes, this does not appear to be Fichte's position. According to an early passage of the *Grundlage des Naturrechts*, Fichte's argument will characterize the principle of right (*Rechtsbegriff*) that would govern a community of free beings *if* such a community is realized. *Whether* such a community is realized is at the discretion of individuals (*ist . . . etwas Willkürliches*).[16] Several pages later, Fichte explicitly affirms the necessity of consent (*Einwilligung*) for obligation to the laws of a particular state:

> That I must adapt myself to just these particular men arises because I live with them in society; but I live with them in society because of my free resolution, and in no way out of an obligation. This is applicable because of the civil contract [*Bürgervertrag*]: it is originally in the free choice [*in der freien Willkür*] of every man whether he wills to live in this particular state, although, if he wishes to live with men [in general], then it is not a free choice whether to enter into some state or other . . . But, as soon as he expresses his will to enter into a particular state, and is accepted into it, he is thereby, through this mere mutual declaration, completely restricted by all the laws required of this group of men . . . Through these few words—I will to live in this state—he accepts all of the laws . . . [The material of the law is given by the law of right] . . . But the form of the law, its binding power, is given for the individual only through his consent.[17]

It is the views expressed in this passage that Hegel wants to challenge. Hegel's claim is that the state is not based on a contract, because individuals already have a duty to belong to, and obey, the state whether or not they have given their consent.

An alternative rejoinder would start by conceding that contractarians do view authority and political obligation as ultimately matters for individual choice (albeit a choice that is constrained by certain rational norms and principles). And this does indeed mean that there is a theoretical possibility that individuals will decide not to enter the state at all or will stubbornly decide to establish a state that is irrational or unstable (although in practice this is unlikely to be the case since the uncertainties and inconveniences of the state of nature,

[15] Neuhouser, 'Fichte and the Relationship between Right and Morality', 169 n. 23.

[16] Fichte, *Grundlage des Naturrechts*, 10–11.

[17] Ibid. 14–16 (cf. p. 107).

together with the fundamental human drive to sociability, give individuals an overwhelmingly powerful motivation to set up a rational state) or that they will not recognize the authority of the state or the corresponding political obligations. But leaving open this possibility is necessary if an account of political authority is to show respect for the value of individual freedom. It is because freedom is the first principle of normative justification for contractarians that they insist that the decision to enter into a state on certain terms is ultimately a matter for individual choice. The implication of Hegel's claim that the rational state is necessary, and that individuals have a duty independently of their consent to belong to and obey it, is to deny the value of freedom and to belie Hegel's claim to have grounded his view in freedom.

This formulation of the contractarian view brings us to the crux of what divides Hegel and social contract theorists. When the argument is put in this form, Hegel thinks, it relies on an untenable analysis of freedom. This is, in part, for a reason I mentioned in §4.1. To the extent that social contract theory equates freedom with the capacity for individual choice (*Willkür*), Hegel maintains that it is working with a false and unattractive conception of freedom (*PR* §258; *VGP* iii. 307/402; *VG* 117–18/99). To equate freedom with the capacity for choice is to allow that an agent who chooses to follow his own unexamined desires and inclinations is fully free. For reasons that I explored in Chapter 2, however, Hegel thinks that 'giving in' to one's desires and inclinations is no more a case of freedom than is submitting to an authority: both are cases of allowing something external to determine for one what one could think through for oneself. Against contractarians, Hegel urges that freedom has an objective dimension: a condition of being free is that one engage in reasonable choice—that one follow one's own thought and reason. Hegel concedes, then, that his view of membership, authority, and obligation neglects individual freedom—but only if freedom is wrongly identified with *Willkür* (*PR* §29; *VG* 117–18/99; *VPR17* 92). If, on the other hand, freedom is understood in Hegelian terms—if it has the structure we examined in the preceding two chapters of this study—then it turns out that the state is no restriction on freedom but rather is the locus of its highest realization.

It follows that at least part of what divides Hegel and social contract theorists is the problem of how best to conceive of freedom. Contractarians such as Rousseau and Fichte share Hegel's view that a form of rational freedom is realized in the state that is not possible outside it,[18] but they also attach great importance to the more open-ended freedom of *Willkür*. By contrast, Hegel thinks that the kind of freedom that is relevant to thinking about the authority of the state and the source of our political obligations is concrete freedom: it is a freedom that includes objective freedom and thus can be tied to specific duties and virtues, including the duty to be a citizen of a rational state. Contractarians may conclude from this that the Hegelian challenge to social contract theory is grounded in too controversial a premiss to be of much concern. They might even go so far as to argue that Hegel can claim to have grounded his communitarian alternative to social contract theory in the value of freedom only by perversely adopting a conception of freedom that is the very opposite of how that term is ordinarily understood.

In Chapter 2 I defended Hegel's general conception of freedom against objections of this form and in Chapter 6 I will examine, again from a broadly sympathetic perspective, his particular thesis about the realization of concrete freedom in the state. In the present chapter, however, I want to challenge the standard assumption that Hegel's main disagreements with social contract theory boil down to the issues of how best to conceive of freedom and whether freedom, adequately conceived, has the duties and virtues of citizenship as its content. Even if a broadly contractarian conception of freedom is conceded, I will argue, Hegel has an interesting critique that ought to be taken seriously by proponents of social contract theory.

The decision to give or withhold the consent that establishes the authority of the state is made from the standpoint of what social contract theorists call the 'state of nature' (*Naturzustand*). A major assumption of social contract theory is that agents are free in the state of nature. It is because of a concern to respect the freedom of individuals in the state of nature that social contract theorists impose the consent requirement. And, of course, if individuals were not free in the state of nature, then they would not be able (validly) to give or withhold their consent. The question is what exactly is being packed into this assumption of natural freedom. It is obvious that social contract theorists would want to avoid the full, Hegelian notion of freedom that is realized only through citizenship, but it does not follow that they would favour reducing freedom to the mere capacity for

[18] See Rousseau, *The Social Contract*, 196, and Fichte, *Grundlage des Naturrechts*, 104.

choice. If freedom is something valuable, if it is worth respecting in the state of nature, then the freedom involved must be something more than arbitrary choice; it must be something like 'autonomy' or 'self-government'.[19] On this view, the freedom being attributed to agents in the state of nature by social contract theorists must comprise some of the capacities that Hegel associates with subjective freedom and that are important for shaping and directing one's own life: capacities for reflection, deliberation, analysis, self-discipline, and so on. These capacities are also important if individuals in the state of nature are to be considered capable of giving their consent. One reason why young children are deemed unable to give their consent is that they lack some or all of these capacities.

Against the assumption that individuals would naturally possess such capacities, Hegel argues that the state of nature would be a state of animal impulse and savagery. 'We are accustomed to starting from the fiction of a state of nature, which is certainly no state of spirit [*Zustand des Geistes*], of rational will, but of animals amongst one another. The true state of nature is a war of all against all, as Hobbes very correctly remarked' (*VGP* ii. 108/92; cf. *PR* §194; *VG* 117/99; *Enz.* iii, §502; *VPR17* 38; *VPR18* 212).

Now on the face of it this seems a rather odd criticism, since (as Hegel's own reference to Hobbes suggests) it is contractarians themselves who tend to emphasize the uncertainties and inconveniences of the state of nature: it is because the state of nature is such an inhospitable environment that free and rational individuals *have reason* to set up authoritative political institutions. Hegel's point, however, cannot be so easily deflected. His claim is not just that the state of nature would be an inhospitable place to live but that the very capacities for freedom and reason that are cherished by social contract theorists would not be present in the state of nature. The attitudes and capacities that make up free and rational agency cannot reliably be developed and sustained in the state of nature but only in the context of social institutions, including the rational state.

This claim is implicit in Hegel's suggestion that human beings in the state of nature are little different from animals. For Hegel, the

[19] This formulation is explicit in A. J. Simmons's sophisticated contemporary defence of consent theory: 'Because many of us agree with Locke about the importance of the individual's right of self-government or autonomy, we are with Locke drawn to the conclusion that consent is the only ground of political obligation and authority that is consistent with the natural moral freedom to which we are committed' (*On the Edge of Anarchy*, 74).

defining feature of animals, as opposed to human beings, is that they are not free: because they lack the mental complexity necessary to evaluate and regulate their impulses, they cannot be said to be self-determining in anything but the weakest sense (*PR* §4A; *VG* 57/50, 175/144; *Enz.* i, §96A; *Enz.* iii, §381A). The argument is more explicitly made in the *Lectures on the Philosophy of World History*:

> Freedom as the ideal condition of what is as yet purely immediate and natural does not itself possess an immediate and natural existence. It still has to be earned and won through the endless mediation of discipline acting upon the powers of cognition and will. For this reason, the state of nature is rather a state of injustice, of violence, of uncontrolled natural impulses, and of inhuman deeds and emotions. It does involve some restrictions imposed by society and the state, but such restrictions are imposed only on those brutal emotions and crude impulses already referred to, on reflected inclinations, on the needs which arise with the progress of culture, and on arbitrariness and passion. Restrictions of this kind are part of that process of mediation whereby the consciousness of freedom and the will to realize it in its true (i.e. rational and essential) form are engendered . . . Such restrictions are the indispensable conditions of liberation; and society and the state are the only situations in which freedom can be realized. (*VG* 117–18/98–9)

Hegel's view is that human beings in the state of nature are, in effect, like children: they have the potential for freedom and reason but that potential has not yet been realized.[20] For that potential to be unleashed they must undergo an often arduous process of self-formation and education, which Hegel occasionally refers to as *Erziehung* (*PR* §174, A; *VPR17* 106), which simply means education or upbringing, but, more often than not, calls *Bildung* (*PR* §§57, 187). *Bildung* is the general term used by the German *Aufklärer* to designate both the process of education and acculturation that an individual or people must go through to achieve freedom and rationality, and the result of that process. An individual undertakes *Bildung* in the schoolroom and at the knee of his parent or *précepteur*, but also, Hegel is claiming, in the broader context of his social, cultural, and even political experience.[21]

[20] Hegel draws the analogy between the state of nature and childhood at *VPR18* 205, 212. For further passages in which Hegel asserts the necessity of society and state for the development of free and rational agency, see *VPR17* 38 and *VPR19* 210.

[21] Hegel describes *Bildung* at *PR* §187 and *VPR19* 57, 63. For two good discussions of the concept, with specific reference to Hegel, see Gadamer, *Truth and Method*, 9–19, and Kelly, *Idealism, Politics and History*, 341–8.

Hegel's most interesting objection to social contract theory, then, is that it operates with an excessively instrumental view of state and society. It imagines that human beings with fully developed capacities for free and rational agency choose to adopt major social institutions in order to advance their ends and interests. For Hegel, this picture makes the 'common error of taking crude peoples to be free' and thus ignores the 'absolute worth of *Bildung*' (*VPR19* 64–5). In the absence of social institutions such as the rational state, human beings could not develop and maintain capacities for freedom and reason and thus could not possibly be in a position to give or withhold their free consent. As Hegel puts it in his *Lectures on the History of Philosophy*, social contract theory assumes that the 'universal' can be separated from the 'individual'—'as if the individual could on its own [*an und für sich*] be what it presently is, and the universal did not make it that which it is in truth' (*VGP* ii. 108/93). Put more plainly, contractarian thought forgets or ignores the important role that social institutions have to play in constituting the free and rational individuals whom they take for granted.[22]

If Hegel's argument can be sustained, then it follows that, far from being the only account of political legitimacy that takes seriously the value of individual freedom, contractarianism risks undermining the very attitudes and capacities that make up free agency. To the extent that social contract theory allows that it is optional for individuals whether they contract into the rational state, the possibility opens up that the individual freedom that contractarians so greatly cherish will not be realized at all. Hegel, by contrast, can argue that, because 'society and the state are the only situations in which freedom can be realized' (*VG* 118/99), we have reasons grounded in the value of freedom to affirm and accept social institutions even if we have not given them our consent. He clearly envisages an alternative to social contract theory that will seek to articulate the social and political arrangements that provide the context in which the capacities for freedom and reason can develop and flourish. Thus, whereas social contract theorists start by asking 'What arrangements, if any, have free and rational individuals consented to be part of?'—leaving open the possibility that they did not consent to be part of the arrangements required to nourish their capacities for freedom and rationality—Hegel, by contrast, can be thought of as asking a somewhat

[22] For a forceful recent statement of this argument, see Taylor, 'Atomism'.

different question: he asks, in effect, 'What social arrangements must be in place if individuals are to develop and sustain their capacities for freedom and rationality?'

As I have already suggested, this whole critique ignores the possibility that the social contract is hypothetical. Hegel's argument turns on the assumption that, for contractarians, a condition of the legitimate authority of major social and political institutions is that those institutions enjoy the actual consent of all of their members. It is this assumption that opens up the theoretical possibility that individuals might undermine the very freedom that contractarians seek to respect by failing to consent to the rational state. At least some social contract theorists, however, notably Kant, never claim that the contract is an actual historical event and thus do not hold, as Hegel implies, that the obligation to obey the state is grounded in actual consent.[23] Instead, these theorists treat the social contract as what Kant calls an 'idea of reason'—an idea that may lack empirical reality but which none the less necessarily regulates our thinking about right and justice. Their idea is to explore what social (and, in particular, political) arrangements it would be rational for individuals to consent to from an appropriately defined initial situation. This emphasis on what it *would* be rational to choose, rather than on what individuals (who often behave irrationally) *actually* choose, means that they can avoid Hegel's objection by arguing that it would be irrational for individuals not to select institutions that foster and encourage their capacities for free and rational agency.[24]

Hegel, it seems to me, can, should, and perhaps does (he never singles Kant out for criticism on this issue) accept this argument, since it effectively concedes the main point that he wants to make. In particular, it concedes the point that the project of grounding political authority in the freedom of the individual is not to be carried out by asking whether institutions enjoy the actual consent of their members but by appealing to certain criteria of reasonableness that are independent of the actual choices and decisions that people make. Moreover, even if Hegel's objection is damaging only against more voluntarist strands of the social contract tradition, he can still claim to have reminded contractarians in the Kantian tradition of

[23] See Kant, *Political Writings*, 79, 143, and 'Metaphysical First Principles of the Doctrine of Right', in *The Metaphysics of Morals*, §42.

[24] Rawls, for example, is sensitive to this kind of consideration in his discussion of the basic liberties in *Political Liberalism*, lecture VIII, pp. 310–24.

the non-instrumental value of social institutions—the ways in which they work not just to advance and protect the interests of free and rational agents but actually constitute agents as free and rational in the first place.

There are several objections to Hegel's position that seem more difficult to handle, however. One possible objection is that Hegel confuses the conditions of the initial acquisition of the capacities for free and rational agency with the conditions of the maintenance of those capacities. It is plausible to think that an individual born and raised outside certain forms of community with others would not develop the attitudes, capacities, and self-understandings associated with free and rational agency. But it does not follow from this that an individual, having developed into a free and rational agent, could not then freely decide to leave the community that made him who he is. There is a passage in Fichte's *Grundlage des Naturrechts* that hints at just such an argument:

> It is indeed proven that, if a rational being is to come to self-consciousness, and so become a rational being, it is necessary that he should be influenced by an other, as someone capable of reason . . . That, however, once self-consciousness has been posited, a rational being must continue rationally to influence the subject is not in this way posited . . . The postulate that community between two free beings should continue to take place appears from this to be arbitrary—as something which each being must freely commit himself to.[25]

Against an objection of this form, Hegel might conceivably respond by arguing that it ignores people who have yet to develop the required capacities, including members of future generations. If the present generation decides to opt out of a community of the required form, then they are denying future generations of conditions under which they can become free and rational agents. A political theory starting from the principle of freedom ought to be concerned with *securing* the freedom of all individuals, including children and members of future generations, and not just with *respecting* the freedom of those who have already managed to develop free and rational agency. Alternatively, Hegel might challenge the assertion that the conditions of the development and maintenance of the required capacities are relevantly different. If he can show that maintaining free and rational agency, and not just developing it, also requires liv-

[25] Fichte, *Grundlage des Naturrechts*, 87–8.

ing in a community of a certain form, then he will still have a reason grounded in freedom for endorsing that community, independent of whether consent has been given or not.

A different objection has the most potential for damage and pushes Hegel to be more forthcoming about the precise character of his alternative to social contract theory. An important assumption of Hegel's argument is that the state is one of the social institutions that is necessary for the development and maintenance of free and rational agency. Without this assumption, Hegel's argument is effective only against those contractarian theories that assume a state of nature that is not just pre-political but also pre-social. However, it is not at all obvious that the assumption is defensible. It is plausible to say that the capacity for free and rational agency is a product of some social institutions or other (and hence that any view that assumes a pre-social view of the state of nature is likely to be unsustainable). But why should we accept Hegel's claim that the rational state is necessary for the *Bildung* of the free individual? He says, for example: 'Man is himself *free*, and in possession of himself, only through *Bildung* . . . The formation [of man] to freedom itself, and the realization and maintenance of this freedom, is the state.'[26] But why does Hegel think that the state plays such a crucial role in the development and maintenance of free and rational agency? Only if he can provide an adequate response to this question can his critique be of real concern to contractarians.[27]

4.3. *Recognition as the Foundation of Hegel's Alternative to Social Contract Theory*

So far I have argued that Hegel's most fundamental objection to social contract theory is that it ignores the social and political

[26] See p. 125 of the German edition of the *Philosophy of Right* for this handwritten note.

[27] Gough objects that Hegel 'fails to distinguish between society and state, and attributes to citizenship what is more truly due to membership of society' (*The Social Contract*, 185). Objections of this form against Taylor's atomism argument are developed by Leslie Green (*The Authority of the State*, 197–200) and A. J. Simmons (*The Lockean Theory of Rights*, 112–14). As Green puts it, 'The crucial step for our purposes therefore remains to be taken. We need to establish, not just that the free individual is a product of a certain kind of society and therefore must support the social conditions of such freedom, but also that such support is not possible, or not complete, without conceding the moral authority of the state' (p. 200).

conditions under which free and rational agency can be developed and sustained. Social contract theory, as Hegel understands it at least, takes it that respecting individual freedom means making it a condition of the legitimacy of major social institutions that they enjoy the consent of all of their members. But, in so doing, it forgets or ignores the role that social and political institutions have to play in constituting free individuals in the first place. Somebody who is committed to the value of human freedom already has reason to feel reconciled to certain social and political institutions, whether or not he has consented to be a part of them.

Hegel concludes from this criticism that a more defensible approach to the problem of reconciliation must focus on the 'substantiality' of the ethical realm rather than starting from the 'isolated individual' (*PR* §156A; *VGP* ii. 108/93, 226–7/208). In saying this, he takes himself to be reviving Plato's idea that an account of justice in the polis is methodologically prior to an account of justice in the individual (*VGP* ii. 105–8/90–3). Just as for Plato an understanding of justice in the individual requires an exploration of the nature of a well-ordered polis, so for Hegel working out the implications of a concern for the freedom of the individual paradoxically requires abandoning the standpoint of the individual in favour of an account of a community of individuals.[28] Hegel's strategy for reconciling his contemporaries to the major institutions and practices of the modern European social world will involve arguing that those institutions and practices are necessary for the development and maintenance of the capacities for free and rational agency. Like social contract theory, this approach starts from a commitment to human freedom, but unlike that theory (in Hegel's view) it is sensitive to the social and political basis of the capacity for freedom.[29]

The problem for the remainder of the chapter will be to try to elucidate the precise way in which Hegel goes about demonstrating that the major institutions and practices of the modern social world are necessary for the *Bildung* of free individuals. As I suggested at the end of the previous section, this problem is especially pressing in the

[28] Hegel also credits Aristotle with this insight: 'Aristotle does not place the individual and his rights first, but recognizes the state as what in its essence is higher than the individual and the family, for the very reason that it constitutes their substantiality' (*VGP* ii. 226/208).

[29] Thus Hegel hopes to integrate Plato's organicism with Rousseau's commitment to human freedom: see *VGP* ii. 129/115. For discussion, see Pelczynski, 'Political Community and Individual Freedom in Hegel's Philosophy of the State', 58–9.

light of a natural contractarian objection to Hegel's project, which concedes that some social institutions may be crucial for *Bildung* but seeks to salvage the social contract project by denying that these institutions must include the state. The focus of the present chapter will be on setting out the framework in which Hegel means to approach objections of this kind. Detailed consideration of Hegel's account of the state will be postponed until Chapter 6.

One way in which Hegel could proceed at this point is to embark upon an empirical investigation of the social conditions under which the capacities for free and rational agency are developed and sustained. Such an investigation might face huge practical difficulties, but it at least seems to be asking the right sort of question. For better or worse, however, this is not Hegel's style: he explicitly denies that the method of his social philosophy will depend on any empirical generalities or on what he terms 'the assertion that various circumstances *are present*' (*PR* §31). Instead, he thinks that he can provide an a priori deduction of the general sorts of practices and institutions (although not the contingent details (*PR*, Preface, p. 25/21)) that are essential to the development and maintenance of the capacity for free and rational agency.[30] This apriorism is clearly a weakness in Hegel's approach, given that he is making what look to be empirically falsifiable claims about the relationship between individual development and social institutions. But even a strict empiricist could concede that Hegel's 'logical' deduction of the necessity of certain institutions and practices helps to suggest new hypotheses about the relationship between individual and society by showing various social arrangements in a new light. This is no doubt a much less ambitious characterization of Hegel's project than he would want to endorse, but it does not contradict what he was trying to achieve (since he assumes that the empirical sciences would confirm his conclusions) and it has the virtue of pinpointing what is of enduring philosophical interest in that project.

The foundation of Hegel's attempt to show the necessity of certain practices and institutions is his theory of recognition. The theory of recognition provides the bridge between the concern for the development of individual freedom and the focus on the social institutions and practices that make up a community of free individuals. It

[30] Hegel holds that 'philosophy has the empirical sciences to thank for its development' and, in exchange, shows the conclusions of those sciences to be necessary by providing them with an a priori basis (*Enz.* i, §12).

constitutes Hegel's explanation of why the development of free and rational agency is ultimately a social and political process.

For Hegel, the problem of how an agent develops and reinforces a capacity for free and rational agency is primarily a problem of how he can arrive at and sustain the right sort of self-understanding. When an agent is unfree, or a 'slave', as Hegel often puts it, this is usually due not to his chains but to his underdeveloped self-conception or self-understanding. The problem with the slave, Hegel claims, lies in his will, which 'does not yet know itself as free and is consequently a will with no will of its own' (*PR* §26A; cf. *VPR19* 73). 'The basic principle of all slavery', he thinks, 'is that man is not yet conscious of his freedom' (*VG* 225/183; *PR* §57). If the slave could only think, or take, himself to be free, then he would become free:

> everything depends on the spirit's self-awareness; if the spirit knows that it is free, it is altogether different from what it would be without this knowledge. For if it does not know that it is free, it is in the position of a slave who is content with his slavery and does not know that his condition is an improper one. It is the sensation of freedom alone which makes the spirit free. (*VG* 56/48; cf. *VPR17* 55)

Individuals remain unfree in the state of nature, Hegel claims, because they lack this 'sensation' or 'thought' of their freedom (*VPR17* 38).

What Hegel seems to have in mind here is the idea, first introduced in §3.5 above, that the possession of a certain set of goals, attitudes, and capacities is an indispensable condition of subjectivity. These include: the capacity and willingness to distance oneself from one's immediate desires and inclinations in order to subject them to critical examination; the awareness of having options and alternatives in one's life; and the self-discipline needed to tear oneself away from one's desires and inclinations in order to pursue one's own true or rational goals. Hegel mentions some of these different capacities and attitudes in a passage in his *Lectures on the Philosophy of World History*: the individual achieves *Bildung*, he says, when he is 'accustomed to adopt a theoretical attitude', 'to control himself', 'to renounce particularity and act in accordance with universal principles', 'to analyse the situation before him', and to 'isolate' different aspects of that situation and 'abstract' from them (*VG* 65–6/57). Unless an agent has this set of attitudes, goals, and capacities, which together form a distinctive self-understanding, he could never engage in the kind of reflective choice that is the hallmark of free and rational agency.

Hegel's account of recognition seeks to explain how individuals could come to have, and to reinforce, this self-understanding or consciousness of their freedom. It is in the account of recognition that Hegel investigates the conditions under which agents can gain a sense of their own subjectivity or achieve what he calls 'self-certainty'. The struggle for recognition, he says, is 'a necessary moment in the *Bildung* of all men' and represents 'the *beginning* of true human freedom' (*Enz.* iii, §435A).[31]

The basic premiss of Hegel's account is that an agent can achieve self-certainty, or confirmation of his freedom and independence, only through interacting with his environment. Simply telling himself that he is free is not enough: 'the assertion that one is free does not suffice to make one so' (*Enz.* iii, §431A; cf. *Ph.G.* 148/113).[32] To establish an identity as free and independent, an agent needs to see that he is actively affecting other things or people—that his will is making a difference in the world—and that he is not dependent on these things—he is not a plaything of outside forces and authorities. Hegel considers three possible ways in which an agent might interact with his environment in order to achieve this self-certainty: (1) he can assert his independence *vis-à-vis* non-human material objects by 'negating' them; (2) he can force other human agents to recognize his independence; or (3) he can enjoy the freely given recognition of other human agents.

On model (1), agents attempt to affirm their independence by demonstrating the nothingness of their material environment. The general thought seems to be that an agent can show that he is independent by maintaining his existence despite altering or destroying

[31] My understanding of Hegel's account of recognition is greatly indebted to Wood, *Hegel's Ethical Thought*, ch. 4. Other good discussions include Kelly, 'Notes on Hegel's Lordship and Bondage'; Taylor, *Hegel*, 148–57; and Williams, *Recognition*, ch. 8. For an interpretation of Hegel's account of recognition that seeks to link the issue of how subjects can confirm and reinforce their sense of independent agency to Hegel's broader philosophical concerns (in particular those of the *Phenomenology of Spirit*), see Pippin, *Hegel's Idealism*, ch. 7, and 'You Can't Get There from Here'.

[32] In discussing Hegel's account of recognition, I have drawn upon relevant passages from the *Phenomenology* as well as the *Encyclopaedia* and lecture materials from the 1820s included in standard editions of the *Encyclopaedia*. The mixing of 'early' and 'mature' work by Hegel seems appropriate in this case, since Hegel explicitly refers the reader back to the *Phenomenology* discussion of recognition at several places in the *Philosophy of Right* (*PR* §§35, 57).

the objects that surround him. I prove that I am not dependent on coffee, for instance, by outlasting the disposal of my coffee beans and the transformation of my *cafetière* into a vase. In fact, Hegel thinks that simply altering, or giving a new form, to an object is not sufficient for an agent to establish his own independence: it shows only that he is not dependent on the object in its present form, not that he is independent of its matter as such (say, in some different form) (*Enz.* iii, §428A). The only fully adequate means of establishing independence, on this model, is for the agent to negate his material environment completely by destroying it.

The obvious problem with model (1) is that it is self-defeating. The complete negation of an agent's material environment can lead only to his own death, which is clearly not the kind of self-confirmation he is after. Even if the agent manages to escape this outcome, the approach is self-defeating in that it requires the destruction of precisely that (the material object) in which he finds his self-certainty. Once the object is eliminated, all that remains is the agent's *memory* of his act of independence, and this seems too much like simply *asserting* to oneself that one is free—which, we have seen, is never, in Hegel's view, sufficient for self-certainty. The very success of the agent's striving for confirmation of self brings about its own frustration and failure: 'the desire is again generated in the very act of satisfaction' (*Enz.* iii, §428). The agent never properly achieves confirmation of his independence but is always forced to find some new object for negation. Because of his 'perpetual relapse into subjectivity from objectification', the agent 'never absolutely attains his goal but only gives rise to the progress ad infinitum' (*Enz.* iii, §§428A–429A).

What is really needed is an object that can be negated, and thereby confirm the agent's independence, without destroying itself in the process—a kind of 'standing negation', as Charles Taylor puts it.[33] This brings us to model (2), which involves one agent forcing another to recognize his freedom and independence. What weakens an agent's sense of independence, we have seen, is his apparent dependence on his surrounding environment. Systematically destroying this environment is not a workable solution, but there is, Hegel wants to argue, an alternative: the elements that make up the environment can themselves negate the apparent ties of dependence by acknowledging the

[33] Taylor, *Hegel*, 152.

freedom and independence of the agent. The only kind of element that is capable of this act of self-negation through recognition is another agent. An agent, Hegel concludes, can achieve the desired sense of independence, or self-certainty, only through the recognition of his fellows: 'self-consciousness achieves its satisfaction only in another self-consciousness' (*Ph.G.* 144/110). 'Self-consciousness exists in and for itself when, and by the fact that, it so exists for another; that is, it exists only in being recognized [*als ein Anerkanntes*]' (*Ph.G.* 145/111). The thought behind this transition is hard to make out, but Hegel seems to have in mind the kind of situation in which an agent lacks a sense of independence, say, because he feels dependent on his friends for support and security. One, ultimately self-defeating, solution to this problem is for the agent to break off his friendships. Another, Hegel appears to be suggesting, is for his friends to treat him in ways that reassure him that he is not dependent on them but rather acknowledge his freedom and independence.

It looks, then, as though an agent can achieve the desired self-certainty by successfully forcing another agent to recognize him as free and independent. Agents, it would seem, have a reason to get others to recognize them in this way, even if it means risking their lives (in fact the risking of life is an essential part of the story, as we shall see in §4.4). This, of course, is precisely what the master seems to have been successful at doing in Hegel's parable of the struggle for recognition and its institutional resolution in the form of the master–slave relationship. In this arrangement, Hegel notes, we find, albeit in a distorted form, 'the emergence of man's social life and the commencement of political union' (*Enz.* iii, §433). Only in the context of social life can an agent be free, Hegel thinks he has shown, because only by living with others does he develop and maintain the capacities, goals, and attitudes that freedom requires.

Famously, however, Hegel goes on to argue that the particular kind of social recognition that is found in the master–slave relationship turns out to be just as self-defeating as the mode of self-certainty proposed by model (1). Part of Hegel's argument involves pointing out that the master remains a passive consumer of the goods prepared for him by the slave and thus cannot satisfy himself fully that he is independent of his desires and inclinations. The slave, by contrast, is driven by his fear of the master to learn how to resist and control his own desires and thus gradually gains a sense of his own agency (*Enz.* iii, §435A). The more direct way in which model (2) turns out to be self-defeating is that it ignores the important truth that recognition, if it is to contribute to self-certainty, must be given *freely*. The recognition by the slave really amounts to nothing more than a mere *assertion* by the master that he is free, for the slave recognizes the master only because the latter coerces him into doing so. But, as we have already seen, it is not sufficient, in Hegel's view, for the achievement of self-certainty that an agent simply assert that he is free. Some kind of independent confirmation is required.

This failure of model (2) brings Hegel finally to (3), in which the agent achieves self-certainty by receiving the free recognition of other agents, whom he acknowledges as free in return. 'I am only truly free', on this view, 'when the other is also free and is recognized by me as free' (*Enz.* iii, §431A).

> The master confronted by his slave was not yet truly free, for he was still far from seeing in the former himself. Consequently, it is only when the slave becomes free that the master, too, becomes completely free. In this state of universal freedom, in being reflected into myself, I am immediately reflected into the other person, and, conversely, in relating myself to the other I am immediately self-relating. (*Enz.* iii, §436A)

Hegel's claim, then, is that the only way in which an agent can conclusively affirm his own sense of agency and independence is as part of a community of mutually recognizing free agents. Only in such a community do agents have truly independent grounds for taking themselves to be free.

This conclusion helps us to see more precisely why Hegel thinks it is so problematic for social contract theory to assume that individuals have the capacities for freedom and rationality in the state of nature. The possession of these capacities presupposes that individuals have a certain self-understanding—that they have what Hegel terms a 'consciousness of their freedom' (*PR* §57; *VPR17* 55; *VG* 225/183). The acquisition of this self-understanding, in turn, requires that individuals participate in stable patterns of mutual recognition. But because the state of nature is a condition of war of all against all, it is a condition in which the struggle for recognition has not yet been resolved. As Hegel puts it in his 1817–18 lectures on *Rechtsphilosophie*:

> When [the individual] does not freely enter into [the state], he places himself in the state of nature, where his right is not recognized and the natural

process whereby he becomes recognized, through the struggle for recognition and through power, must still come about . . . If the individual has the particular will not to be in the state, then he wills an immediate existence, and he puts himself against the state in the state of nature; he must enter into a struggle with the state. The free agent must have his knowledge in another self-consciousness; this is his higher existence . . . The individual can only have this existence through being recognized by the will of another. (*VPR17* 145–6)

For Hegel, the mistake made by contractarians is to overlook the fact that it is only through the state that the struggle for recognition can be resolved and thus that agents can acquire the very capacity for free and rational agency that social contract theory presupposes. 'Only in the state is the recognition of freedom complete' (*VPR19* 74).

We can also see more clearly the direction in which Hegel's alternative to social contract theory is meant to proceed. His claim that reconciliation must start from the substantiality of the ethical order rather than the isolated individual is grounded in the thought that it is only in a community of free individuals, in which stable patterns of mutual recognition have been established, that it is possible to talk of human freedom at all. The proper aim of a philosophy committed to the value of human freedom is not to investigate what arrangements individuals have consented to, but to work out what a community of mutual recognition must be like—what social and political arrangements it must contain. If Hegel can show that certain arrangements—for example, certain institutions, practices, rights, duties, virtues, and so on—are necessary features of such a community, then he is in a position to provide his contemporaries with good reasons to feel reconciled with those arrangements.

4.4. *Social Institutions as Mediating and Stabilizing Recognition*

What remains unclear is just how Hegel proposes to derive the necessity of particular social and political arrangements from the general requirement that a community of mutual recognition be established and maintained. It seems especially unclear why the *state* should be considered a necessary feature of such a community, and yet Hegel seems committed to showing that it should be if his critique of social contract theory is to be valid against versions of the theory that assume a pre-political but not a pre-social state of nature. Otherwise contractarians can argue that the state of nature *is* sufficiently constituted as a community of mutual recognition for the capacities to be developed that allow individuals to make an intelligent and free choice about entering into the state.

The crucial step in Hegel's argument that mutual recognition has specific institutional implications is his idea that mutual recognition needs to be *mediated* by institutions and practices. Hegel's claim is that two or more individuals can recognize each other as free and rational agents only *through* specific institutions and practices in which they are participating. To this extent, a community of mutual recognition can be realized only if it has a certain objective institutional structure. This is one reason why Hegel thinks that *Geist* is necessarily embodied (*PR* §66): *Geist* cannot fully realize itself without giving itself some 'existence' (*Dasein*) that mediates the mutual recognition of the individuals who constitute it.[34]

To locate in Hegel's thought the idea that recognition must be mediated, we need to return briefly to an unresolved problem that remains from his initial treatment of recognition. In the struggle for recognition, agents are led by a need to affirm their sense of agency to attempt, through force, to extract the recognition of their fellows (I referred to this earlier as model (2)). This attempt involves the risking of life in a deadly combat with the other. The combat arises, in part, because *both* agents are concerned to achieve the desired sense of their own agency: neither is willing to give up the goal of liberation without putting up a fight.

But the risking of life in combat is important for Hegel's account for another reason as well. In order to *attract* the recognition of the other, the agent needs to do something to *show* the other that he is free: each self-consciousness has, as Hegel puts it, the 'drive to *show* [*zeigen*] itself as a free self, and to be as such for the other' (*Enz.* iii, §430). The other's recognition that I am free needs to be *mediated* by some demonstration by me of my freedom and independence. Risking my life in combat is this kind of demonstration: it shows that I am indifferent to, and not dependent on, my natural existence. 'At this stage', Hegel explains, 'man demonstrates his capacity for freedom only by risking his own life and that of others' (*Enz.* iii, §431A; cf. *Ph.G.* 149/114).

[34] For discussion of Hegel's 'principle of necessary embodiment', see Taylor, *Hegel*, 80–94.

The violent struggle between agents is clearly of limited duration. It leads eventually either to the death, or to the surrender, of one of the combatants, the latter case setting up the master–slave relationship. This relationship raises an important problem: now that the combat is in the past, what mediates the recognition of the master by the slave? Now that he is no longer risking his life, what *existence* does the master give his freedom, such that the slave can recognize him as free? How does he *demonstrate* his freedom to the slave?

The answer, of course, is that the master does *not* adequately demonstrate his freedom and this is exactly the defect of the master–slave relationship: having won the battle, he slips back into a passive life of consumption and sensuous pleasure. The slave recognizes the master because he is forced to, not because there is something indicative of free agency in the master's activity. It is the slave, if anyone, who gives an objective recognizable existence to his agency through his disciplined activity of formative work (*Ph.G.* 153–5/117–19).

The failure of the master–slave relationship is resolved by the transition to 'universal self-consciousness' (model (3)) (*Enz.* iii, §436), which is Hegel's term for a community of mutually recognizing free agents. It is important to note, however, that even in this community the need for recognition to be mediated still arises. Given that agents are no longer risking their lives in battles with one another, they need to find some alternative means of demonstrating to one another that they are free. They need to manifest their agency in ways that can attract the recognition of the other. Hegel acknowledges this problem and gestures at the solution in a lecture version of his account of recognition. The individual, he claims, 'makes himself worthy of . . . recognition' by showing himself to be a rational being: he does this by obeying the law, by filling a post, by following a trade, and by other kinds of working activity (*Enz.* iii, §432A).

It seems to me that there is also a second, equally important way in which recognition requires mediation for Hegel, although it is harder to find general formulations of this requirement in Hegel's texts. Just as mutual recognition requires that individuals find ways of attracting the recognition of the other, it also demands that they find ways of *expressing* their recognition of the other—something that may require specific institutions and practices. The claim that '*X* recognizes *Y* to be a free and rational agent' necessarily entails, for Hegel, at least three different sub-claims: (*a*) that *Y* demonstrates to *X* that he is free and rational; (*b*) that *X* has a thought or representation of *Y* as free and rational, *and* (*c*) that *X* manages to express or communicate this thought to *Y*. Without element (*c*), recognition could not possibly have the beneficial impact on *Y*'s sense of himself as a free and rational agent that Hegel anticipates. Of course, it might be argued that recognition is expressed simply through language and thus that the expression requirement has no specific institutional or practical implications. But Hegel's assumption is that, since actions can, on the one hand, belie words and, on the other, reinforce them, the expression requirement does show that recognition needs to be mediated by specific institutions and practices. Part of the rationale behind the institution of contract, the practice of showing love for one's partner, friends, or children, and the requirement that the state treat its members as equals before the law, to mention just a few of Hegel's examples, is that these are all means by which recognition is expressed and in this sense mediated.

Hegel claims that the standpoint of the *Philosophy of Right* is beyond the stage at which spirit must attain a consciousness of its freedom through the struggle for recognition (*PR* §57). However, it would be a mistake to conclude from this that the derivation of social arrangements in the *Philosophy of Right* will have nothing to do with recognition. (An equally natural way of understanding Hegel's claim is to take it as saying that the *Philosophy of Right* is beyond the standpoint where spirit attempts to attain a consciousness of its freedom through a struggle for supremacy or through the master–slave relationship.) In the *Philosophy of Right*, and the associated lectures, Hegel returns to the theme of recognition time and time again, emphasizing in particular the ways in which the institutions and practices he discusses work to mediate mutual recognition and thus reinforce individuals' consciousness of their freedom.

For instance, in the published version of 'Abstract Right', Hegel notes that 'I am free for the other only in so far as I am free in my existence' (*PR* §48) and explicitly relates this assumption to his accounts of property and contract (*PR* §71; cf. §§40, 51). He makes much the same point in his 1819–20 lectures ('In order to become recognized as free, I must also show myself to be free in my existence' (*VPR19* 73–4)) and is even more explicit there and elsewhere about the ways in which this requirement underlies his accounts of property and contract (*Enz.* iii, §§490–1; *VPR17* 48, 56–7; *VPR18* 231).[35] Hegel also sees crime as

[35] I discuss Hegel's justification of property in Chapter 5 below.

a form of negative recognition in which the criminal denies, rather than affirms, that his victim is a free and rational being and thinks that punishment is a way of negating this negation (*VPR17* 68, 71, 130). He holds that civil society is the domain in which mutual recognition is most fully realized (*PR* §238; *VPR17* 125, 130; *VPR18* 264; *VPR19* 72), in part because it secures the freedoms of property and contract, but also because it is the sphere in which individuals can attract the recognition of others by taking a position in an estate and showing industriousness, skilfulness, rectitude, honour, and so forth, in performing the functions of that position (*PR* §§244, 253; *Enz.* iii, §432A; *VPR17* 124; *VPR19* 194–6).[36] He thinks that the rule of law is another way in which the validity of the rational will is recognized by others (*PR* §217A), he maintains that love and friendship are forms of mutual recognition (*PR* §158A; *Aesthetics* 562),[37] and he even claims at one point that fashion and imitation are ways in which individuals attract the recognition of others (*VPR17* 113; *VPR18* 260–1).

Thus it seems that one way in which Hegel proposes to move from the general idea that a community of mutual recognition must be established to an attempt to reconcile his contemporaries with specific social and political arrangements is by arguing that certain particular arrangements are required to mediate recognition and, to that extent, to make a community of mutual recognition possible.[38] A

[36] The connection between being a member of an estate and attracting the recognition of others is one of the main reasons why Hegel worries that the poor and unemployed will be reduced to a 'rabble' (*Pöbel*): 'The poor man feels excluded and mocked by everyone, and this necessarily gives rise to an inner indignation. He is conscious of himself as an infinite, free being, and thus arises the demand that his external existence should correspond to this consciousness . . . Self-consciousness appears driven to the point where it no longer has any rights, where freedom has no existence. In this position, where the existence of freedom becomes something wholly contingent, inner indignation is necessary. Because the individual's freedom has no existence, the recognition of universal freedom disappears. From this condition arises that shamelessness that we find in the rabble' (*VPR19* 194–6). I have used the translation included in Wood's editorial notes in the English translation of *PR*, pp. 453–4. See also *PR* §253.

[37] For a good discussion of 'love as a form of recognition', see Williams, *Recognition*, 180–5.

[38] Cf. Benhabib, 'Obligation, Contract and Exchange', 173: 'Hegel does not resort to methodological thought experiments, but proceeds from the standpoint of a community of individuals who have come to recognize one another as persons to specify the form of social interaction through which such recognition is concretized as a practice.' I disagree, however, with Benhabib's suggestion that Hegel does not employ 'thought experiments'. Given Hegel's explicit advice that the *Philosophy of Right* not be read as a historical reconstruction (*PR* §§3, 32, A), it is hard to know how to interpret its arguments except as a series of thought experiments aimed at showing the inner logic of the actual social world.

social world without property, contract, punishment, love, fashion, civil society, the state, and so on could not be a community of mutual recognition, since it would lack the necessary mechanisms by which individuals attract and express recognition. Someone who agrees with Hegel that human freedom ought to be the principle of all moral and political justification thus has reason to endorse and affirm these institutions and practices whether or not they have been consented to: if Hegel's claims are correct, then these arrangements are necessary for mutual recognition and thus are necessary for the development and maintenance of free and rational agency.

Of course this is only a partial reconstruction of Hegel's alternative to the social contract method of argument in that it fails to explain what might be called the 'developmental structure' of the argument of the *Philosophy of Right*: the fact that it presents a sequence of shapes or determinations of spirit, each of which is supposed to develop necessarily out of the previous one. I want to delay detailed consideration of this (for Hegel, very important) aspect of the argument until §6.3 below, but it is worth mentioning something briefly here to complete the argument of this chapter. The method by which the book attempts to identify and elaborate the necessary structure and content of a community of mutually recognizing free agents is the dialectical, or speculative, method borrowed from logic. The argument begins by specifying a conception of what such a community would be like whose basic features seem indispensable or minimally necessary. By 'basic features' I mean, for example, the self-understandings of agents in the community, the institutions and practices in which agents interact together, and the rights, duties, and virtues that make up the normative framework in which they operate. The argument then proceeds with a kind of thought experiment that attempts to reconstruct the experience of a social world having those features. The aim of this reconstruction is to show that a social world with just those features would not, in fact, be self-sufficient (*selbständig*) but rather would in some sense be self-defeating, unless it also had certain additional features. Since the features of the initial conception are indispensable for mutual recognition, and they turn out to depend on a richer conception with additional features for their possibility, these further features can be regarded as indispensable as well. The argument then examines whether the newly characterized social world would, on its own, be self-sufficient, and so on. The outcome, if Hegel can sustain the argument, is a complex and highly differentiated picture of the necessary structure and content of a community of mutual recognition—one that he thinks would correspond in its essentials with the modern European social world in which he lives. If we are willing to affirm the first, simple social world as necessary for the mediation of mutual recognition, then we have reason to affirm and feel reconciled with our own social world as well.

We might summarize the main steps in Hegel's argument for the contemporary social world, then, as follows:

1. Human freedom is the basis of social and political legitimacy.
2. The capacity for freedom is not something that every adult human being automatically has, but is developed and sustained only in the context of a community of mutual recognition: it is the recognition of other free agents that reinforces the idea of oneself as free that is essential to being free.
3. A community of mutual recognition is possible only if it contains certain mediating institutions and practices: it is through these institutions and practices that individuals attract and express recognition.
4. The set of institutions that make up the modern social world, and that include the state, represent the minimum self-sufficient institutional structure that is capable of mediating mutual recognition.

Like social contract theory, Hegel's alternative approach seeks to ground the legitimacy of the major institutions of the social world in freedom. For social contract theory (as Hegel understands it) this is done by imposing a requirement that those institutions enjoy the consent of all of their members. For Hegel, however, this argument presupposes that individuals outside institutions such as the state could have and maintain the capacities for subjectivity involved in making a free and rational decision about joining the state—an assumption he disputes. Rather, he argues, it is ultimately only in a social world containing the state that individuals develop these capacities, because such a social world is the minimum self-sufficient social world that is capable of mediating mutual recognition. For Hegel, then, we have a reason grounded in freedom to affirm and endorse the modern social world—including the modern state—whether or not we have consented to it.

4.5. *Concluding Remarks*

One of the great attractions of the social contract tradition is that it seems to offer the possibility of an independent standpoint from which the legitimacy of major social institutions can be assessed. Even if social contract theory has occasionally been aligned with absolutism, it can at least claim that its method seeks to abstract from the contingencies of power and domination that might prevail in a social order at any given time in order to evaluate and criticize that order from the perspective of the freedom and well-being of the individual. In some versions of the theory, the adoption of this independent perspective may even ground an individual right to disobedience and active resistance. One frequently articulated worry about communitarian political thought is that it cannot achieve this objectivity or independence. Of course, many communitarians seek to make a virtue out of looking for the norms of social and political legitimacy in the context of the social order itself, but, as we noted at the start of Chapter 1, the obvious worry is that they will end up endorsing an uncritical acceptance of existing social structures and power relations.

Hegel's social philosophy is often contrasted with the social contract theory along just such lines. It is suggested, for instance, that Hegel's political thought represents little more than an attempt to defend the status quo of early nineteenth-century Prussia;[39] that he does not grant individuals rights *against* institutions but instead views institutions as embodiments of right (or talks of the rights of institutions against individuals);[40] and that he fails to allow any space for individual reflection about, criticism of, or resistance to existing social structures.[41] It should, I think, be conceded that there is a grain of truth in each of these charges—even if none of them is quite correct as it stands. Hegel was essentially a conservative politi-

[39] Haym, *Hegel und seine Zeit*, ch. 15, is the classic statement of this view. See also Tugendhat, *Self-Consciousness and Self-Determination*, 317: 'Hegel's philosophy is consciously and explicitly the philosophy of the justification of the existing order, quite irrespective of how this existing order may be constituted.'

[40] See e.g. the Editor's Introduction to *VPR19* 31.

[41] Again, see e.g. Tugendhat, *Self-Consciousness and Self-Determination*: Hegel demands 'unconditional obedience to the state' and 'the surrender of responsibility on the part of the citizens' (p. 319). And Hegel allows 'no independent and critical relation to the community' (pp. 315–16; see also p. 320).

cal thinker who, despite backing the rather modest package of reforms that was partially introduced to Prussia in the first two decades of the nineteenth century, remained highly sceptical about the democratic aspirations of the French Revolution. He harboured a deep fear of the consequences of a culture of dissent and criticism for the maintenance of social order and insisted that the main task of political philosophy was not to criticize (let alone to incite people to revolt) but to seek reconciliation with actuality.

All this being said, it should, I hope, be clear from the argument of this chapter that Hegel's communitarian alternative to social contract theory *does* offer the possibility of an independent standpoint from which the legitimacy of major social institutions can be assessed. Hegel's major claim about the modern social world, as we have seen, is that it constitutes the minimum self-sufficient set of institutions and practices that can mediate the mutual recognition needed to develop and sustain individual free agency. This is clearly a claim that can fail to hold true for certain sorts of social structures and power relations, even if Hegel did think it was broadly true of his own social world. Despite the methodological priority it accords to the social order over the individual, Hegel's procedure leaves open the possibility that oppressive social orders can be condemned for failing to actualize the capacities for free and rational agency of their members.

At the beginning of this chapter I suggested that the standard picture of Hegel's relationship with social contract theory has two main elements. First, it sees the disagreement between Hegel and contractarians as mainly a dispute about how best to conceptualize freedom, with Hegel favouring a view of freedom as rational self-determination against a more open-ended contractarian conception. Secondly, it is argued that Hegel can claim to have preserved the will as a principle of political legitimacy only in the weak sense that people in a Hegelian state tend to affirm or assent to the existing political order in which they find themselves. Throughout the chapter I have challenged this standard picture. I have argued that, even if Hegel's argument does at times rely on a crude and distorted picture of what contractarians believe, it is an argument that should be taken seriously by anyone starting from contractarian premisses. Moreover, Hegel's alternative to social contract theory has an impressive logic and coherence to it that should not be too quickly dismissed: it takes seriously the value of human freedom and reminds us of the great variety of ways, some of them quite subtle, in which the institutions and practices of the social world work to develop and sustain free agency, thus giving us a standpoint from which we can endorse or criticize our social world.

5
Hegel's Justification of Private Property

5.1. *Introduction*

Hegel subscribes to one of the oldest and most common justifications of private property in the history of political thought: the claim that there is an important connection between private property and freedom. 'The true position', he asserts, 'is that, from the point of view of freedom, property, as the first *existence* of freedom, is an essential end for itself' (*PR* §45). Because property gives 'existence' to freedom, it grounds a right (*Recht*) both in Hegel's technical sense of the term (*PR* §29), and in the everyday sense that it imposes various duties and obligations—for example, of non-interference, on others.[1]

That there is some sort of connection between freedom and private property is a thesis that has been interpreted and elaborated in a number of quite different ways by the defenders of private ownership. According to what is perhaps the simplest version of the thesis, private property expands the liberty of the individual property-holder by removing certain obstacles to the realization of his ends and/or by providing him with a medium in which to express himself and to pursue his conception of the good life. This view is essentially a *constitutive thesis* about the relationship between freedom and private property: it assumes that individual freedom is marked by the absence of interference, and the presence of options, and notes that a right to some piece of private property both prevents others from interfering in certain ways and gives one certain options that would not otherwise be available.[2] A second view, which might be called the *social-stability* thesis, holds that the institution of private property is instrumental to the maintenance of a liberty-protecting social system. This view is often supported by pointing to the ways in which

[1] On the correlation between rights and duties, see *Enz.* iii, §486.

[2] For critical discussion of this kind of justification of private property, see Cohen, 'Capitalism, Freedom and the Proletariat', 11–17, and Christman, *The Myth of Property*, ch. 4.

the decentralization of power that is entailed by a system of private property acts as a check against tyranny.[3]

In this chapter, however, I want to explore a third interpretation of the relationship between freedom and private property, which I believe finds its most philosophically interesting expression in Hegel's mature social philosophy. Hegel elaborates and defends what I shall call a *developmental thesis* about the connection between individual freedom and private property. According to this thesis, having at least a minimal amount of private property is essential to the development and maintenance of the capacities and self-understandings that make up free personality. Hegel insists that it is only in possession of property that I 'become an actual will' (*PR* §45) or 'give my will existence' (*PR* §46A). 'Property', he claims, 'is a possession which belongs to me as a certain person, and in which my person as such comes into existence, into reality' (*VGP* ii. 126/111). 'The rational aspect of property', he adds, 'is to be found . . . in the superseding of mere subjectivity of personality. Not until he has property does the person exist as reason' (*PR* §41A).[4]

My aim in this chapter will be to develop a philosophical interpretation of Hegel's developmental thesis. Such an interpretation needs to address at least three different kinds of issues. I look at the first, which concerns Hegel's conception of free personality, in §5.2. What does he mean by 'personality'? Is it something that we should be concerned to develop today? The second issue, which I examine in §5.3, concerns why Hegel thinks that private property encourages the development of free personality. What is it about the relationship between an agent and his private property that causes him to develop

[3] For a defence of this view, see Friedman, *Capitalism and Freedom*. For a good discussion, see Ryan, *Property*, 3–4 and ch. 3.

[4] For the claim that Hegel defends a subtle version of the social-stability thesis, see Ryan, *Property and Political Theory*. Ryan's suggestion that 'Hegel is obsessed by getting rational man to feel an adequate loyalty to his own state' (p. 141) seems to be what lies behind his assertion that 'the point of there being property rights is to be seen in a variety of ways in which people anchor themselves and their purposes in the world' (p. 124). The main problem I see with Ryan's interesting interpretation is that it downplays the kinds of passages that I just cited, in which Hegel emphasizes the role played by property in developing will and personality. A second problem with the social stability thesis as an interpretation of Hegel is that it cannot cope with Hegel's important claim that 'everyone ought to have property' (*PR* §49A). Even if it is true that a system of private property, unlike other property regimes, has beneficial consequences for the maintenance of the system of liberties, it hardly seems likely that private ownership has such consequences only when everyone has some property—a point that is acknowledged by Ryan (p. 124).

and maintain the capacities and self-understandings that make up personality? The third, related problem concerns why, in Hegel's view, the development of personality would not be encouraged under alternative property regimes. Why, for instance, would *any* form of interaction with material objects not be sufficient for the development of the relevant capacities and self-understandings? Why is private property uniquely qualified to perform this task? In §§5.4 and 5.5 I attempt to answer these questions.

The most recent attempt to resolve these problems in a philosophical way can be found in Jeremy Waldron's book *The Right to Private Property*.[5] Like the present chapter, Waldron starts from the assumption that 'Hegel argues that individuals need private property in order to sustain and develop the abilities and self-conceptions definitive of their status as persons'.[6] Much of Waldron's chapter on Hegel is then devoted to explaining, in a generally sympathetic way, how Hegel seeks to defend this claim.

The central thrust of Waldron's interpretation is that a private-property system, unlike other property arrangements, works to inculcate individuals with the self-discipline required for them to be properly functioning persons.[7] Waldron illustrates his interpretation with the example of a carpenter building a chair. Once the carpenter has done certain things to the wood, there are certain other things that he cannot then go on to do. This means that he must learn to plan and to be stable and disciplined in his willing.[8] The argument points to the need for private property, Waldron thinks, because, if others were constantly intervening in the carpenter's material interchange with the world, then there would be no point in his engaging in self-disciplining long-term projects at all; others would just upset them.[9]

Waldron's interpretation is impressive in its attempt to put together a philosophically interesting justification of private property that draws on distinctively Hegelian themes such as the relationship between discipline and freedom. But I believe that the argument can be faulted both as an attempt to justify private ownership and as an interpretation of Hegel.

As an attempt to justify private property, it fails to appreciate that private property is neither sufficient nor necessary for the learning of self-discipline, nor even central to it. That it is not *sufficient* is

[5] Waldron, *The Right to Private Property*, ch. 10. [6] Ibid. 353.
[7] Ibid. 370–4. [8] Ibid. 372. [9] Ibid. 373–4.

demonstrated by familiar examples of wealthy property-holders who, far from developing the various capacities that Waldron associates with property, lead a thoroughly dissolute and undisciplined lifestyle. Waldron surely exaggerates when he says that the possession of property 'forces' an agent to impose consistency, coherence, and stability on his projects.[10] If anything, it is the condition of propertylessness that forces people to become resourceful, imaginative, forward-looking, and so forth. As this last point suggests, private property is not *necessary*, because there are other ways of developing the abilities in question that do not involve working on objects over which one has exclusive access and control. Raising a child, or fulfilling the duties of many jobs and professions, encourage planning, self-discipline, consistency, and so on, but do not seem to presuppose a system of private property.[11] Presumably a central way in which we learn self-discipline is by being told that we cannot have something we want unless we do something unpleasant first (for example, 'You can't have your pudding until you finish your peas!').[12]

The weakness of Waldron's account as an interpretation of Hegel lies in the way in which it sidelines two themes that are central in Hegel's own argument. The first is Hegel's emphasis on the idea that the person is an object to himself in his property (*PR* §45).[13] Waldron tries to capture this idea by suggesting that it is the fact that the material object (say, the chair) registers the effects of the person's actions that forces him to plan and to be disciplined. But the fact that it is my actions which bring about changes in the object is incidental to the need for me to be disciplined in my approach to the object. I would equally need to be disciplined if it were nature acting on the object (for example, I might need to act to prevent mould from spreading across my walls). Hegel's claim that I am an object to myself in my property thus plays no essential role in Waldron's reconstruction at all. The second important theme that is downplayed by Waldron's

[10] Waldron, *The Right to Private Property*, 373.

[11] Hegel laments the fact that Plato denies private property to his Guardians (*PR* §46, *VGP* ii. 125–6/110). But, given the rigorous education that Plato subjects his Guardians to, it would be strange of Hegel to deny that the Guardians have the capacities for planning and self-discipline.

[12] An important theme in Hegel's work is that we learn the self-discipline required for freedom through being subjected to the will of another. Although in some circumstances this subjection may take the form of a master–slave relationship (*Enz.* iii, §435A), Hegel holds that in modern European societies it occurs in the context of the family (*PR* §174, A; *VPR18* 257; *VPG* 487/407).

[13] I discuss this idea in §5.3 below.

interpretation is that of mutual recognition.[14] As we shall see in §5.5, this theme is less prominent in the published *Philosophy of Right* version of Hegel's argument than elsewhere, but it is important nevertheless and needs to be integrated into any satisfactory interpretation of Hegel's position.

In this chapter I develop an alternative approach to Hegel's justification of private property, one that restores to a central place the two important themes that are marginalized by Waldron.[15] Although I believe that the argument I end up attributing to Hegel is stronger than the one developed by Waldron, I am sceptical, for reasons I suggest in the concluding section, about whether it is an adequate defence of private ownership. This being said, even if Hegel's defence of private property is ultimately unsatisfactory, his argument may help us to assess other, perhaps more broadly defined, property regimes and arrangements. For the most part, in any case, my aim will be to make the most out of Hegel's argument and not to criticize it.

The attempt to clarify Hegel's account of property is a worthwhile project in its own right—especially in the light of the revival of interest in Hegel that can be found in contemporary discussions of property—but it should also serve to illustrate, and thereby to support, the more general account of Hegel's approach to legitimation and 'reconciliation' that I introduced in Chapter 4. In particular, my interpretation in this chapter will help to confirm my claim (in §4.4) that a central part of Hegel's attempt to reconcile his contemporaries to their social world is the idea that the institutions and practices of that world work to mediate the mutual recognition required for individuals to become and remain free.

5.2. *Personality*

In all of the mature versions of Hegel's social philosophy, the main discussion of property can be found in the section entitled 'Abstract

[14] Waldron argues that the need for recognition could be satisfied by *any* system of property, not just private property. See *The Right to Private Property*, 303–4, 375. I suggest why Hegel may have thought differently in §5.5 below.

[15] Two papers that are quite congenial to my position are Stillman, 'Property, Freedom, and Individuality in Hegel's and Marx's Political Thought', and Knowles, 'Hegel on Property and Personality'. Unlike these papers, but like Waldron's book, I shall explicitly focus here on how, and to what extent, the argument developed by Hegel constitutes a justification of *private* property, rather than property more generally.

Right'. The central assumption of 'Abstract Right' is that the agents, or wills, who make up the social world are *persons* or possess *personality* (*PR* §§33, A, 35). This assumption distinguishes the social world of abstract right from the worlds of morality and the ethical life, where agents are assumed to be not only persons but also subjects and members respectively; they possess not only personality, that is to say, but also subjectivity and substantiality (*PR* §§33, A, 35).

'Abstract Right' has two main aims relating to its central assumption—one positive, the other negative. The positive one is to determine what basic institutions and practices the social world must contain, given the assumption that agents in that world are persons. Hegel's methodological assumption here is that, if we accept the value and importance of personality, then the argument he shall develop should give us good reasons to feel reconciled to the institutions and practices in question and to think that they are justified.[16] The second, negative aim of 'Abstract Right' is to show that a social world containing only persons, and the institutions and practices grounded in personality, would not be viable: unless agents possess subjectivity and substantiality in addition to personality, the social world they inhabit would be self-undermining (for example, property rights would be regularly violated, contracts would not be observed, and punishment would take the form of revenge) and even the personality of agents would be at risk. It is the first aim that shall concern us here, for central amongst the institutions which Hegel thinks necessary for personality is private property.[17]

Three features of Hegel's conception of personality are worth remarking on, all of them emphasized in the opening paragraphs of 'Abstract Right'. The first point is that to be a person, or to possess personality, is to have a sense of independence from one's given situation and ends: 'It is inherent in *personality* that, as *this* person, I am completely determined in all respects (in my inner arbitrary will, drive, and desire, as well as in relation to my immediate external existence (*Dasein*)), and that I am finite, yet totally pure self-reference, and thus know myself in my finitude as *infinite, universal,* and *free*.' Personality, Hegel adds, 'begins only at that point where the subject

[16] On Hegel's project as an attempt to *reconcile* modern Europeans to their social world, see Hardimon, *Hegel's Social Philosophy*, ch. 3. Waldron, *The Right to Private Property*, 344–7, contains a good defence of the claim that Hegel seeks to justify private property and not *merely* to understand it. See also Ryan's sensitive remarks in *Property and Political Theory*, 139–40.

[17] I shall have more to say about the second aim in §6.3 below.

has not merely a consciousness of itself in general as concrete and in some way determined, but a consciousness of itself as a completely abstract "I" in which all concrete limitation and validity are negated and invalidated' (*PR* §35). An agent can be said to be a person if and only if he (*a*) perceives that he has certain empirical features—for example, certain wants, desires, and so forth—*but also* (*b*) conceives of himself as independent of these empirical circumstances, in the sense that they do not dictate to him what he must be or do. Personality thus involves an understanding of oneself as an independent, self-determining agent and therefore a capacity to reflect on, and critically scrutinize, one's given situation and ends (cf. *PR* §35A).

The second feature of Hegel's conception of personality worth noting is that it is not tied to the pursuit of any particular ends or goals, but is essentially open-ended:

> The *particularity* of the will is indeed a moment within the entire consciousness of the will (see §34), but it is not yet contained in the abstract personality as such. Thus, although it is present—as desire, need, drives, contingent preference, etc.—it is still different from personality, from the determination of freedom.—In formal right, therefore, it is not a question of particular interests, of my advantage or welfare, and just as little of the particular ground by which my will is determined, i.e. of my insight and intention. (*PR* §37)

Hegel does, as this passage suggests, have a more full-blown conception of freedom in which the content of one's ends becomes important, but this is different from free personality. As we saw in Chapter 2, the fully free will, in Hegel's view, is the will that, in determining what to do, does not take any of its contingently given wants or desires as authoritative, not even the system of all of its wants and desires, but rather attempts to determine its activity completely out of its own thought and reason (*PR* §21). To be free in this sense, we saw in Chapter 3, means only acting in certain ways; ultimately, it means adopting the duties and virtues of the various institutions of *Sittlichkeit*, including the state. This is not the case with free personality: being a person is consistent with acting in any particular way, so long as one preserves a sense of oneself as independent in so doing. Personality implies a sense of distance between oneself and one's ends and life situation. It involves the ability to evaluate and reflect on one's ends that is central to our everyday idea of individual autonomy. Unlike full Hegelian freedom, it need not imply that our determinations are rooted in thought and reason 'all the way down', nor that there is some set of rational ends to be discovered once we embark on a course of radical reflection.

Thirdly, Hegel assumes that personality is a distinctively *human* capacity (it helps to distinguish human beings from animals), but not one that human beings necessarily have (*PR* §35, A) (in this sense, some human beings are *merely* animals). As with all forms of free agency, personality involves a set of capacities and self-understandings that are acquired only through *Bildung*—the process of education and acculturation achieved through one's social experience (see §4.2 above). In certain types of social worlds, the individual is able to develop the capacities and self-understandings that are integral to personality; in other types, he cannot.[18] The central claim of Hegel's account of property is that it is only in social worlds containing the institution of private property that an agent can become a person; it is only in such a world that he can 'become an actual will'.[19]

5.3. *A Puzzle*

This brings us to the central problem that I want to address in this chapter. How, according to Hegel, does the institution of private property encourage the development of free personality? What is it about private ownership that causes the agent to develop the capacities and self-understandings that make up personality or to reinforce them once they have already been developed? This section represents an initial attempt to answer these questions. By examining some of Hegel's claims about property in the *Philosophy of Right* I shall attempt to reconstruct the rationale, as he saw it, of a private-property system. We shall see that this reconstruction at best shows why private property is sufficient for the development of free personality; it does not show why private property is necessary and thus fails to constitute an adequate justification of that institution. My conclusion, therefore, will be that there is a puzzle about how Hegel

[18] For instance, Hegel thinks that individual personality did not develop in Asian civilizations, and did so only to a limited extent in Ancient Greece (*PR* §185; *VPG* 177/141, 339/278; *VGP* i. 372/323).

[19] Hegel backhandedly credits Plato with having perceived this connection between private property and the development of personality. According to Hegel, it is because Plato sought to forestall the emergence of free personality in his republic that he was careful to proscribe private ownership (for the Guardians). See *VGP* ii. 125–6/110–11.

might attempt to complete his argument for private ownership. The remainder of the chapter then tries to solve this puzzle.

Hegel's central assertion about property is made at §45: 'the circumstance that I, as free will, am an object [*gegenständlich*] to myself in what I possess and only become an actual will by this means constitutes the genuine and rightful element in possession [*Besitz*], the determination of *property* [*Eigenthum*].' This passage in fact makes two important claims that need to be unpacked. The first is the claim that, in property, I, as a free will, am an object to myself. In his 1818–19 lectures, Hegel expresses this point more directly when he says that 'I look at myself in my property' (*ich schaue mich in meinem Eigenthum an*) (*VPR18* 225) and that in property 'I regard myself as free' (*VPR18* 224). The second claim is that it is this experience of being an object to myself that allows me to 'become an actual will'. It is through looking at myself in my property that I develop and reinforce the capacities and self-understandings that make up personality. I shall call these the *self-perception* and *self-development* claims respectively and examine them in turn.

At first glance the self-perception claim might seem somewhat puzzling. Of course we often say that a person's possessions reveal a great deal about her personality,[20] but it is not clear that, when we say this, we mean personality in the special Hegelian sense of the term. How might a person's possessions reveal her personality in the sense of her capacity for independent reflection and agency?

A clue to Hegel's meaning can be found in the 1822–3 Addition to §44 of the *Philosophy of Right*, where Hegel suggests that, by appropriating an object, I manifest or demonstrate the supremacy of my will *vis-à-vis* the object. I do this by giving it a configuration that it did not have before, a configuration that reflects my end or 'soul':

> to appropriate something means basically only to manifest the supremacy of my will in relation to the thing and to demonstrate that the latter does not have being in and for itself and is not an end in itself. This manifestation occurs through my conferring upon the thing an end other than that which it immediately possessed; I give the living creature, as my property, a soul other than that which it previously had; I give it my soul.

Much of Hegel's subsequent discussion of taking possession and using property returns to this theme of manifesting or demonstrating

[20] As Knowles illustrates in the opening pages of 'Hegel on Property and Personality'.

the supremacy of one's will in relation to the object. Physically seizing and giving a form, which are both ways of taking possession of an owned object, are, Hegel thinks, simply variations on a third way of taking possession—making a sign. And 'it is precisely through the ability to make a sign and by so doing to acquire things that human beings display their mastery over the latter' (*PR* §58A). Using or consuming an object is also a way of demonstrating one's supremacy: '[With use] the thing is reduced to a means of satisfying my need. When I and the thing come together, one of the two must lose its [distinct] quality in order that we may become identical. But I am alive, a willing and truly affirmative agent; the thing, on the other hand, is a natural [negative] entity' (*PR* §59A).[21]

These passages suggest a way of understanding the self-perception claim. They suggest that a person looks at himself in his property in the sense that he sees concrete evidence that he is independent of his given circumstances or situation. By interacting with the object in various ways—by grasping it, giving it a form, marking it, consuming it, and so on—the person manifests or demonstrates his supremacy over his natural environment; he thus sees that environment need not dictate to him what he shall be or do, that he can impose his own plans and purposes on his situation and make a difference. Or, in terms of the passage I just referred to, he gains a concrete perception of the fact that he is 'a willing and truly affirmative agent'.[22]

The self-development claim is the claim that this experience of perceiving his independence and agency helps the individual to develop and sustain his personality itself. The claim is not explicitly defended by Hegel in his discussion of property, but it can be quite easily explained in terms of several themes that were explored in Chapter 4. The first of these themes, which Hegel often returns to, is that having a conception of oneself as free, or taking oneself to be free, is an indispensable condition of being free (see §4.3). This requirement becomes quite transparent when it comes to the freedom of personality, for, as

[21] See *PR* §59: '*Use* is the realization of my need through the alteration, destruction, or consumption of the thing, whose selfless nature is thereby revealed . . .'.

[22] This point is nicely expressed by Waldron: 'By investing a natural object with purpose an individual becomes aware of the priority of will in a world composed largely of objects that cannot actively possess it. Thus he ceases to regard himself as a mere animal part of nature and begins to take seriously the special and distinctive features of rationality, purpose, and will' (*The Right to Private Property*, 302). See also Taylor, *Hegel*, 8: 'Manipulability of the world confirms the new self-defining identity.'

we have already seen, part of being a person, for Hegel, is having a certain self-understanding—a sense of oneself as independent of one's given situation and ends. The second Hegelian theme, which completes the argument, is that one cannot arrive at a sense of oneself as free simply by asserting it to oneself: the assertion that one is free does not suffice to make one so (*Enz.* iii, §431A). To come to think of oneself as free, and to sustain this self-understanding, one needs to receive some kind of objective confirmation from one's surroundings of one's free and independent agency (see §4.3 above).

So the self-development claim is simply the claim that the experience of having a concrete perception of one's independent agency helps to develop and confirm the sense of oneself as independent that is an integral part of being a person. Hegel's justification of private property, then, might be expressed as follows: it is important that an individual have private property because it is important that he develop and sustain his personality—his capacities for independent reflection and agency. Private property helps to develop personality because it gives the individual a concrete perception of his independence, a perception that confirms the sense of himself as independent that is an essential part of being a person.

An obvious objection to this attempt to justify a private-property system, however, is that, at best, it establishes only that private property is a *sufficient* condition for developing and sustaining one's personality. It does not show that a similar argument could not be made on behalf of a system of common property.[23] And surely the primary challenge faced by the defenders of private ownership is to demonstrate the *relative* superiority of private property *vis-à-vis* other kinds of property arrangements.

Hegel's only explicit attempt to meet this challenge is not particularly satisfying. He argues that, 'since my will, as personal and hence as the will of an individual, becomes objective in property, the latter takes on the character of *private property*' (*PR* §46). But this inference from the individuality of the person's will to the need for *private* property is not, without further argument, valid, for it ignores the important possibility that the individual person could develop and

[23] Hegel assumes that the principal alternative to private property is common property (*gemeinschaftliches Eigentum*), the form of property relations found, for instance, in monasteries and recommended by Plato in his *Republic* (*PR* §46, A). As I suggest in §5.6 below, one of the weaknesses of Hegel's account of property is that he fails to recognize that there is more than one alternative to a private-property system.

sustain his sense of independent agency by interacting with objects that are common property.[24]

This brings me to the puzzle that will occupy us for the remainder of this chapter: how might Hegel complete the argument? Unfortunately, there are very few clues to be found in the published text of the *Philosophy of Right*, and so it might be thought that we have taken Hegel's argument for private property as far as it can go. But I want to try to take it a little further by examining two important features of the background to Hegel's account. One is an argument by Fichte, which Hegel and his readers would almost certainly have been familiar with; the other is a set of pre–1820 (the year of the completion of the *Philosophy of Right*) versions of Hegel's account of property, which all emphasize the important relationship between private property and mutual recognition. By combining material from these two different sources, I will attempt to reconstruct the final steps in Hegel's defence of private ownership.

5.4. *Property and Personality in Fichte's Social Philosophy*

A number of recent books and articles have emphasized the importance of appreciating the Fichtean background to Hegel's political philosophy. This is not only because of the profound influence exercised by Fichte's writings on the development of the young Hegel,[25] but also because Fichte's *Grundlage des Naturrechts* remained the single most important work of contemporary political philosophy in Germany throughout the time that Hegel was developing his mature political theory.[26] In Chapter 4 we looked briefly at Hegel's confrontation with Fichte's social contract theory. Recent work has also emphasized the extent to which Hegel's account of recognition was influenced by Fichte's *Grundlage des Naturrechts*.[27] Less attention has been given to the relationship between Fichte's discussion of

[24] For further discussion of this point, see Waldron, *The Right to Private Property*, 373.

[25] See e.g. *DFS*, which includes a seven-page discussion (pp. 142–9) of Fichte's *Grundlage des Naturrechts*.

[26] For a sustained attempt to argue for the relevance of Fichte to understanding Hegel's ethical and political thought, see Wildt, *Autonomie und Anerkennung*, 19–23 and part III.

[27] e.g. Wildt, *Autonomie und Anerkennung*; Williams, *Recognition*; and Wood, *Hegel's Ethical Thought*, ch. 4.

property and Hegel's own account. This is unfortunate for several reasons.

First, although there is only one explicit reference to Fichte in the published text of 'Abstract Right' (*PR* §79), Hegel does mention Fichte several more times in the corresponding sections of his various lectures on *Rechtsphilosophie* (e.g. *PR* §52A; *VPR17* 48, 55, 59, 104). It seems clear from these references that Hegel was familiar with Fichte's doctrine on property and that to a considerable extent he was sympathetic with it.[28]

Secondly, both Fichte and Hegel discuss property in the context of the same basic problematic. The two thinkers assume a conception of agents as individual *persons* and think that a central problem of social and political philosophy is to identify the social conditions of the possibility of personality.[29] Private property, for both philosophers, is one such condition and is justified on this basis.

Finally, an important common theme runs through the justifications of property offered by each writer in that each emphasizes the way in which property allows the subjection of nature to the will's ends and purposes and the manifestation thereby of the supremacy of the will. Just as, for Hegel, 'to appropriate something means basically only to manifest the supremacy of my will in relation to the thing and to demonstrate that the latter . . . is not an end in itself' (*PR* §44A), so, for Fichte, 'the final ground of property in a thing is . . . the subjection of that thing to our purposes'.[30]

Like Hegel, Fichte considers property in the context of a theory of 'right' (*Recht*) more generally.[31] Anticipating Hegel, he uses the term 'right' to refer broadly to any kind of social institution or arrangement that is a condition of the possibility of personality and also, more narrowly, to what we think of as rights—that is, claims that we have that place others under duties to treat, or refrain from treating, us in certain ways.[32] Like Hegel, Fichte hopes to establish that

[28] For instance, at *VPR17* 55, Hegel approvingly cites Fichte's 1793 critique of Rehberg in which the discussion of property anticipates Fichte's account three years later in the *Grundlage des Naturrechts*. For the 1793 account, see J. G. Fichte, *Beiträge zur Berichtigung der Urteile des Publikums über die Französische Revolution*, esp. pp. 117–18.

[29] See J.G. Fichte, *Grundlage des Naturrechts*, 94, 111–13. All translations from Fichte's *Grundlage des Naturrechts* are my own. For an excellent discussion of Fichte's conception of personality, and its relationship to Fichte's understanding of right and morality, see Neuhouser, 'Fichte and the Relationship between Right and Morality'.

[30] Fichte, *Grundlage des Naturrechts*, 117.

[31] Ibid. 111–17.

[32] Ibid. 94–5.

private property is *rechtlich* in both of these senses: it is an institution that makes personality possible; and it is therefore something that warrants placing others under certain duties—for instance, duties of non-interference. In particular, Fichte wants to show that private property is a natural or 'original' right (*Urrecht*)—one that has its basis not in any positive enactments of the political community, nor in the terms of any covenant or agreement that individuals may have entered into with one another, but only in the conditions of the possibility of free personality.[33]

The identification of specific *Urrechte*, then, including the right to property, involves tracing out the social conditions of free personality. As we saw in reconstructing Hegel's theory, and as Fichte himself recognizes, this exercise presupposes that we have some idea of what is meant by free personality: 'the concept of freedom . . . gives the concept of an *Urrecht*, that is, of that right [*Recht*] to which every person as such is absolutely entitled'.[34] To be a free person, Fichte assumes, is to be only cause, and never effect, in the external world; a free person is any agent who has the 'capacity to be absolute first cause'.[35]

Fichte recognizes several ways in which an agent can fail to enjoy this freedom. One problem might be that his ends and purposes are determined externally rather than *self*-determined; he may lack the power to formulate ends and purposes spontaneously.[36] Another is that there may be external interventions, either by nature or by other agents, which produce changes in the world he is acting on, thereby upsetting his free efficacy (*Wirksamkeit*). Something more needs to be said about why this second case represents a problem for freedom and I shall return to it in a moment.

Fichte, in fact, holds that, strictly speaking, nature never changes, since it is governed by unvarying mechanical laws: 'all change conflicts with [nature's] concept.'[37] When nature *appears* to us to change or 'intervene', it is in fact we who have misunderstood or misjudged the relevant laws of nature. This kind of misunderstanding, he thinks, is preventable and when it occurs is 'our own responsibility'.[38] The main social condition of the possibility of free personality, he concludes, is that others not intervene in the external world on which an agent is acting: 'It is only other free beings that could produce an unforeseen

[33] Fichte, *Grundlage des Naturrechts*, 94–5, 111–13.
[34] Ibid. 112–13.
[35] Ibid. 113.
[36] Ibid. 113.
[37] Ibid. 115.
[38] Ibid. 116.

and unpreventable change in our world—that is, in the system of that which we have come to know and related to our purposes; then, however, would our free efficacy [*Wirksamkeit*] be disturbed.'[39]

From this premiss, and from the premiss that anything that is a social condition of free personality can give rise to a right, Fichte draws the conclusion that a person has a right to a sphere of the external world that is free from the interventions of others: 'The person has the right [*Recht*] to demand that, in the whole world known to him, everything should remain just as he knew it, because he depends for his efficacy on his knowledge and would immediately be disoriented, and would find the course of his causality [*Causalität*] blocked, or would obtain other results than those he intended, as soon as a change took place.'[40] This right, however, is nothing other than a right to private property: 'Here lies the ground of all right of property. That part of the sensuous world which is known to me, and has been subjected by me, even if only in thought, to my purposes, is originally . . . my property. No one can influence it [*auf denselben einfliessen*] without hindering my free efficacy.'[41]

Fichte's deduction of an original right to private property, then, can be summarized as follows: an agent has a right to whatever constitutes a social condition of the possibility of his personality. The main such condition is that there be no interventions by others into the sphere of the external world in which he is acting. But this is just to say that a social condition of the possibility of personality is that the agent have access to, and control over, a sphere of the external world from which others are barred from intervening. Since private property is, in essence, a right to exclusive access and control over some material object in the external world, it follows that individuals have a right to private property.

Although this argument raises a number of issues, the key question, it seems to me, concerns why interventions by others in the world on which I am acting can be said to thwart my free personality. Why, for example, might the fact that I am forced to share a garden in common with others frustrate my freedom as a person? I can think of two ways of construing Fichte's argument: one resembles the constitutive thesis that I mentioned at the beginning of the chapter; the other anticipates, but also extends in an interesting direction, the argument I attributed to Hegel in the previous section.

[39] Ibid. 116. [40] Ibid. 116. [41] Ibid. 116.

On the first reading of Fichte's argument, interventions by others frustrate my freedom as a person because they constitute obstacles to the realization of my ends and purposes in the world. To be a free person, we saw earlier, is, according to Fichte, to be a cause, and never an effect, in the world. This means that, among other things, there should be a causal connection between my having a certain purpose and a certain state of affairs (the object of my purpose) being realized. Interventions by others can thwart my freedom simply by frustrating this causal connection. For instance, if my purpose is to cultivate roses in the garden, others might frustrate the realization of this purpose by digging up the soil for their own gardening projects.

On this reading of the argument, Fichte's justification of private property is a familiar one. To be a free person, one must have the opportunity to pursue one's purposes, unhindered by the actions of others. But this means—so the argument goes—that one must be the bearer of private-property rights, for these rights secure an opportunity to realize one's purposes by excluding others from access.

The flaw in the argument is equally familiar. In so far as the opportunity to realize one's purposes is concerned, a system of private property cuts both ways. It is, of course, true that my private-property rights to certain material objects enable me to realize certain ends that might be frustrated by others were those objects common property. But it is equally true that the fact that other material objects are privately owned by other people, rather than commonly owned, thwarts the realization of certain of my ends. Whether a private-property system best enables some agent to realize his ends depends on how much property he has and what his ends are. It may well be the case that the agent does better under a common-property system than under a private-property one.[42]

There is, however, an alternative way of construing Fichte's argument that makes better sense of the text and that aligns it more closely with the argument that I have been attributing to Hegel. Immediately following the passages from the *Grundlage des Naturrechts* that I have been quoting, Fichte continues:

To say that the person wants his activity in the sensuous world to be a cause [*Ursache*] is to say that he wants a perception [*Wahrnehmung*] to result which will correspond to his own concept of the purpose of his activity . . . It has

[42] The objection sketched in this paragraph is made by Cohen, 'Capitalism, Freedom and the Proletariat', 11–17.

already been mentioned that, if this is to be possible at all, the natural course of things in the future, that is, either after the active influence [*thätigen Einwirkung*] of the person, or after the purposeful omission [*zweckmässigen Unterlassung*] of an activity, must be left undisturbed.[43]

The significance of this passage lies in its suggestion that free personality requires not only that one's purposes *have* causality, but also that one have a *perception* of their causality. A similar claim is made by Fichte in the Introduction to the *Grundlage des Naturrechts*:

In the concept of freedom lies, first and foremost, only the capacity to formulate, through absolute spontaneity, concepts of our possible efficacy . . . But something else is required for a rational individual, or person, to find himself as free, namely, that the object [*Gegenstand*] referred to in this concept of his efficacy should correspond with [his] experience, and thus that something in the world outside of him should result from the thought of his own activity. Now, should the effects of rational beings occur in the same world, so that they can influence and mutually disturb and hinder one another, as is indeed the case, then freedom—in the above sense—would only be possible for such persons under the condition that their efficacy should be enclosed within certain limits, and that the world, as the sphere of their freedom, should be divided, so to speak, amongst them.[44]

Here again Fichte argues from the need for the person to perceive his own efficacy as an agent ('to find himself as free') to the conclusion that the world should be divided up amongst different people into separate spheres of influence.

The argument is most clearly made as part of Fichte's deduction of the relationship of right (*das Rechtsverhältnis*) in general.[45] There Fichte seeks to identify the conditions under which a subject 'determines himself to be a free individual' and 'constitutes his freedom and self-sufficiency'.[46] He claims that a subject can constitute himself as free only to the extent that he can see various effects taking place in the world around him as grounded in his own agency. For this to happen, the subject must be able to distinguish how far the effects taking place around him have their ground in his own agency and how far they are grounded in the agency of other rational beings: in order to 'posit himself as an absolutely free being' the subject must be able to 'separate himself completely from the free being outside of

[43] Fichte, *Grundlage des Naturrechts*, 117.

[44] Ibid. 8–9. For discussion of this passage, see Neuhouser, 'Fichte and the Relationship between Right and Morality', 164–5.

[45] Fichte, *Grundlage des Naturrechts*, 41–56.

[46] Ibid. 42.

him and attribute his free efficacy only to himself'.[47] Fichte claims that, if the subject is to be in a position to conclude that *his own* agency was the ground of the effects he sees around him, then he must have a sphere in which only he, and not the other rational being, is free to choose: 'But in this sphere, now, only the subject can have chosen and *not the other* [rational being], for he [the other] has left it undetermined, according to our assumption. What exclusively chooses in this sphere is *his* self, is the individual, who in setting himself in contrast to another rational being determines himself as a rational being.'[48] So here again Fichte argues from the need to perceive one's own agency (in order to constitute oneself as a free agent) to the conclusion that the world should be divided up into separate spheres of influence.

These passages suggest that the reason why interventions by others upset free personality is not only that they constitute obstacles to one's causality or efficacy but also that they make a perception of one's efficacy impossible. In part, of course, interventions by others make this perception impossible *because* they constitute obstacles to that efficacy. But they may also make perception of one's efficacy difficult even where this is not in fact the case. Throughout his discussion of property, Fichte stresses the ways in which the agent's knowledge of the situation conditions his sense of himself as efficacious: 'Free efficacy and determinate knowledge condition one another mutually.'[49] The problem posed by interventions by others is that they can throw off our knowledge of the situation by introducing what Fichte terms 'unforeseen and unpreventable changes . . . in our world'.[50] Where others have intervened, I can no longer be confident that alterations in the object are due to *my* will; my perception of the object is not, as far as I can tell, a perception of my own efficacy. Where there are no interventions by others, on the other hand, changes in the object can be explained only by my purposes. Under these conditions, I should be able to connect certain changes in the object with the plans and projects that were present in my will. (Recall that, for Fichte, nature does not change or 'intervene'; it only *appears* to when we misunderstand or misjudge it. He seems to be assuming that the agent is sufficiently knowledgeable about the workings of nature to avoid this kind of problem.[51])

[47] Fichte, *Grundlage des Naturrechts*, 41–2. [48] Ibid. 42.
[49] Ibid. 114–15. [50] Ibid. 116. [51] Ibid. 115–16.

Consider, for instance, the gardener who plants and tends some tomatoes until one day they are ripe for picking. He knows that this is not something that happens without human intervention and he is confident that no one else has intervened in the garden. He also knows that the project of cultivating the tomatoes just this way had been in his will all along. With the success of the tomatoes, he therefore has an objective confirmation of the causal efficacy of his own plans and projects. He sees himself as someone who does not, or need not, take his situation as a given, but who can impose his own will—his own plans and projects—on that situation. By contrast, if others come and go as they please in the garden, and perhaps work on it themselves, he cannot be so confident that the successful tomatoes are the result of his own efficacy. Someone else may have been taking the important measures all along.

Two comments need to be made concerning Fichte's argument, on this second interpretation of it. The first is that, to a very considerable extent, it anticipates Hegel's argument in the *Philosophy of Right*, as I set this out in the previous section. For both thinkers, the rationale behind a private-property system centres on the way in which private property provides the individual property-holder with a concrete perception of his own agency and in this way helps to constitute him as a free person.

Secondly, however, Fichte goes even further than Hegel in attempting to explain why it is that only a private-property system, and not some other set of property arrangements, can facilitate this self-perception. The problem with common property is that interventions by others make it difficult for the agent to be confident that the alterations and transformations in the material objects he has been interacting with are the result of *his* agency. He cannot be sure that they are his plans and purposes that have been imposed on the world, for they may have been somebody else's. We cannot be certain, of course, but Hegel may have been taking something like this account, which both he and his readers would have been familiar with, for granted in developing his own version of the argument.

5.5. *Property and Recognition*

No doubt a number of possible objections, both interpretative and substantive, might be made to the argument I have been developing.

At this point, I want to draw attention to two in particular, which will help me to introduce the final piece in Hegel's defence of private ownership.

The first objection is that Hegel's argument, at least on my interpretation of it, seems strongly individualistic and to that extent in conflict with other more communitarian tendencies in his thought (see Chapter 4).[52] The argument I have been sketching suggests both that an isolated individual could develop and sustain a free personality and that the presence of others makes it more difficult for him to do this. Elsewhere, as we have seen, however, Hegel argues that an individual can develop his capacities for freedom and agency only in the context of a community with others that provides for mutual recognition.

The second objection is simply that there is something deeply unconvincing about the Fichtean attempt to establish the necessity of *private* property that I described in the previous section. The central thrust of that argument was that, in the context of common property, an agent could not be confident that changes and alterations in the material world were evidence of *his* plans and purposes, for they might have been the result of somebody else's. An obvious objection to this, however, is that I know what my purposes are and if I see that the material world comes to reflect these purposes then surely I can be confident that it was I who made a difference. It seems far-fetched to worry that somebody else might have had exactly the same plans in mind as me. Consider, for example, the case of a sculptor who spends a few hours of each day working on a sculpture in the town square. Why should there be any serious doubt in his mind that the final product reflects his own plans and purposes?[53] Or consider Hegel's own example of the boy who 'throws stones into the river and now marvels at the circles drawn in the water as an effect in which he gains an intuition of something that is his own doing' (*Aesthetics* 31). Surely the river need not be the boy's own private property for him to have this intuition.

To see how Hegel might respond to these objections we need to introduce one final element into his account, an element that is not very prominent in the published *Philosophy of Right* discussion of property, but that is central in earlier versions of the argument. These

[52] For the claim that Hegel's conception of personality is 'individualistic', see Munzer, *A Theory of Property*, 82.

[53] I am indebted to G. A. Cohen for suggesting this example to me.

earlier versions are found in the Heidelberg *Encyclopedia* (*VPR* i), published by Hegel in 1817, and also in the transcripts of Hegel's 1817–18, 1818–19, and 1819–20 lectures on *Rechtsphilosophie*. These versions of the argument explicitly emphasize the important relationship that Hegel sees between private property and recognition. They indicate that it is important, for Hegel, that human beings possess private property primarily because of the way in which private property mediates the recognition of others—a recognition that is essential to the development of the capacities and self-understandings that are integral to free personality. It is this element of recognition that can help Hegel to respond to the objections raised above.[54]

In the Heidelberg *Encyclopedia* of 1817, for example, Hegel argues that 'As a person . . . I have my realization only in the being of other persons, and only in this realization am I an actual person for myself' (*VPR* i. 146). The object of property is the 'medium' (*Mitte*) that makes this recognition possible. Through property, my will has, for others, a 'determinate recognizable existence' (*VPR* i. 146).[55] In his 1817–18 lectures, he argues: 'Possession is essentially the externalization [*Äußerlichkeit*] of the will: through the sphere of existence, I externalize my personality . . . Through the will's existence, or external being, there arises being for others and in this way my will becomes recognizable by others' (*VPR17* 48).[56] And in 1818–19 he notes: 'Property only contains existence when the person becomes for another, that is to say, is recognized' (*VPR18* 265).

This emphasis on property as a mediator of recognition is less prominent but not altogether absent from the published *Philosophy of Right* version of Hegel's account. Hegel writes, for instance, that 'my inner idea and will that something should be *mine* is not enough to constitute property, which is the *existence* of personality; on the

[54] For other commentaries emphasizing the importance of recognition for Hegel's account of property, see Ritter, 'Person and Property: On Hegel's *Philosophy of Right*, Paragraphs 34–81'; Stillman, 'Property, Freedom and Individuality in Hegel and Marx', 137, 148; Knowles, 'Hegel on Property and Personality', 56–7; and Benhabib, 'Obligation, Contract and Exchange', 172.

[55] The claim that property mediates recognition is made even more explicitly in the 1827 and 1830 editions of the *Encyclopedia*; see *Enz.* iii, §§490–1.

[56] See also *VPR17* 56–7: 'Through the sphere of my freedom, which I have in property, I come into a relation with other persons . . . The essential existence of property is the existence of its rightful, absolute side, and this is that, in property, persons recognize one another . . . My existence in my property is a relation to other persons; here mutual recognition is created; the free is for the free.'

contrary, this requires that I should *take possession* of it. The *existence* which my willing thereby attains includes its ability to be recognized by others' (*PR* §51). And he says that 'A person, in distinguishing himself from himself, relates himself to *another person*, and indeed it is only as owners of property that the two have existence [*Dasein*] for each other' (*PR* §40).

Once recognizability is seen as central to the 'existence' that property gives to personality, Hegel's justification of property becomes much clearer. Through property, Hegel is arguing, I can confirm and reinforce my sense of being a person and of possessing the capacities that are constitutive of my personality—the capacities for independent reflection and agency. Property has this effect because it is not only a sphere in which the person can exercise his agency, but also one that records those manifestations of agency in a way that can be discerned and admired by both the agent himself and by others. If an object is the property of some person, we can look at the alterations and transformations that it has undergone and believe that it was his agency that brought them about. We thus have grounds for attributing agency to him and for extending the recognition to him that we reserve for everyone that we take to be free. By manifesting the activity of his will, property mediates the recognition of the agent—both his self-recognition and his recognition by others—and thus fosters and sustains the self-understanding that he requires in order to be a person.

This final reformulation of Hegel's defence of private ownership suggests how he might respond to the two objections I raised at the beginning of this section. Against the first objection, that his argument for property seems strongly individualistic, it is now possible to point to an important communitarian dimension in the account: a central part of Hegel's approach, it would seem, is to ask what sorts of institutions and practices must be in place if a community of mutually recognizing free agents is to be possible. Private property, Hegel is claiming, is one such institution.

To the second objection, that the argument does not really establish the necessity of *private* property, Hegel might now respond as follows. It may be true that I know what my purposes are and that if I see that the material world comes to reflect these purposes then I can be confident that it was I who made a difference. To this extent, *private* property is not necessary; other property arrangements might do as well. But it is not the case that other people can associate changes and alterations in the material world so easily with my purposes and plans.

In a world in which material objects are common property, all others see is evidence of somebody's purposive activity (for example, they see an igloo built in the snow). They have no particular reason to link this evidence of purposive activity with me. If the igloo were on a piece of land that is my private property, however, then they can regard it as evidence of the efficacy of my plans and purposes. They thus have reason to recognize me as a free person. In so far as recognition by others, and not just self-recognition, is a condition of developing and sustaining one's free personality, the argument recommends private property and not just any form of property arrangements.

In §4.4 I advanced the hypothesis that one of the central ways in which Hegel seeks to reconcile his contemporaries to the institutions and practices of their social world is by showing them that those institutions and practices are required to mediate the mutual recognition they need to develop and sustain their capacities for free and rational agency. The interpretation of Hegel's justification of private property that I have been developing in this chapter helps to confirm this hypothesis by suggesting that part of the rationale behind a private-property system, for Hegel, lies in the way in which private property, unlike alternative property regimes, allows individuals to demonstrate their free personality to one another and thereby facilitates mutual recognition. A social world that lacks the institution of private property could not be one in which individual personality is able to develop and flourish because it could not be a community of mutual recognition.

5.6. *The Limits of Hegel's Argument*

I have to confess at this point that, even after trying my best to present Hegel's theory in a favourable light, I find the final product rather unconvincing as a defence of private ownership. It does not follow from this, however, that there is nothing of value in Hegel's discussion. Let me conclude, then, by mentioning two important problems I see with the argument together with some more positive implications that might be drawn out of the discussion.

The first point is that, at best, Hegel's argument shows that common ownership would make mutual recognition difficult and thereby hinder individuals from developing and sustaining their personalities. It seems less convincing as a critique of collective ownership, which is a second possible alternative to private property. By a system of collective ownership I mean a system of allocating resources according to centralized procedures and mechanisms that make reference to the collective interest.[57] It seems possible that some such system could be devised that allocated to individuals the degree of exclusive access that they require to manifest their agency, but that, in other respects, falls short of a system of private property (for example, in its rules concerning the alienation of property or concerning the enjoyment of profits flowing from ownership). To the extent that such a system is possible, Hegel's defence of private property remains incomplete; he would need to adduce further reasons for preferring private to collective ownership. On the other hand, Hegel might claim to have shown that *some* degree of privacy and exclusivity will need to be built into property arrangements, even if full private ownership is not necessary. Notice, for instance, that there seems to be some degree of exclusivity assumed in the public-sculpture and stone-throwing examples mentioned earlier: the examples would not have the same force if it were permissible for just anyone to come along and add their contribution to the sculpture or if a whole crowd of boys were throwing stones into the river.[58]

The second more serious problem with Hegel's argument lies in its resolutely a priori character. Whereas Hegel is making a priori philosophical claims about the ways in which people develop certain self-understandings and capacities, what really seems appropriate here is empirical psychological investigation (see §4.3 above). It might well turn out that there is a great variety of ways in which people actually develop these self-understandings and capacities, some of which do not presuppose any degree of exclusivity or privacy. Having said this, Hegel's discussion helps us to formulate new hypotheses for empirical investigation and we should not assume in advance that empirical research will falsify his claims any more than we should assume that such research will support them.[59]

[57] For the distinction between private-, common-, and collective-property systems, see Waldron, *The Right to Private Property*, 37–46.

[58] I am grateful to Peter Stillman for pressing me on this point.

[59] For a discussion of recent psychological studies supporting the contention that property works to reinforce a person's sense of agency, see Christman, 'Distributive Justice and the Complex Structure of Ownership', 235–8.

6

A Civic Humanist Idea of Freedom

6.1. *Introduction*

One of the keys to Hegel's political philosophy is a distinction between two ways of understanding the relationship between freedom and life in a political community. The prevailing view, which Hegel associates with contractarianism,[1] sees the state as a kind of compromise: each person agrees to diminish his freedom by submitting to the rule of right in exchange for others agreeing to do the same (*PR* §29; *VG* 111/93–4; *VGP* iii. 307/401; *Enz.* iii, §539). On this view, individual freedom is diminished by life in a political community but less so than it would be in a state of nature: the state restricts our ability to do as we please, but without the state the violent and unpredictable actions of others would restrict this ability to an even greater extent. An implication of this view is that, if human nature were different, then there might be no need for a state at all and we could all enjoy that much more freedom.

A central aim of Hegel's political philosophy is to challenge this contractarian picture of the relationship between freedom and the state and to propose an alternative way of understanding that relationship in its place. Hegel denies that the state should be considered a limitation on freedom and instead claims that a kind of freedom is realized in the state that, by its very nature, could not be enjoyed outside the state. 'Man is free, this is certainly his substantial nature', he argues, 'and not only is this freedom not given up in the state, but it is actually in the state that it is first constituted' (*VGP* iii. 307/401). 'To imagine that freedom is such that the individual subject, in its co-existence with other subjects, must limit its freedom in such a way that this collective restriction, the mutual constraint of all, leaves everyone a limited area in which to act as he pleases, is to interpret freedom in purely negative terms; on the contrary, justice, ethical life,

[1] For texts in which Hegel associates the view in question with contractarians such as Fichte, see *VPR19* 152, *VPR17* 139, and *DFS* 144–5.

and the state, and these alone, are the positive realization and satisfaction of freedom' (*VG* 111/93–4).

Although the picture of Hegel as some kind of authoritarian or proto-totalitarian thinker that is often associated with his claims about freedom and the state is now widely rejected,[2] most commentators have been reluctant to endorse Hegel's position more positively. Even a writer such as Allen Wood, who is generally sympathetic to Hegel's account of freedom, expresses scepticism about the claim that the state is the realization of freedom: 'our best reason for resisting Hegel's assertion that "duty liberates" ', he argues, 'is a healthy scepticism concerning Hegel's view that the fulfilment of our duties in a modern social order really contributes to a concretely free and rational life'.[3] An aim of the present chapter is to challenge this standard assessment of Hegel's claims about freedom and the state by offering a reinterpretation of Hegel's position. I develop a generally sympathetic account of why Hegel thinks that freedom is realized in, rather than limited by, the state and I try to defend his arguments against certain natural objections.

An important part of the foundation for exploring Hegel's claims about freedom and the state was laid in Chapter 4, where we explored Hegel's confrontation with social contract theory. The argument there was that a major reason why Hegel rejects the contractarian model of the state is that he takes it to be too instrumental. By imagining that human beings with fully developed capacities for free and rational agency choose to adopt major social institutions in order to advance their ends and interests, contractarians tend to neglect the important role that social institutions have to play in constituting free and rational individuals in the first place. For Hegel, one reason why the state should be viewed, not as a limitation on freedom, but as its first realization is that the state belongs to the minimum self-sufficient institu-

[2] An exception is Tugendhat, who talks of the 'totalitarian character of Hegel's philosophy of objective spirit'. See *Self-Consciousness and Self-Determination*, 320, and 312–23 more generally. The classic reading of Hegel as an authoritarian defender of Restoration Prussia is Haym, *Hegel und seine Zeit*, ch. 15. For good criticisms of this reading, see Ritter, *Hegel and the French Revolution*; Wood, *Hegel's Ethical Thought*, 41–2, 51, 257–8; Taylor, *Hegel*, 449–61; Avineri, *Hegel's Theory of the Modern State*, chs. 6–9; and Westphal, 'The Basic Context and Structure of Hegel's *Philosophy of Right*', 234–44. See also the exchange between Knox and Carritt in Kaufmann (ed.), *Hegel's Political Philosophy*.

[3] Wood, *Hegel's Ethical Thought*, 51. See also p. 30: 'it is only too evident to us that the political state cannot play the role, whether in the life of the individual or in the collective life of the human race, which Hegel tried to assign it.'

tional structure capable of developing and sustaining the capacities and self-understandings associated with free and rational agency.

The present chapter seeks to extend and complete the discussion of Chapter 4 in three different ways. First, it explores Hegel's conception of the state and explicitly contrasts it with the conception of the state that Hegel associates with contractarianism. As we shall see, Hegel has a fairly idiosyncratic understanding of the state and thinks that it is only when the state is understood in his terms that it represents the full realization of freedom. Secondly, the chapter attempts to fill in more concretely why Hegel takes the state to be a necessary part of the institutional structure needed to foster and encourage free and rational agency. The discussion here draws on the general framework introduced in Chapter 4, and the account of property given in Chapter 5, to explain why, in Hegel's view, a social order hospitable to subjectivity, but lacking the Hegelian state, would not be stable and self-reproducing. And, third, the chapter examines an important claim about freedom and the state that was bracketed in Chapter 4 (§4.2): the claim that the state not only facilitates the development and maintenance of the capacities associated with subjective freedom but also provides the locus for objective freedom. Bringing objective freedom into the picture, alongside subjective freedom, will enable us to make sense of Hegel's important assertion that 'the state is the actuality of concrete freedom' (*PR* §260).

My discussion of Hegel's position will be limited in two different respects. First, it presupposes the arguments of the previous chapters of this study and, in particular, the account of Hegel's general conception of freedom developed in Chapters 2 and 3. My argument is that, if Hegel's general conception of freedom turns out to be correct, then his claims about freedom and the state are actually more coherent and plausible than is often thought. This will strike some readers, who remain sceptical about Hegel's general approach to freedom, as a serious limitation indeed, but it should be pointed out that there are a number of commentators who accept something like Hegel's conception of freedom but doubt that it supports his claims about the state.[4] On the other hand, there are also some people who oppose Hegel's general conception of freedom *because* it leads—absurdly in their view—to his claims about the state. One aim of this chapter is to suggest that this link is less absurd than is often supposed.

[4] e.g. Wood; see references in n. 3 above.

Secondly, the discussion to follow is a limited one in the sense that it will not be considering whether the state with exactly those features described by Hegel in the *Philosophy of Right* represents the realization of freedom. I will try to give enough of a flavour of the institutional detail of Hegel's account of the state to bear out my interpretation. But, like almost all contemporary readers, I am sceptical about whether all of the particular institutional arrangements endorsed by Hegel really are needed for the actualization of freedom. Hegel's insistence on the necessity of a monarchy, the weak and unrepresentative character of the legislative power he favours, his faith that the powerful bureaucracy he defends would promote the common good, and his ambivalence about the value of public opinion are all highly questionable aspects of his account of the state. My interest will be in the claim that the *broadly Hegelian state* represents the full realization of freedom.[5] By this I mean the state that has some of the most fundamental features assigned by Hegel to the state but may differ from Hegel's account of the state in a number of particular respects.

My hope is that the argument of this chapter will help to justify attaching the label 'civic humanist' to the reading of Hegel's idea of freedom that has been developed in this study. As I noted in §1.6, there are obviously a number of respects in which Hegel departs from themes commonly associated with civic humanism: his insistence that the contemplative life of art, religion, and philosophy represents a higher form of freedom and goodness than that available through a life of citizenship, and his general lack of enthusiasm for active political participation by ordinary citizens, are only two of the most obvious examples of this. Still, there are three good reasons for using the label 'civic humanism', which I have noted already in §1.6, and which will be central to the argument of the present chapter. First, the label draws attention to the humanist character of the position being attributed to Hegel: that Hegel's claims about freedom and the state can be understood without reliance on the idea that God is the agent of, or provider of content for, freedom. Secondly, it also draws attention to the civic humanist character of one of Hegel's central claims about freedom and the state that will be considered below: the claim that individuals achieve a fully rational or 'objective' existence only as good citizens of the state. And, thirdly, it aligns the inter-

[5] The phrase 'broadly Hegelian state' is adapted from Hardimon, *Hegel's Social Philosophy*, 254.

pretation to be developed here with a number of philosophical and sociological themes commonly associated with civic humanism. In particular, we shall see that a central part of Hegel's analysis of freedom and the state rests on the civic humanist thought that a free society is a fragile construction that can be sustained only if certain objective and subjective conditions are met. The objective conditions include the rule of law, the division of political authority into separate but interlocking spheres of responsibility, mechanisms to ensure the accountability of public officials, and an emphasis on public education. The subjective conditions centre on the idea that citizens must be animated by certain dispositions and virtues if the institutions of their freedom are to be guaranteed.

6.2. *Two Conceptions of the State*

For Hegel, the disagreement about whether the state is best viewed as limiting or as actualizing freedom rests in part on a prior disagreement about the concept of the state. The two different views about the relationship between freedom and the state, he thinks, correspond to two distinct understandings of the basic nature and purpose of the state (*PR* §258; *VPR17* 144). Hegel generally uses the term 'state' (*der Staat*) to refer to his own preferred conception of the state and contrasts this with what he variously calls the 'necessity-state' (*der Notstaat*), the 'police-state' (*der Polizeistaat*), the 'external-state' (*der äußere Staat*), or the 'understanding-state' (*der Verstandesstaat*) (*PR* §183). Although each of these terms captures some facet of the distinction that Hegel wishes to draw, I shall generally use the term *Notstaat*, which nicely draws attention to the unfreedom of the sphere in question, to refer to the alternative conception of the state that Hegel wishes to oppose. It is important to note, as critics of Hegel's account of freedom and the state have typically not done, that Hegel *concedes* that, if the state is equated with the *Notstaat*, then it does indeed represent a limitation on individual freedom (this is part of the reason why he calls it a *Notstaat*) (see *PR* §186; *VPR17* 145; *VPR18* 250; *VPR19* 147). It is only the state in Hegel's specialized sense of the term that is said not to restrict freedom at all, but to actualize it fully.

To be in a position to understand and evaluate Hegel's claims about freedom and the state, then, it is necessary to come to terms with this distinction between two conceptions of the state. Since Hegel closely identifies the *Notstaat* with the sphere of civil society, this suggests that we must address one of the perennial questions in Hegel interpretation—namely, how to understand his distinction between state and civil society. Indeed, as we shall see shortly, at the root of many objections to Hegel's claims about freedom and the state is a misunderstanding of how he draws this fundamental distinction.

Although the basic thrust of Hegel's state/civil-society distinction is clear enough, understanding the precise way in which the distinction is drawn is notoriously difficult. The main exegetical difficulty arises from the fact that Hegel's general formulations of the distinction are often not clearly illustrated by, and at times seem at odds with, the particular judgements he makes about which institutions and activities belong in each sphere. To point to only the most obvious example of this, it has puzzled commentators for generations why Hegel assigns the administration of justice and the police to the sphere of civil society and not, as we do in ordinary parlance, to the state. In what follows, I offer a formulation of Hegel's distinction that can account for much of what he has to say about the two spheres, but I should admit from the start that I am sceptical about whether *any* account of the distinction can explain all of Hegel's particular judgements.

The prevailing late-twentieth-century understanding of the distinction between civil society and state contrasts a voluntary sphere containing a plurality of independent centres of decision-making, on the one hand, with a public, authoritative, overarching framework of institutions that individuals find themselves in independently of their own choices and decisions, on the other.[6] Thus civil society is standardly identified with two characteristic features of modern liberal democracies: the network of groups and partial associations, such as trade unions, churches, pressure groups, protest movements, clubs, and so on, that bring together like-minded individuals for the achievement of some particular purpose; and, in some versions at least, the market economy.[7] By contrast, the state is taken to be the set of legislative, executive, and judicial institutions that make,

[6] See e.g. Gellner, *Conditions of Liberty*, esp. chs. 1, 22; Walzer, 'The Civil Society Argument'; and Cohen and Arato, *Civil Society and Political Theory*, pp. ix–x.

[7] Cohen and Arato (*Civil Society and Political Theory*) argue, however, that the market economy should not be considered part of civil society.

implement, and apply authoritative decisions affecting the whole community. The distinction is being used in roughly this sense, for instance, when it is argued that the emerging democracies of Eastern Europe need to foster and encourage the development of civil society in order to counterbalance their strong state traditions: the point here is that the centralized, authoritative institutions that make up the state in these countries need to be supplemented and checked by autonomous networks of voluntary groups and associations through which individuals can develop and pursue their own independent agendas in a solidaristic context.[8]

This way of understanding the distinction certainly has some historical roots in Hegel's formulation of the distinction and to a considerable extent does capture the spirit of the contrast he has in mind.[9] Unfortunately, formulating the distinction this way makes it very difficult to see how Hegel could hold that freedom is best identified with the state rather than with civil society: if the contrast between state and civil society is essentially a contrast between an obligatory and authoritative sphere, on the one hand, and a sphere of independent will formation and voluntary exchange, on the other, then it seems much more natural to think of civil society as realizing freedom and of the state as a (perhaps necessary) limitation on it. To this extent, the state/civil-society distinction, and the corresponding distinction between two conceptions of the state, does not, as Hegel intends, strengthen the case for his claims about freedom and the state but, if anything, seems to undermine it.

Fortunately for Hegel's argument, however, this contemporary formulation of the distinction does not, as most careful commentators have perceived, quite do justice to Hegel's position.[10] Indeed it is probably no exaggeration to say that the key to understanding Hegel's claim about freedom and the state is to try to forget our usual way of understanding the state/civil-society distinction and to attend closely to what Hegel actually has to say about the two spheres. One

[8] See e.g. Walzer, 'The Civil Society Argument', and Gellner, *Conditions of Liberty*.

[9] An excellent discussion of the Hegelian roots of contemporary thinking about civil society is Cohen and Arato, *Civil Society and Political Theory*, ch. 2.

[10] Good discussions of Hegel's state/civil-society distinction to which I am greatly indebted include: Avineri, *Hegel's Theory of the Modern State*, 141–7; Pelczynski, 'Introduction' to *State and Civil Society*, and 'The Hegelian Conception of the State', 10–12; Plant, *Hegel: An Introduction*, ch. 9; Riedel, *Between Tradition and Revolution*, ch. 6; and Hardimon, *Hegel's Social Philosophy*, ch. 6.

problem with the contemporary formulation of the distinction is that it obscures Hegel's contention that civil society is easily confused with the state and his corresponding tendency to refer to civil society as the *Notstaat*: for it is very hard to see why anyone would be apt to confuse either the market economy or a society's network of private groups and associations with the state. A second problem is that Hegel allocates to civil society two sets of institutions—the administration of justice and the 'police' (perhaps better translated as 'public authority')[11]—that on the contemporary formulation would be considered part of the state.[12]

Careful attention to what Hegel actually has to say about the distinction suggests that the main contrast he seeks to draw between the two spheres is this: whereas civil society is the domain in which individuals and groups have as their end and object the 'particular', and relate only indirectly and unconsciously to the 'universal', the state is the domain in which individuals, groups, and institutions consciously and directly have as their end and object the 'universal' (*PR* §§181–7; *VPR17* 108–9; *VPR19* 147–52). In civil society the universal is an unintended consequence or by-product of the actions of agents for whom 'the particular . . . is the primary determining principle': in civil society I think I am pursuing only the particular, 'but I am in fact simply under a misapprehension, for, while I believe that I am adhering to the particular, the universal and the necessity of the [wider] context nevertheless remain the primary and essential factor' (*PR* §181A). By contrast, in the state, the universality of the will is 'manifest' (*offenbare*) and 'self-transparent' (*sich selbst deutliche*) (*VPR17* 145), so that agents are 'living in the universal *for* the universal' (*VPR17* 109). That is to say, in the state agents directly and explicitly seek to identify and consciously bring about the universal: the universal is both 'in itself'—it is the outcome of everyone's actions—*and* 'for itself'—it is the object of reflection and the intended consequence of action (*PR* §256). 'The state therefore *knows* what it wills, and knows it in its *universality* as something *thought*. Consequently, it acts and functions in accordance with known ends and recognized principles, and with laws which are laws not only *in themselves* but also for the consciousness' (*PR* §270).

[11] Hegel's use of the term 'police' (*Polizei*) is discussed by Wood in his notes to the English translation of *PR*, p. 450, and by Riedel, *Between Tradition and Revolution*, 152–3. (Cf. *VPR18* 259.)

[12] Although at *PR* §287 he complicates things further by suggesting that they are part of the state.

The obvious question raised by this formulation of the distinction concerns what Hegel means in the context by 'particular' and 'universal'. One interpretation of this terminology would identify the particular with associations of which only some people in society are members and the universal with an association to which everyone in society belongs: on this view, civil society would be the sphere of the particular in the sense that it is a sphere of partial groups and associations, and the state would be universal in the sense that it provides an overarching framework that regulates and oversees the particulars. Although this is certainly part of what Hegel has in mind, on its own it leaves us back with the contemporary formulation of the state/civil-society distinction and the problems it raises. A closer look at Hegel's discussion of state and civil society, however, suggests that the particular/universal distinction he is operating with works along two further dimensions.[13]

The first dimension refers to the *kind of good* that individuals, groups, and institutions in each sphere seek to realize. A good is particular, for Hegel, if and only if it involves the well-being (*Wohl*) of the agent who enjoys it: a particular good always relates to the satisfaction of some empirically given need, desire, inclination, or so on (*PR* §189; cf. *PR* §§45, 71, 182, 185; *VPR17* 111, 145; *VPR18* 250, 258; *VPR19* 70, 147). By contrast, a universal good is something that is good for an agent independently of what needs, desires, etc., he experiences: it is universal in the sense that it is not peculiar to agents having certain needs or desires, but is good for all free and rational agents as such. Obvious candidates for universal goods, in Hegel's philosophy, include the goods associated with the spheres of art, religion, and philosophy: Hegel thinks that these are goods independently of the desires and needs that agents happen to have (*VPR17* 189–90). But in the practical sphere, explored by Hegel in the *Philosophy of Right*, the chief examples of universal goods are the capacities for free and rational agency together with the conditions for the development,

[13] Here my account of Hegel's state/civil-society distinction diverges somewhat from Hardimon's excellent discussion in *Hegel's Social Philosophy*, 205–14. Hardimon identifies the 'universality' of the state with the fact that it promotes the 'common good' and argues that what makes a good 'common' is the fact that it is agreed upon 'through a collective deliberative process in which the community attempts as a community to determine what its ends are' (p. 211). This gloss strikes me as far too Rousseauian to be an accurate reflection of Hegel's position and in the text below I suggest an alternative way of understanding the senses in which Hegel takes the state to be 'universal' *vis-à-vis* civil society.

maintenance, and exercise of these capacities. Since one of the most important conditions of developing and sustaining free and rational agency is, as we have seen, to live in a stable and effective community of mutual recognition, Hegel sometimes says that social union is a universal good and contrasts it with 'the interest of individuals [*der Einzelnen*] as such' and their 'particular satisfaction': 'union as such', he asserts, 'is itself the true content and end' (*PR* §258; cf. *PR* §163).

The second dimension of Hegel's contrast between particular and universal concerns the degree to which agents are *self*- or *other-regarding* in their actions, motives, and dispositions. Individual ends and actions are said to be particular when they are essentially self-regarding: they aim at the good of the individual performing them or at the good of his close circle of family, friends, and colleagues (*PR* §§181A, 182–3; *VPR17* 108–9; *VPR19* 147). Universal ends, on the other hand, aim at the good of others or the good of the community as a whole. Hegel holds that the two dimensions along which particularity and universality can be distinguished tend to converge into one. Ends that are particular in the first sense—their goodness resides in the needs and desires they satisfy—are often particular in the second sense—they are often selfish and unethical; on the other hand, ends that are universal in the first sense are typically other-regarding. This convergence thesis is not due to equivocation on the terms 'particular' and 'universal' but reflects the idea, explored in Chapter 3 of this study, that agents who abstract from their given needs and desires as possible reasons-for-action still have one reason-for-action left—they have reason to participate in and support relationships of community with others in the context of which they can develop and sustain their capacities for free and rational agency.

Hegel, we have seen, defines the relationship between civil society and state in terms of three distinct propositions. He stipulates that:

(1) civil society is the sphere in which agents have the particular as their end and object;
(2) the universal is an unintended consequence of this pursuit of the particular in civil society; and
(3) the state is the sphere in which agents consciously have the universal as their end and object.

Having analysed Hegel's twofold distinction between particularity and universality we are now in a position to make sense of this characterization of the state–civil-society relationship.

Proposition (1) says most basically that civil society is the sphere in which individuals seek to achieve *their own welfare*—that is, the satisfaction of their own empirically given needs and desires. In Hegel's words, 'the concrete person who, as a *particular* person, as a totality of needs and a mixture of natural necessity and arbitrariness, is his own end, is *one principle* of civil society' (*PR* §182). Proposition (1) thus defines civil society as that sphere in which two assumptions made by classical political economy hold true: (i) that individuals are basically self-seeking (animated by *Selbstsucht*); and (ii) that individuals are basically utility-maximizing. It also affirms that, in so far as civil society is made up of institutions such as the administration of justice and the police, as well as individuals and groups competing in the market place, the basic rationale or purpose of these institutions is to be understood in terms of the satisfaction of individuals' self-regarding needs and desires. The point of these institutions, that is to say, lies both in the way in which they help to establish, regulate, and stabilize a market economy in which individuals can seek maximal fulfilment of their ends and desires and in their function of providing resources to people who lack the means or capacities to satisfy their own needs and desires through market transactions (*PR* §§208, 217, 221, A, 230, 235–40, 249).[14] Hegel may also have meant to suggest, although this is less clear, that, in so far as these institutions are considered part of civil society, the people who manage and control them are basically self-regarding and utility-maximizing.

Proposition (2) again borrows from classical political economy but also goes beyond it. It suggests that the pursuit by individuals of their own welfare, as mediated by the institutions and arrangements of civil society, has two unintended consequences. The first of these, and the one that is most strikingly emphasized by classical economists,[15] is that self-regarding utility maximization works to the benefit of other people: as Hegel puts it, '*subjective selfishness* turns into a *contribution towards the satisfaction of everyone else*' so that 'by a dialectical movement, the particular is mediated by the universal [and] each individual, in earning, producing, and enjoying on his own account, thereby earns and produces for the enjoyment of others' (*PR* §199). Here Hegel clearly has in mind the ways in which individuals in the context of a market economy are forced to provide

[14] See also Plant, *Hegel: An Introduction*, 225, and Hardimon, *Hegel's Social Philosophy*, 189–205.

[15] See e.g. Adam Smith, *The Wealth of Nations*, 118–19.

benefits for others if they are to obtain benefits for themselves: the good of others is not the aim of the individual in the market place, but it is the by-product of his self-seeking utility-maximizing activity. 'The individual provides [*sorgt*] only for himself and has only himself as his end; however, he cannot provide for himself except by providing for others and by having others provide for him' (*VPR19* 108). A second and distinct by-product of individuals seeking their own particular welfare, less emphasized by classical political economy, is the achievement of a more universal *kind* of good. This is most clearly set out at *PR* §187, where Hegel argues that through work individuals achieve both practical and theoretical *Bildung*: through work they learn to plan and to be disciplined and they have concrete evidence of the efficacy of their own purposes and agency, evidence that helps to reinforce their sense of themselves as free and rational agents (cf. *PR* §197, A; *Ph.G.* 153–4/118–19). This idea is also implicit in Hegel's account of the recognition and self-respect that individuals gain from being members of an estate and corporation: by taking up a position in civil society in this way, individuals attract the recognition of their fellows, which further reinforces their sense of themselves as free and rational agents (*PR* §253; *Enz.* iii, §432A). Proposition (2) further suggests that institutions associated with civil society, such as the administration of justice and police, indirectly work to foster and nourish the individual's capacities for freedom and rationality. By securing private property, and enforcing contracts, for instance, these institutions cater directly to individual particularity but indirectly to the development of the individual's free personality.

Finally, proposition (3) says that the state shares in common with civil society the fact that it is a sphere in which individuals (*a*) work for the benefit of others and (*b*) develop and reinforce their capacities for free and rational agency. But it claims additionally that, whereas in civil society this fact is an unintended by-product of the self-regarding utility-maximizing behaviour of individuals, the state is the sphere in which individuals directly, explicitly, and intentionally work for the good of others, or for the whole community, and seek to preserve and promote a community of mutual recognition in which all can develop and sustain their free and rational faculties. The state, then, is a sphere of institutions—the sovereign, executive, and legislative powers—that have the maintenance of the conditions of freedom for the whole community as the object of their knowledge and deliberation and make, implement, and apply decisions on this basis (*VPR19* 144). It is also a sphere in which the fundamental dispositions of individuals are other-regarding ones including 'political virtue' (*PR* §257) and 'patriotism' (*PR* §268). It is thus a sphere that can embrace a wide range of activities and relationships in which these dispositions are appropriate, including, for instance, voting for a deputy in the context of one's corporation, informing oneself about and obeying the law (including paying taxes), doing military service on behalf of the community, contributing to public opinion, acting as a deputy in the Assembly of the Estates, and performing one's role as a civil servant in an impartial and conscientious manner.

As I noted earlier, the contemporary formulation of the state/civil-society distinction sees it as primarily a distinction between the market economy and the network of private partial associations, on the one hand, and an overarching authoritative set of institutions, on the other. Although Hegel's formulation of the distinction has some affinities with this view, we can now see that it is constructed in a quite different way: The allocation of different relationships, activities and institutions is, for Hegel, primarily a question not of whether they are private, partial, authoritative, and so on, but of their fundamental purpose and of the aims, knowledge, and dispositions of the individuals who are involved. If the individuals who are involved in some relationship are primarily self-seeking utility-maximizers, and/or the relationship caters to this orientation, then Hegel assigns the relationship to the sphere of civil society. If, however, the relationship is primarily concerned with preserving and promoting the freedom of agents (rather than their welfare), and agents are disposed to act not just for their own good but for the good of the community as a whole, then Hegel assigns it to the state. This way of understanding Hegel's distinction can explain not only why the market economy is assigned to civil society and the legislature and executive are assigned to the state, but also more difficult cases, such as why the administration of justice and the police appear as part of civil society and then reappear again in the sphere of the state (*PR* §287).

More importantly for the argument of this chapter, it is now possible to see why Hegel holds that state and civil society can be regarded as two rival conceptions of the state. This is because it is possible to view the state as having two quite different sorts of relationships with its citizens. On one view, the contractarian view, which in effect makes the state part of civil society, the state is primarily an instrument with which self-seeking utility-maximizing individuals seek to secure and further their own welfare. As I noted earlier, Hegel concedes that, if this view of the state is adopted, then the state does indeed constitute a limitation on individual freedom as ordinary consciousness tends to assume. On a second view, however, what might simply be termed a 'Hegelian' view of the state, the state's primary function is not to promote the welfare of citizens but to secure and maintain their freedom; moreover, citizens are conceived of as having a less instrumental, more affirmative and patriotic attitude towards their political institutions, regarding them not as a necessary evil but as a constitutive component of their identity and good. It is when the state is understood in this second way that Hegel insists that it represents not a restriction on but the full actualization of individual freedom.

6.3. *The Rationality of the Hegelian State*

Hegel's deeper point, of course, is not just that there is this alternative to the prevailing contractarian conception of the state but that his conception better characterizes the nature of the state as it actually is (recall that Hegel's aim is to reconcile us to our own world and not to posit some better world 'beyond') and that it better captures the distinctive rationality of the state. We misunderstand the state, and miss out an important dimension of social experience, he is suggesting, if in characterizing it we abstract from the phenomenon of patriotism or ignore the ways in which being a citizen is central to many individuals' identities and self-understandings. We fail to perceive the rationality of the state, moreover, if we focus exclusively on the ways in which the state is instrumental to the security and welfare of individuals and neglect its function of developing and sustaining the capacities for human reason and freedom. The advantage of the Hegelian view of the state is that it avoids both of these mistakes.

At this point a contractarian is likely to pose a question of the following sort: why exactly is the Hegelian state rational in this sense? As I noted at various points in Chapter 4, it is by no means self-evident that the state *is* necessary for the development and maintenance of the capacities for free and rational agency. This step in the argument now seems especially in need of defence in the light of Hegel's idiosyncratic conception of the state. Why should the existence of a political community in which individuals are patriotic, and being a citizen is central to their identities and self-understandings, be such an indispensable condition of becoming and remaining free?

Much of the work of reconstructing Hegel's position on this issue was done in Chapter 4. My argument there was that a central task of Hegel's social philosophy—one that distinguishes it from social contract theories—is the elaboration of the social and political conditions under which the capacities for free and rational agency are developed and sustained. Hegel argues that one such general condition is that individuals participate in what I termed a 'community of mutual recognition'—a community in which institutions and practices are established through which individuals can recognize one another as free and rational agents and thereby solidify the self-understandings that are integral to *being* free and rational. Although Hegel thinks that a wide range of different institutions and practices have a part to play in this mediation of mutual recognition, central amongst them, as we saw in detail in Chapter 5, is the institution of private property. Private property mediates recognition—both self-recognition and recognition by others—and thus plays an essential role, in Hegel's view, in constituting individuals as free agents.

Although the institutions of property, and, Hegel swiftly adds, contract (*PR* §§71–81), are necessary conditions of the development of freedom and rationality, Hegel thinks that they represent just one particularly 'abstract' stage in that development. The full actualization of freedom, he maintains, calls for a 'richer', 'more concrete', 'more truly universal' set of institutions and practices, including the family, civil society, and the state (*PR* §30). In Chapter 5, I gave some reasons why a claim about the need for property arrangements providing some degree of privacy and exclusivity might be plausible, even if it is far from clear that Hegel's defence of full private ownership is successful. To vindicate Hegel's claim about the distinctive rationality of the state, we need now to investigate why something *more* than property is required for the development of freedom. If property and contract mediate the mutual recognition that is required to constitute individuals as free agents, then why should it matter what further institutional structure a community has, so long as it contains these institutions?

One reading of Hegel's position is that property and contract represent just one 'abstract' stage in the development of freedom because they actualize only a very poor and incomplete kind of freedom in individuals. Whereas true freedom consists in rational self-determination, property and contract foster and nourish only the arbitrary freedom of personality that Hegel occasionally deprecates (e.g. at *PR* §149, A). A community must contain a 'richer', 'more concrete' institutional structure in order to provide a context in which agents can actualize, as subjects and members, the fuller and more authentic freedom of rational self-determination as well.

This interpretation is correct in one sense but not in another. What is correct about it is that Hegel does hold that at each stage in the development he describes in the *Philosophy of Right* the self is more fully actualized than at the previous stage: the member of ethical institutions is more 'concrete' and 'actual' than the subject of morality, who in turn is more fully actualized than the person of abstract right (*PR* §104).[16] The interpretation is misleading, however, in so far as it purports to explain *why* Hegel holds that the initial stages he describes in the book are less concrete and rational than the final set of institutions and practices (that is, those that constitute the state). It is true that Hegel thinks that the self of abstract right is less fully actualized than the moral and ethical selves, but this is not what accounts for the irrationality or defect of abstract right.

To see this one need only consider Hegel's strictures about the method and structure of the *Philosophy of Right* in the book's Introduction. He describes the development from the abstract sphere of property and contract to the concrete sphere of the state as 'an *immanent* progression and production of its own determinations' (*PR* §31). He insists that the dialectical method that he follows is 'not an *external* activity of subjective thought, but the *very soul* of the content which puts forth its branches and fruit organically' (*PR* §31). And he says that the reason why we do not begin straightaway with 'the highest instance' or 'concretely true' is that 'we wish to see the truth precisely in the form of a result, and it is essential for this purpose that we should first comprehend the abstract concept itself' (*PR* §32A). These comments, which summarize methodological assumptions that Hegel feels he has established in his logic, suggest that the reason why further development is required after the initial stage of property and contract is not so much due to the failure of property and contract to live up to some externally imposed criterion (full self-actualization) as it is to some internal defect, or inadequacy, or con-

[16] This is emphasized by Wood, in *Hegel's Ethical Thought*, 21–2, 30–2.

tradiction, in the initial abstract determination itself. The problem with property and contract cannot *just* be that they fail fully to actualize the self (although Hegel believes this to be the case), because this would not constitute an *immanent* critique of those institutions. To be true to his own methodological requirements Hegel needs somehow to show that such an institutional structure is self-frustrating or defective on its own terms. Likewise, to see the truth (that is, the rationality of the state) as a *result* he cannot merely show that the state more fully actualizes the self than do other institutional structures, for this again is an appeal to an external criterion; he needs to demonstrate that it provides a 'solution' or adequate 'response' to the contradictions inherent in other institutional structures that have been shown to be necessary.[17]

Consistent with these methodological strictures, Hegel characterizes the abstract stages (such as property, contract, morality, civil society, etc.) as not 'self-sufficient' (*selbständig*) (*PR* §§32A, 182A; *VPR17* 86; *VPR18* 222) or able to exist 'independently' (*für sich*) (*PR* §§32A, 141A). The state in particular, and *Sittlichkeit* more generally, by contrast, are compared with a living organism that is able to reproduce itself continuously over time, despite being subject to various shocks and deprivations (*PR* §§142, 146, 267–9, 270A, 278; *VPR17* 89, 91, 148, 150). Hegel's suggestion, then, is that property and contract are necessary conditions of the development and maintenance of free and rational agency but that a community containing only these institutions would not be viable and self-reproducing. The state is an indispensable condition of the development and sustaining of the capacities for freedom and rationality because it is part of the minimum self-sufficient institutional structure that is effective at fostering and reinforcing these capacities. 'It is necessary to look in the state for right in its highest actuality. Right only comes to actuality in the state. It is not contingent that men have entered into the

[17] This distinction between 'externalist' and 'immanent' readings of the method and structure of the *Philosophy of Right* is similar to Pinkard's distinction between 'backward' and 'forward' readings (*Hegel's* Phenomenology, 280 n. 10). A backward reading views Hegel as comparing each determination in the sequence developed in the book with the structure of freedom and right deployed in the full-blown social order achieved by the end of the book. A forward reading, by contrast, investigates how each determination in the sequence breaks down on its own terms and thereby leads to, or generates, the social order reached at the end of the book. I agree with Pinkard that a forward reading more closely conforms to Hegel's guidelines concerning methodology and structure.

state, [since] it is only in the state that the concept of freedom comes to its self-sufficient existence [*selbständigen Dasein*]' (*VPR18* 222).

As with so many key concepts in his social philosophy, Hegel does not provide us with an easily accessible account of 'self-sufficiency'. What does seem clear is that he associates it closely with his notion of dialectic: something that is unable to exist on its own, or lacks self-sufficiency, is something that is subject to dialectical reversals and internal contradictions. A structure lacks self-sufficiency, that is to say, when it reveals itself to be self-undermining or self-frustrating: its very success at fulfilling its purpose leads to its own failure to achieve that purpose (*VG* 65/56).[18] Applied to institutional structures, Hegel seems to have the following idea in mind: an institutional structure is self-sufficient or self-reproducing when its normal operation works to secure and reinforce the conditions under which it can continue to operate effectively over time. An institutional structure lacks self-sufficiency, by contrast, when its normal operation works over time to undermine its ongoing effective operation.[19]

Notice that this conception of self-sufficiency does not say that the continued effective operation of a self-sufficient structure is *guaranteed*, come what may. Even the most rationally articulated organism or state, Hegel recognizes, will have a natural life span and may even have its life cut short by extreme shocks or deprivations (*PR* §§30, 340; *VG* 68–71/59–60). The point about self-sufficient structures is that they do not actively encourage the conditions of their own destruction but, rather, tend to bring about the conditions that work to secure their own self-reproduction against a range of ordinary shocks and deprivations.

Why might an institutional structure lack self-sufficiency in this sense? The precise mechanism by which the dialectic undermining each structure considered by Hegel operates varies from case to case, but one idea seems central to most of them. An institutional structure operates effectively only if the established rules of conduct that partly constitute it are generally accepted and followed. If, for example, a system of private property is to be established and maintained that has the beneficial consequences for individual development

[18] Cf. Hegel's examples of dialectic at *Enz.* i. §81A and *VG* 67–8/58–9.

[19] Consider e.g. Hegel's suggestion that 'extreme anarchy and extreme despotism lead to one another' (offered as an example of dialectic) (*Enz.* i. §81A). The point seems to be that the normal operation of a structure characterizable as 'extreme anarchy' would, over time, lead to its own self-destruction and replacement by 'extreme despotism' (and the same is true in reverse).

anticipated by Hegel, then people must, in general, respect the property and person of others, keep their contracts, and so on. Following such rules of conduct, however, often means accepting burdens and sacrifices or at least forbearing from actions that are in one's immediate self-interest. A system of private property can operate effectively, for example, only if at least most people impose on themselves a duty not to help themselves to others' goods as soon as they get a chance. One major reason why an institutional structure may lack self-sufficiency, this suggests, is if that structure fails to imbue people with the disposition to accept the burdens and sacrifices needed for its own maintenance and effective operation. When a failure of this sort occurs, the maintenance of the institutional structure in question is a matter of 'contingency' (*Zufälligkeit*): individuals may have ends conducive to the maintenance of the institutions that they are part of, but they may just as likely not have them.

It seems clear that the argument takes this form in the case of the institutions of property and contract. In the latter part of 'Abstract Right' Hegel argues that property and contract imbue people with motivations and dispositions that lead them to act in ways that actually undermine the institutions of property and contract (see especially *PR* §81, A). In particular, as we saw in Chapter 5, he thinks that these institutions encourage agents to think of themselves as persons—that is, as independent of their given situation and capable of acting on their own ideas and purposes. The problem arises because a person as such could decide that *any* particular idea or purpose is his own: the notion of personality is neutral with respect to the content of an agent's ends (for this reason Hegel associates it with *Willkür*) (see §5.2 above). This is a problem because, as we have seen, the effective operation and survival of the institutions of property and contract depend on agents having certain ends and not having others: they must keep their contracts and not violate the property of others (including their personal security). If agents are only persons, and have no further incentives, or possess no deeper self-understanding, then it is contingent whether they will actually will the ends necessary for the survival of the institutions required to maintain their personality.[20] In this sense, the very success of a social

[20] This argument is most clearly made at *PR* §81A: 'In contract, we had the relationship of two wills as a common will. This identical will, however, is only relatively universal—a posited universal will—and is thereby still in opposition to the particular will. The contract or agreement nevertheless contains the right to require its

structure consisting of property and contract at turning agents into persons seems to guarantee its own demise.

This argument is one particular instantiation of a persistent theme in Hegel's social and political thought: the idea that a culture of independent personality and subjectivity has potentially destabilizing implications for the established institutions and practices of a society. For instance, Hegel famously holds that the pre-Socratic Greeks enjoyed a harmonious social existence in which they habitually fulfilled the tasks and functions that allowed their social order continuously to reproduce itself. It was only when the sophists introduced the principle of critical reflection, and this principle gradually permeated Greek culture, that the maintenance of the social order was threatened. When individuals began to consult their own particular beliefs and convictions about what to do, rather than reflexively following the customs and conventions of their community, their willingness to accept the burdens and sacrifices needed to keep the community going could no longer be counted on. Hegel goes so far as to read Plato's *Republic* as a profound philosophical attempt to describe what his community would have to do (for example, ban private property, occupational choice, and the family) in order to forestall the development of the principle of independent personality that threatens it with disintegration (see *PR* 185, A; *VGP* ii. 105–30/90–115; *VPG* 306–10/250–3).

Hegel's own project, however, is not the Platonic one of finding ways of stifling individuality and subjectivity. Quite to the contrary, his concern is to identify what features of the modern social world make a spirit of independent personality and subjectivity realizable in a stable and self-sustaining way. Indeed, one way of understanding the structure of the remainder of the *Philosophy of Right* is as an attempt to develop a solution to the contradiction set up by the institutions of property and contract. Property and contract are necessary conditions of the development and maintenance of free and rational agency but on their own they are self-undermining and so some further elaboration of the institutional structure needed for freedom is required. Because this first 'structure of recognition [*Anerkanntsein*] is contingent' (*VPR17* 73), right must be 're-established' as 'valid', 'actual', and 'effective' (*PR*

performance; but this again is a matter for the particular will, which may, as such, act in contravention of that right which has being in itself' (cf. *VPR17* 64).

§82A).[21] One institution introduced by Hegel to this end is punishment: punishment is supposed to orient individuals away from certain ends and towards others by expressing society's condemnation of wrong-doing. Hegel thinks that this is part of the solution to the contradiction he identifies in 'Abstract Right' but not the whole story: so long as agents possess only personality, and not some deeper self-understanding as well, punishment will remain indistinguishable from revenge and destabilizing conflict will be impossible to avoid (*PR* §102).

The second part of the *Philosophy of Right*, 'Morality', proposes a quite different sort of corrective to the self-sufficiency problem introduced by property and contract. It suggests that the problem of stabilizing the institutional structure needed to develop free personality could be solved if agents possessed not just personality but also subjectivity (*PR* §§103–6). A subject, in Hegel's technical sense of the term, is an agent who conceives of himself not only as independent of his given situation but also as a bearer of certain ends and purposes that are distinctively *his own*.[22] He thinks of himself as free, and as leading a good life, not just to the extent that he exercises his capacities for reflection and choice, but to the degree that he determines his life according to his own projects and purposes and, in particular, as Hegel emphasizes in the final section of 'Morality', according to his own *conscience*. The idea behind Hegel's proposal seems relatively clear: if the fundamental disposition of individuals is not just one of independent personality but also revolves around willing certain specific ends, and those ends are the ones that lend self-sufficiency to the institutional structure needed for the development of personality (and now subjectivity as well), then the contradiction that afflicts 'Abstract Right' would be resolved. As Hegel puts it at the end of 'Abstract Right', what is required is 'a will which, as a particular and *subjective* will, also wills the universal as such', and this is exactly what morality aims to provide (*PR* §103).

[21] As H. B. Nisbet points out in his translator's footnote to *PR* §82A, Hegel's term-of-art *Wirklichkeit* (actuality) is closely related to the verb *wirken* (to be effective). One idea that Hegel wishes to convey with his famous dictum that 'what is rational is actual; and what is actual is rational' is that a social order is rational only if it is stable, effective, and self-reproducing (cf. *PR* §270A).

[22] I have not always used 'subject' and 'subjectivity' in this technical sense (nor do I think that Hegel always does so) but have often used the terms to mean roughly 'agent' and 'agency'. A 'subject' or 'agent' in this looser usage is someone who possesses certain capacities, self-understandings, and attitudes, e.g. for reflection, self-examination, and so forth.

As with punishment, however, Hegel holds that morality and subjectivity are part of the resolution to the contradiction introduced in 'Abstract Right' but not the complete solution. He thinks that there are two separate problems with the attempt to resolve the contradiction in the way suggested by 'Morality': one concerns the *content* of conscience, the other the *motivation* of individuals. The content problem is simply the problem of whether the ends and duties that individuals find they are committed to after searching their consciences really will be the ones that provide support for the institutional structure needed for the development and maintenance of personality and subjectivity (*PR* §§135–41). The motivation problem concerns whether individuals will be disposed to follow their consciences or whether they will prefer to pursue their own personal interests and satisfaction instead.[23] Hegel claims that, on its own, morality is unable to provide either of these guarantees needed to lend self-sufficiency to an institutional structure in which individuals can develop and sustain their capacities for free and rational agency. In 'Morality', as in 'Abstract Right', it is entirely contingent whether individuals will have the specific ends and motives needed to secure the development of freedom and rationality.

Underlying this argument is the assumption that an individual's deepest convictions, values, and motivations are shaped by the social practices and institutions in which he participates. Thus we might expect that, given the 'right' social environment, individuals would find the 'right' ends in their consciences and the motivation to follow those ends. The problem, however, is that morality, as Hegel understands it, makes no assumptions about what social practices and institutions are established beyond the assumption of property and contract (the institutions that introduced the contradiction in the first place).[24] Morality is in effect an attempt to resolve the contradiction arising in 'Abstract Right' in a non-institutional way, but is for this very reason bound to fail because, unless certain institutions are in place, there is no reason to suppose that individuals searching their consciences and considering their motives will make practical

[23] Hegel is less explicit about this problem in his discussion of morality itself, but it is clear that he thinks that one advantage of *Sittlichkeit* over *Moralität* is that in the former individuals have a disposition to act ethically: 'the habit of the ethical appears as second nature' (*PR* §151; cf. *PR* §§142, 150).

[24] Holding people responsible and showing concern for the welfare of others might be considered moral practices but they remain too formal and indeterminate to resolve the contradictions initially introduced in 'Abstract Right'.

decisions that work to stabilize the institutional structure that makes personality and subjectivity possible.

Hegel's conclusion, which he reaches in Part Three of the *Philosophy of Right*, 'The Ethical Life' (*Sittlichkeit*), is that, if freedom is to be actualized, then agents must be not only persons and subjects but also *members*. Only if agents are participating members of certain modern social institutions—notably the family, civil society, and the state—can they be expected to have the convictions, values, motivations, and dispositions that stabilize an institutional structure in which they can develop and maintain the capacities involved in personality and subjectivity.[25] This is because, in contrast to the arbitrariness of individual ends and motives in 'Abstract Right' and 'Morality', each of these institutions encourages individuals in different ways to act for the good of others. The family works through sentiment and affection, civil society through an invisible hand mechanism and the honour and comraderie of being a member of an estate and corporation, and the state through various institutional structures together with the dispositions of patriotism and civic virtue.

Freedom is actualized in modern *Sittlichkeit*, then, because a community containing the institutions and practices of modern *Sittlichkeit* is the minimum self-sufficient institutional structure in which agents can develop and reinforce the capacities for freedom and rationality. Modern *Sittlichkeit* is an indispensable part of such an institutional structure because it is the only environment in which individuals can be reliably expected to acquire the other-regarding ends and dispositions that will encourage them to accept the burdens and sacrifices presupposed by a self-reproducing social order that is hospitable to personality and subjectivity. Hegel's response to the ancients' worries about the destabilizing effects of subjectivity is thus to argue that a social order *can* tolerate a high degree of independent personality and subjectivity but *only* if a crucial condition is met. Its citizens must be members of ethical institutions that imbue them with goals, values, convictions, and so forth, such that, when they consult their own opinions and consciences about what to do, the answers

[25] Hegel is ambivalent about the contribution of the Christian religion to a general culture of freedom. Religion can imbue people with a disposition to respect the state and its laws, but it can also have extremely destabilizing implications, e.g. where it teaches that 'laws are not made for the pious', or where it sets Church and state up as rival authorities (*PR* §270).

they arrive at reinforce that order rather than ripping it apart, as happened (in Hegel's view) in the ancient world and as recently as the French Revolution.[26]

The claim that the Hegelian state is rational amounts to the proposition that the ties of sentiment and affection that characterize the family, and those of mutual advantage and collegiality that are found in civil society, are not on their own sufficient to guarantee that people will accept the sacrifices and burdens needed to support a freedom-developing institutional structure.[27] The model of the family is not generalizable because the bonds of affection and sentiment extend only as far as one's close relations and friends, whereas the maintenance of the required institutional structure requires some willingness to accept burdens and sacrifices on behalf of the countless strangers with whom one shares a community. Mutual advantage, the principle of civil society, can have a tremendous integrative effect within the context of an established market economy, but it is much less able to support the norms, rules, and institutions that create such an economy in the first place.[28] Hegel argues that the effective operation of a market economy presupposes a political authority that administers justice, regulates the market, and looks after the welfare and education of people who are unable to provide for themselves. If the individuals who oversee and control this authority are simply seeking their own advantage, the authority is unlikely to fulfil the functions for which it is established and unlikely to be seen as legitimate by the people affected by its decisions. Moreover, as Hegel points out in his 1822–3 lectures, it is naïve to think that the coercive power of the political authority would on its own be capable of securing individual property and contractual rights. What does the real work here is self-discipline and a sense of respect for the freedom of others: 'representational thought often imagines that the state is held together by force; but what holds it

[26] Good discussions of Hegel on *Sittlichkeit* include Taylor, *Hegel*, ch. 14; Wood, *Hegel's Ethical Thought*, chs. 11–12; and Hardimon, *Hegel's Social Philosophy*, chs. 5–6. However, none of these accounts emphasizes the dimension of Hegel's idea of *Sittlichkeit* that I have been drawing attention to in the text—namely, the way in which *Sittlichkeit*, by imbuing people with certain attitudes and dispositions, stabilizes and makes self-reproducing an institutional structure in which individuals can develop and sustain the capacities involved in personality and subjectivity.

[27] See Taylor, 'Hegel's Ambiguous Legacy for Modern Liberalism', 70.

[28] A good discussion of both the integrative and disintegrative dimensions of Hegel's account of civil society can be found in Cohen and Arato, *Civil Society and Political Theory*, ch. 2.

together is simply the basic sense of order which everyone possesses' (*PR* §268A).

The ties of comraderie and collegiality characteristic of the corporation do come closer to stabilizing and unifying a social order hospitable to subjectivity and so Hegel views it as a transitional institution between the market economy and the state. The corporation orients its members to a common good, works to inform its members about issues of concern to their particular sphere of working life, and helps to structure and canalize its members' political views and opinions so that they are not wildly capricious or arbitrary but reflect pressing and serious concerns that members might have. Still, Hegel thinks that the corporations are not, on their own, sufficient to stabilize a social order conducive to subjectivity. Because their ends remain 'limited and finite' (*PR* §256) and involve only '*particular* common interests' (*PR* §288), there are forms of conflict and instability that they will not be able to address.

It is only when a social order seeking to accommodate and promote subjectivity includes as its central and overarching institution the Hegelian state that Hegel expects it to be stable and self-sufficient. The Hegelian state performs this function because its central institutions—the sovereign, executive, and legislative powers—effectively and reliably pursue the universal interest: the interest that all have in living in a stable and self-reproducing community of mutual recognition that develops, nourishes, and respects individual subjectivity. These institutions are *effective* in the sense that they have the capacity to stabilize and preserve a social order hospitable to subjectivity against a range of destabilizing shocks and deprivations of both an internal and external nature. The institutions of the Hegelian state are *reliable* in the sense that they do tend to exercise this capacity rather than abusing their power and authority by promoting their own particular interests.

Hegel thinks that the state is effective and reliable in these ways in virtue of two sets of conditions that it meets: a set of objective conditions relating to the institutional and constitutional articulation of the state; and a set of subjective conditions relating to the dispositions of citizens. These two kinds of conditions, and their importance in stabilizing a social order hospitable to subjectivity, are nicely captured in a passage where Hegel situates his own discussion of the state in the context of Montesquieu's famous account of the principles of different forms of government:

as the condition of society grows more advanced and the powers of *particularity* are developed and liberated, it is not enough for the heads of the state to be virtuous; another form of rational law is required apart from that of the disposition if the whole is to have the strength to maintain its unity and to grant the forces of developed particularity their positive as well as negative rights. In the same way, we must avoid the misunderstanding of imagining that, since the disposition of virtue is the substantial form in a democratic republic, this disposition thereby becomes superfluous, or may even be totally absent, in a monarchy. (*PR* §273)

Here Hegel identifies as the problem the question of 'how the whole is to have the strength to maintain its unity' in a context where 'the powers of particularity are developed and liberated' and 'granted their positive as well as negative rights'. The answer, he claims, involves both a 'rational law' and a 'disposition' requirement: the state must be articulated into a system of rational law and its citizens must be animated—whether the state is a democratic republic or monarchy—by a disposition of virtue.

The objective or 'rational-law' conditions are described in detail in the lengthy discussion of the state's 'political constitution' (*PR* §269) in the *Philosophy of Right* (*PR* §§273–320) (and corresponding lectures). In general, Hegel thinks that the constitution should articulate the state into different tasks and functions such that the state takes on the character of an 'organism' that 'continually produces itself in a necessary way and thereby preserves itself' (*PR* §269A; cf. *PR* §269). More concretely, Hegel holds that the state should be divided into sovereign, executive, and legislative powers: 'This is a highly important determination which, if understood in its true sense, could rightly be regarded as the guarantee of public freedom' (*PR* §272). As the qualification 'if understood in its true sense' hints, however, Hegel worries that this division of functions and responsibilities could, if it is not determined correctly, set up rival centres of authority that end up destabilizing or paralysing the state. He thinks that the state can avoid these outcomes but still enjoy the advantages of the division of powers if a number of precautions are taken: the executive and legislative powers should be made clearly subordinate to the sovereign power (the monarch), for instance, and the sovereign and executive powers should participate actively in the law-making function of the legislative power. Other objective conditions emphasized by Hegel include: the use of a hereditary principle based on primogeniture to determine the succession in the monarchy (*PR*

§280); a highly trained civil service, appointed on the basis of merit (*PR* §291), and monitored by both the sovereign from above and the 'communities' and 'corporations' of civil society from below to ensure that it does not misuse its power (*PR* §§295, 297); and a system of selecting deputies for the lower house of the legislative power that works through elections held in individual corporations rather than directly through general elections (*PR* §308).

The subjective conditions of an effective and reliable state involve, in general, what Hegel terms 'political virtue' (*PR* §257) and 'patriotism' (*PR* §268). The political virtues include a 'sense of order', a willingness to obey the law and to pay one's taxes, the integrity of public officials, and a general orientation to the universal on the part of officials, deputies, and (to a lesser extent) the general public. In times of military crisis, these virtues extend also to the disposition of 'valour' (*PR* §§326–8). 'Patriotism' normally involves a disposition to recognize and accept the state as the context in which one's substantial and particular interests are preserved and contained, although it can occasionally imply (presumably in the context of a military crisis) 'a willingness to perform *extraordinary* sacrifices and actions' on behalf of the community (*PR* §268).

It is worth emphasizing that the satisfaction of the subjective and the objective conditions is, in Hegel's view, a single package. 'Disposition', Hegel insists, 'takes its particularly determined *content* from the various aspects of the organism of the state'—that is, from the different tasks and functions into which the state is articulated by the constitution (*PR* §269). The idea seems to be that citizens acquire and retain the dispositions considered to be subjective conditions through participation in the institutions and practices associated with the objective conditions. Civil servants and deputies are socialized into the virtues of integrity and orientation to the universal, for example, because of the objective character and structure of the executive and legislative powers. And ordinary citizens acquire and continuously reinforce an orientation to the universal through their participation in the corporation, which channels and structures their attitudes and dispositions, and through exposure to the institutions of 'public opinion' (*PR* §§315–19), which educates them about universal interests and concerns. On the other hand, the institutions and practices set out as objective conditions will operate effectively and reliably only if the citizens who participate in them are animated by the dispositions identified as subjective conditions.

When these subjective and objective conditions are satisfied, and thus the Hegelian state is fully in place, then Hegel thinks that a social order hospitable to subjectivity becomes realizable in a stable and self-sufficient way. Individuals have acquired an orientation to the universal that was missing in the previous, more 'abstract' stages discussed in the *Philosophy of Right*, and this orientation is shaped and continuously reinforced by the various supporting constitutional and institutional structures that are in place. Hegel's affirmation of the modern state (and of modern *Sittlichkeit* more generally) is rooted in thought that these conditions (or at least their 'principle') *are* satisfied in the modern world: 'The principle of modern states has enormous strength and depth because it allows the principle of subjectivity to attain fulfilment in the *self-sufficient extreme* of personal particularity, while at the same time *bringing it back to substantial unity* and so preserving this unity in the principle of subjectivity itself' (*PR* §260).

6.4. *The State as the Actuality of Concrete Freedom*

We are finally in a position to do justice to Hegel's important claim that 'the state is the actuality of concrete freedom' (*PR* §260). We know from §2.1 above that he understands *concrete* freedom to be the unity of two distinct kinds of freedom: *subjective* freedom and *objective* freedom. Concrete freedom is attributable to an agent pursuing some determination if and only if (*a*) the agent has reflected on the determination in question and found some subjective satisfaction in pursuing it, and (*b*) the determination is prescribed by reason. These two dimensions of subjectivity and objectivity are clearly at issue when Hegel elaborates his claim that the state is the actuality of concrete freedom by adding,

> *concrete freedom* requires that personal individuality and its particular interests should reach their full *development* and gain *recognition of their right* for itself (within the system of the family and of civil society), and also that they should, on the one hand, *pass over* of their own accord into the interest of the universal, and on the other, knowingly and willingly acknowledge this universal even as their own *substantial spirit*, and *actively pursue it* as their *ultimate end*. (*PR* §260)

The state is the actuality of concrete freedom because it caters to its members' 'personal individuality' and 'particular interests' (their subjectivity) *and* provides a universal or rational way of life (giving them objectivity) that they 'knowingly and willingly acknowledge' (subjectivity).

To unpack fully Hegel's claim about concrete freedom and the state, then, we need to explore why each of subjective and objective freedom are realized through participation in the Hegelian state. Let us start with the more straightforward of these sub-claims, the proposition that subjective freedom is realized through the state. The passage quoted above is, in fact, careful to distinguish three different senses in which subjective freedom is realized through the state and it is worth emphasizing all three: it says that subjective freedom (or what he terms 'personal individuality and its particular interests') is *developed* through the state, that its *right is recognized*, and that it *passes over* 'on its own accord' to the universal realized in the state, which it 'knowingly and willingly acknowledges'. Subjective freedom is developed in the state because, as we saw in detail above, the state is an important part of the minimum self-sufficient institutional structure that works to develop and sustain the capacities and attitudes associated with subjectivity. The right of subjective freedom is recognized in the state because the state respects and protects spheres of individual choice (chiefly) in the family and civil society: individuals can choose whom to marry, with whom to trade, what occupation to pursue, and so on.

The third sense in which subjective freedom is realized in the state—that the subject passes over on his own accord to a universal that is knowingly and willingly acknowledged—can be divided into two parts corresponding to the words 'knowingly' and 'willingly'. The suggestion that individuals *knowingly* acknowledge the state as the universal reflects Hegel's view (examined in §§2.3 and 2.5 above) that individuals fully realize concrete freedom only if they achieve a full degree of reflective awareness with respect to their determinations (in this case the duties and virtues of citizenship). The passage from *PR* §260 is thus expressing Hegel's confidence that this reflective awareness will indeed be achieved by many citizens of the Hegelian state.

The suggestion that individuals *willingly* acknowledge the universal is slightly more puzzling, but I think it starts to make sense if we recall a crucial feature of the Hegelian state. As we saw in §6.2, it is integral to Hegel's idea of the state that individuals are disposed to act for the good of the community as a whole—that they are animated by the various dispositions associated with 'patriotism' and 'political virtue'. In obeying the law, paying taxes, voting, and deliberating in the context of the corporation, acting as a conscientious civil servant or deputy, doing military service in times of crisis, and so on, individuals in a Hegelian state are not working for the good of something alien to their own purposes and identity but are helping to realize something—the good of the community as a whole—to which they are subjectively committed. To this extent, individuals enjoy subjective freedom in the state in the sense that they are habitually affirming, and giving expression to, an important aspect of their identity.

It is easy to miss this last point because it is easy to forget that Hegel operates with a highly idiosyncratic conception of the state. He effectively reverses the commonplace identification of the state with the exercise of force and coercion by defining it more affirmatively as a sphere of other-regarding dispositions and virtues. The state, Hegel says, 'is the spirit which is present in the world and which *consciously* realizes itself therein . . . Only when it is present in consciousness, knowing itself as an existent object, is it the state' (*PR* §258A).[29] If individuals do not subjectively identify with the good of the community as a whole—that is, if the state is not 'present in consciousness'—then it is not strictly speaking a state at all but a quite different form of political community—a *Notstaat*. As I have noted several times now, Hegel concedes that individuals are not free in a *Notstaat*, precisely because the ends and duties of citizenship in such a state appear to individuals as something alien and imposed (*PR* §186). Indeed, in his 1817–18 lectures, Hegel explicitly allows that the state can exercise force and violence but then immediately goes on to add that 'such a necessity is not a necessity of freedom' (*VPR17* 148–9).

A much more difficult task is to understand why Hegel thinks that objective freedom is realized in the state. The claim here is that the ends and activities of citizenship that the individual pursues in the state are, in some sense, prescribed by reason. It is this step in the argument that many commentators have been most sceptical about. Why should we accept Hegel's claim that there is anything peculiarly rational or valuable about a life of citizenship in the modern state? In

[29] For instance, Hegel holds that in oriental despotism 'there is no state in the sense of that self-conscious configuration of right, of free ethical life, and of organic development which is alone worthy of the spirit' (*PR* §270, p. 428/301; cf. *VPG* 201/161).

particular, why should we accept it if we abstract, as Hegel would have us do, from the contingent fact that citizenship is central to the identity and self-understanding of many people? This is obviously a crucial question, not just for understanding and assessing Hegel's position, but also for evaluating the prospects for civic humanism more generally: unless civic humanists can answer something like this question, then their thesis that a life of citizenship is a central constituting component of a good and free life seems very hard to accept.

The problem is seriously complicated by the fact that Hegel has relatively little to say explicitly about the issue, surprising as this may seem given his repeated association of the state with objective freedom. Indeed, it is tempting after an initial encounter with Hegel's discussion of the state to be sympathetic with Marx's comment that Hegel's real interest is not with politics but with logic.[30] Hegel devotes remarkably little attention to elaborating what is universal about the state but often seems just to dance around in circles, relating the universality of the state to other ideas and bits of jargon from his logic. Not surprisingly, many commentators offer only the vaguest of interpretations of why the state is for Hegel the realization of objective freedom or ignore the issue altogether.[31]

The quite sensible approach of more ambitious commentators has typically been to interpret Hegel's claims about freedom and the state in the light of whatever view of freedom they attribute to him more generally. Thus, for example, Charles Taylor emphasizes the importance of Hegel's doctrine of Cosmic Spirit both to his theory of freedom in general and to his claim that freedom finds its highest expression in the state in particular.[32] And Robert Pippin interprets Hegel's claims about freedom and the state in the light of his more general view that Hegel's concept of freedom issues into a historicized

[30] Marx, *Critique of Hegel's 'Philosophy of Right'*, 12, 18.

[31] For instance, Walsh (*Hegelian Ethics*, 46–7), does a good job of explaining how subjective freedom is realized in the Hegelian state but overlooks the question of objective freedom. Another commentator who largely ignores the issue in an otherwise excellent discussion is Schacht ('Hegel on Freedom', 320–7). Parkinson ('Hegel's Concept of Freedom', 165) and Inwood (*Hegel*, 486) both suggest that the state is rational, for Hegel, because it provides a moral/legal code expressed in universal propositions. Although this is undoubtedly one sense in which the Hegelian state is rational, I doubt that it helps much to explain why individuals realize objective freedom in the state, since nothing about what ends an agent should adopt follows from rationality in this sense.

[32] Taylor, *Hegel*, ch. 14.

notion of rationality.[33] My own approach to understanding Hegel's claims will be similar in that I will draw upon the general framework I developed in Chapter 3 of this study to illuminate Hegel's understanding of the relationship between objective freedom and the state. After doing this, however, I will also examine what Hegel actually does say about the issue, because I think that this provides independent support for the position I argue for.

I argued in Chapter 2 that objective freedom, for Hegel, involves pursuing a determination that has its basis, not in any contingently given desire or inclination, but only in pure thought and reason alone. This is a very strong condition, which will strike some readers as too strong, but, as I suggested in Chapter 2, it does seem to be an implication of our intuition that freedom and authority are opposed. If to accept something on authority—that is, without thinking it through and endorsing it for oneself—is a mark of unfreedom, then the same must be true of acting unreflectively on some desire or inclination: in both cases, one would be simply accepting some external instruction about how to act that one could think through and decide about for oneself. We would thus expect the determinations of objective freedom to be ones that could be endorsed independently of any appeal to a contingently given desire or inclination. As we saw in Chapter 3, however, this reflective endorsement condition seems to suggest that freedom is subject to a regress: the reasons that agents could appeal to in reflecting upon their goals and desires themselves need to be reflected upon, and so on. I argued that Hegel's solution to this regress problem involves the idea that appeals, in the context of one's practical deliberations, to the end of developing and maintaining one's own freedom would be conclusive. It would be no limitation on an agent's freedom if he neglects to subject *this* end to critical examination, because a commitment to this end is the very basis of his subjectivity in the first place.

Hegel seems to have thought that many of our ordinary ends are not capable of being endorsed 'all the way down' in this way. The ultimate reason or justification for why I choose to marry this person rather than that one, or embark on this career rather than some other, is not the promotion and preservation of my own freedom but something much more prosaic, such as my own welfare or happiness. I might enjoy subjective freedom in making these decisions—a free-

[33] Pippin, *Idealism as Modernism*, 126–7.

dom highly valued by Hegel—but not objective freedom. Hegel's claim, however, is that citizenship (and commitment to the duties and virtues of *Sittlichkeit* more generally) is different: 'in the state', he thinks, 'the individual has for the first time objective freedom' (*VPR19* 209–10). The suggestion here, then, if my analysis of Hegel's conception of freedom is correct, is that a life of citizenship is reflectively endorsable in a way that ordinary private ends are not: it is endorsable all the way down. The fundamental reason or justification that a citizen can appeal to in deliberating about his activity is not some brutely given desire or goal capable of further examination but the end of establishing and maintaining his own freedom itself, the end that partly constitutes his status as a free and rational agent.

But why are the activities associated with citizenship, unlike the agent's private ends and goals, capable of this form of total endorsement? The answer, I suggest, lies in the civic humanist analysis of the conditions of liberty we examined in the previous section. An agent can develop the capacities and attitudes that make up free and rational agency only in the context of a community of mutual recognition. If the interpretation of the previous section is correct, then the minimum self-sufficient or self-reproducing community of mutual recognition is one in which individuals approach the ideal of citizenship that Hegel builds into his conception of the state: unless individuals adopt the ends and dispositions of the good citizen, an institutional structure that preserves and promotes their freedom could never be maintained. This means that an individual reflecting about whether to endorse a life of citizenship can appeal, as a reason for so doing, to the fact that such a life contributes to the development and maintenance of his own freedom. And this is just to say that an individual in this position is objectively free: his activity as a citizen can be endorsed from the perspective of an end that partly constitutes his status as a free and rational agent—the end of establishing and maintaining his own freedom.

We can express this point in Hegel's own language by recalling his assertion, in the Introduction to the *Philosophy of Right*, that the free will has *itself* as its object, content, and end (*PR* §21), and his claim, in the 1817–18 lectures, that 'the will . . . is only *free* . . . in so far as it wills to be free' (*VPR17* 39). These claims have a paradoxical, even circular, ring to them, but we can make sense of them if we understand them as saying that an agent is fully free only to the extent that the ultimate rationale of his determination is to develop and sustain the capacities and attitudes that help to constitute his freedom and subjectivity: the capacities for independent reflection and self-discipline, for instance, and the sense of self-worth needed to employ these capacities. When the agent acts on this reason, then, as Hegel puts it, 'freedom is willed by freedom' (*PR* §21A). The state is the domain in which individuals achieve objective freedom, because in acting as citizens they are, in effect, willing their own freedom.[34] By virtuously deliberating about the common good, voting, obeying the law, serving in the military, and so on, the individual is helping to secure an institutional structure in which his capacities for freedom and subjectivity are fostered and nourished. This is to be contrasted with his private ends, which may indirectly contribute to the promotion and preservation of his freedom, but which, from his point of view, are directed at other less universal goals.

This interpretation of why the state, in Hegel's view, represents the first realization of objective freedom finds support in a number of passages from Hegel's discussion of the state itself. He argues for instance that,

> The political *disposition*, i.e. *patriotism* in general . . . is in general one of *trust* (which may pass over into more or less educated insight), or the consciousness that my substantial and particular interest is preserved and contained in the interest and end of an other (in this case, the state), and in the latter's relation to me as an individual. As a result, this other immediately ceases to be an other for me, and in my consciousness of this, I am free. (*PR* §268)

[34] Frederick Neuhouser proposes a similar account of why Rousseau holds that individuals achieve moral freedom in obeying the general will ('Freedom, Dependence, and the General Will', 391–2). He writes: 'By restructuring human dependence such that subjection to the will of others ceases to be a virtually inevitable consequence of dependence, the general will brings about the objective social conditions that must be present if individuals are to be able to avoid subjection to a foreign will. The general will, then, can be said to be the individual's own true will, even when she does not consciously recognize it as such, because the general will wills the conditions necessary in order for her freedom (along with the freedom of all others) to be realized. Identifying the general will with the true will of each individual is based on the idea that the individual will, apart from whatever particular ends it may embrace, necessarily, and most fundamentally, wills its own freedom. But in willing a certain end (its freedom) it must also will the conditions that make the end attainable. A will that chooses to act in ways that are inconsistent with what is required for the realization of its own freedom cannot be regarded as "doing its own will" and therefore cannot be considered truly free. Such a will—one which in effect wills its own subjection—is a self-negating, therefore contradictory, will.' If the main argument of this study is correct, then one advantage of Hegel's account over Rousseau's as reconstructed by Neuhouser is that it can explain why 'the individual will . . . necessarily, and most fundamentally, wills its own freedom'. See §3.5 above.

Here Hegel asserts that an agent overcomes the otherness of the state, and thereby achieves freedom, when he becomes conscious (through patriotism) that the state preserves and contains both his particular and his substantial interest. I argued earlier that particular interests, for Hegel, are interests that individuals have in virtue of their needs, desires, and so forth, whereas universal or substantial interests are the interests they have in being free and rational and in the conditions of freedom and rationality (see §6.2 above). Hegel's claim, then, is that an agent is free when he comes to see the state as both working for the satisfaction of his needs and desires and as guaranteeing his freedom and rationality. Individuals are free in the state, in other words, because, in acting as citizens in the state, they are working not just to satisfy their needs and desires but to develop and secure their own capacities for freedom and rationality.

This interpretation finds further support from passages in which Hegel claims that there is an *organic* relationship between the will of the individual and the state. As we noted earlier, 'the [political] disposition', for Hegel, 'takes its particularly determined *content* from the various aspects of the organism of the state' (*PR* §269; cf. §278 and *VG* 144/121). Hegel's conception of an organism has two features that are relevant here. First, an organism is an entity that is articulated in such a way as to ensure its own survival: its parts, or, to be more precise, its 'members', are determined to be as they are according to their contribution to the maintenance of the whole. Hegel's suggestion, then, is that the different tasks and functions that citizens perform as members of the state are determined in such a way as to allow the state continuously to reproduce itself. Secondly, the parts or members of an organism do not just serve the whole but have, in exchange, their own maintenance guaranteed by the survival of the whole and thus, indirectly, are serving themselves: 'In an organic relationship, the units in question are not parts but members, and each maintains the others while fulfilling its *own* function; the substantial end and product of each is to maintain the *other* members while simultaneously maintaining itself' (*PR* §286). Thus, Hegel's suggestion is that the individual's 'substantial end and product' involves maintaining himself by performing the tasks and functions that work to preserve and promote the state. And this dovetails neatly with the view I have been attributing to him in this section: individuals are objectively free in the state, for Hegel, because, in acting as citizens in the state, they are working to support an institutional structure that in turn develops and secures their own capacities for freedom and rationality.

To summarize, Hegel's thesis is that 'the state is the actuality of concrete freedom'. Hegel's defence of this thesis involves the claim that an individual is both subjectively and objectively free in playing the role of the good citizen. He is subjectively free in the state because his subjective freedom is developed and recognized in the state. Moreover, as a member of the Hegelian state, being a good citizen is central to his identity and self-understanding and he has achieved a condition of reflective awareness such that he perceives and understands that his determinations as a citizen are objectively rational. He is objectively free because he is engaging in an activity that, unlike his private ends, he can reflectively endorse 'all the way down': he can endorse it from the perspective of an end—developing and sustaining his own freedom—to which he is inescapably committed in virtue of being a free and rational agent.

I started this chapter by observing that Hegel distinguishes between two different ways of understanding the relationship between freedom and life in a political community. On the contractarian view, the state is a kind of compromise in which each individual agrees to diminish his own freedom in exchange for others doing the same. On the other view—Hegel's own civic humanist view—freedom is not given up in the state but is actually constituted there for the first time. We are now in a position to see why Hegel rejects the contractarian view in favour of his own position. The problem with the contractarian picture is twofold. First, it misconceptualizes the state as a largely instrumental form of political community and thus neglects the important dimension of patriotism and citizen identity in the modern state. This leads it to overlook at least two of the important senses in which subjective freedom is realized in the state: the state is part of the necessary institutional structure that develops and maintains their subjectivity; and, by acting as good citizens, individuals give expression to their own values and identity. Secondly, the contractarian picture misconceptualizes freedom by ignoring the dimension of rational or objective freedom: the freedom one enjoys in not accepting anything from outside on authority but in being able to endorse everything that purports to be a reason-for-action from the standpoint of one's own thought and reason. This freedom is first constituted in the state, and not outside it, because it is only in the state that individuals have ends that they can fully endorse on a rational basis.

6.5. *Two Objections*

The argument I have been developing helps to explain why two intuitive objections to Hegel's claim about freedom and the state cannot be sustained. The first is that, if freedom consists in obeying only oneself and not anybody or anything else, then it seems perverse to conclude that this freedom is most fully and truly realized in obeying the state. Only by some dangerous 'sleight of hand', to use Berlin's phrase,[35] could obeying oneself come to be identified with obeying the state. The second objection is simply that there have been many states in history, arguably including Hegel's own Prussian state, that have treated their citizens in an oppressive manner that, far from realizing individual freedom, could only be said to have suffocated it. The Prussian state of the 1820s, for instance, tolerated relatively little freedom of religion, did not permit any of the liberties normally associated with democracy, and did very little to address the unfreedom inherent in poverty and economic inequality. How in the face of this historical experience could one possibly endorse Hegel's claim that freedom is most fully and truly realized in the state?

In response to the first objection, the argument of this chapter shows why, in acting as a good citizen (and this includes obeying the law), there are for Hegel two important senses in which I am obeying myself alone. I am obeying myself, first of all, in the subjective sense that I am pursuing ends and goals to which I attach subjective value and importance.[36] To the extent that I do not subjectively comprehend and affirm what is being asked of me by the state, Hegel accepts the objection and concedes that I am not fully free. Secondly, I am obeying myself in the objective sense that I am acting rationally: I am not uncritically accepting some externally given reason-for-action (as is usually the case in my private life) but am pursuing an end that I can reflectively endorse 'all the way down'. As we have seen, this is because, in acting as a good citizen, I am contributing to the establishment and maintenance of my own freedom.

[35] Berlin, *Four Essays on Liberty*, 134.
[36] See Pelczynski, 'The Hegelian Conception of the State', 26–7.

The second objection is slightly more difficult to deal with. The difficulty is that Hegel does hold that something broadly, although by no means exactly, like his own Prussian state does represent the full actualization of freedom.[37] Although the Hegelian state was fairly liberal by the standards of its own time, it is likely to strike most contemporary readers as providing a less than secure basis for individual freedom. It could be argued, for instance, that the state as characterized by Hegel has too weak and unrepresentative a legislature, too enclosed and powerful a bureaucracy, and allows too limited a role for public opinion, to be considered the full actualization of freedom. One need not accept all of Marx's criticisms of Hegel to agree with him that the Hegelian state seems better designed to promote the powerful and entrenched interests of civil society than the freedom of ordinary citizens, let alone of the poor and dispossessed.[38] And one need not be a contractarian to think that what is missing in the Hegelian state is precisely the participatory, Rousseauian democratic mechanisms that Hegel explicitly repudiates (*PR* §§303, 308).

To concede these points, however, is not to concede the objection under consideration. It does not follow from the fact that Hegel has an implausible view of what constitutes a rational state that he thinks that just *any* state, including states that *he* would consider oppressive, actualize freedom. The disagreement with Hegel that I have just outlined concerns whether the state that he admires is oppressive, not whether individuals are free in oppressive states. It is implicit in the argument of this whole chapter that Hegel would deny that oppressive states do actualize freedom. A state represents the actualization of freedom *only if* its members are both subjectively and objectively free in acting as citizens of that state. Oppressive states would typically fail to satisfy either condition. Individuals would not be subjectively free with respect to such a state, because it would not develop and recognize their subjective freedom. Moreover, they would probably regard it not as integral to their own identities and values but as an alien power that is at best a necessary evil. Individuals would not be objectively free with respect to such a state because it would not

[37] For discussion of the differences between the Prussian state of the 1820s and the state Hegel describes in the *Philosophy of Right*, see e.g. Knox, 'Hegel and Prussianism', 21–2; Westphal, 'The Basic Context and Structure of Hegel's *Philosophy of Right*', 234–44; Avineri, *Hegel's Theory of the Modern State*, chs. 6–9; and Wood's notes to the Nisbet translation of the *Philosophy of Right*.

[38] See e.g. Marx, *Critique of Hegel's 'Philosophy of Right'*, 44–9.

typically be the case that, in acting as good citizens, they are helping to secure the conditions under which they can develop and maintain their own freedom: to the contrary, they would be supporting an institutional structure that suffocates their capacities for free and rational agency rather than actualizing them.

7
Conclusion

The landscape of modern social life is dominated by the institutions of the family, civil society, and the state. These institutions define various duties and virtues for us and shape and structure more broadly the norms, meanings, and understandings with which we reason together about social and political questions. Although there is much that divides us in modern societies, we almost all participate, in some way or other, in the family, civil society, and the state. By appealing to the shared understandings latent in these institutions of our common social life, it becomes possible to exchange reasons with those with whom we disagree with some hope of convergence.

This is a comforting picture of practical reason and yet there is something very unsettling about it. How do we settle ethical questions when the different understandings that we share pull us in conflicting directions? Or what if the pluralistic character of modern societies means that there are certain key understandings that we do not share—understandings that are local to one group's experience of the family, civil society, and the state, and not to the experience of others? More troublingly still, what do we say to the radical critic in our midst who questions the authority of our shared understandings by disputing the legitimacy of the family, civil society, or the state?

With the revived popularity of 'communitarian' political theory, these concerns nag at us more than ever today. They are not, however, *new* concerns. A major assumption of this study has been that Hegel was aware of these challenges and offers us a philosophically rigorous and original response to them. He not only identified the family, civil society, and the state as the major institutions of modern social life and claimed that the duties and virtues they incorporate provide the content of everyday practical reasoning. By insisting on the need for a rational reconciliation to modern *Sittlichkeit*, he also recognized the problem of indeterminacy threatened by this account and acknowledged the concerns of the radical critic.

The overarching aim of this study has been to try to understand Hegel's solution to these challenges through an examination of his 'idea of freedom'. Hegel's basic strategy, I have argued, is to respond to the challenges through an exploration of human subjectivity and its conditions. His claim is that a social world containing modern *Sittlichkeit* is necessary for the full enjoyment of human subjectivity and freedom. A social world that includes the institutions of the family, civil society, and the state, and in which citizens actively recognize and are committed to the duties and virtues that are defined by these institutions, represents the minimum self-sufficient form of social order that is hospitable to human subjectivity. Unless a social order contains these institutions, and unless the duties and virtues they define enter into the concrete life of their members, that order will not be able to foster and respect subjectivity in a stable, self-perpetuating way. Faced with an indeterminacy problem, then, Hegel would send us back to modern *Sittlichkeit*'s foundations in human freedom and its conditions. These foundations can help us to prioritize the conflicting claims of different institutions and practices. Faced with the radical critic of modern social life, Hegel would patiently explain that the institutional life of modern *Sittlichkeit* is necessary for the full expression and realization of human subjectivity.

What, then, should we make of Hegel's solution? Could it be of any relevance today in thinking about the challenges to our own modes of practical reasoning? I hope to have shown in these pages that there is at least something 'living' in Hegel's approach. If my interpretation is right, Hegel's solution does not start out from any fantastical notion of cosmic spirit or dubious assumptions about reason and history (even if these commitments are part of his philosophical system more generally). Instead, Hegel's strategy for warranting modern *Sittlichkeit* starts from a concern that will seem compelling to many of us today: a concern for human freedom and subjectivity and the conditions of their full expression and flourishing. This is a concern that *could* help to overcome indeterminacy and to reconcile or reassure the radical, alienated critic.

Still, there are two broad kinds of worries about Hegel's solution and it seems appropriate to conclude by mentioning them, if only to underline the unsettled, untidy nature of the problems we have been wrestling with. The first worry concerns whether Hegel is right to think that modern *Sittlichkeit* is really necessary for the full development and expression of human subjectivity. There are, after all, countless places in which the argument might have gone off the rails.

In particular, as I noted in several places, Hegel seems to be making a priori claims about the social and institutional conditions under which human personality and subjectivity can be developed and sustained. But what if these claims are not confirmed by experience? To give just a couple of examples, what if experience shows that a social order does not need institutions such as property or contract to mediate mutual recognition or, indeed, that mutual recognition is much less important to human development than Hegel maintains? Any account appealing to fictional struggles for supremacy resulting in master–slave relationships has to raise questions of a hard-headed empirical kind. The worry, in short, is that Hegel has not decisively shown that modern *Sittlichkeit* really is necessary for human freedom and subjectivity.

The second worry is deeper, since it has force even if Hegel is broadly correct to think that the stable enjoyment of human freedom and subjectivity does ultimately depend on modern *Sittlichkeit*. The worry is that the appeal to human freedom and subjectivity does not fully assuage the concerns of certain kinds of critics or estranged opponents of modernity. Sure, they might say, modern *Sittlichkeit* can be defended by appeal to human subjectivity and its conditions. This is hardly surprising, given that human subjectivity and freedom are the central defining ideals of modernity. But why should we think that *these* ideals are authoritative? Do they not, in a way, also reflect our experience of the institutions of modernity? After all, they have not been the dominant ideals at all times and in all cultures.

At this point, I think that Hegel *would* fall back on a story about God's self-realization through the historical process. Human freedom and subjectivity are the correct ideals for thinking about social and political questions ultimately because God wants, or even needs, to be freely known and worshipped. To this extent, the civic humanist reading defended in this study cannot stand entirely on its own. For us today, of course, it seems hard to accept such a metaphysical story at its face value. But, in sensing the need for such a story, Hegel can at least claim to have identified a problem that is no less relevant today than it was in Hegel's own time.

BIBLIOGRAPHY

ALLISON, HENRY E., *Kant's Theory of Freedom* (Cambridge: Cambridge University Press, 1990).

—— 'On a Presumed Gap in the Derivation of the Categorical Imperative', *Philosophical Topics*, 19/1 (1991), 1–15.

—— 'Kant on Freedom: A Reply', *Inquiry*, 36 (1993), 443–64.

AMERIKS, KARL, 'The Hegelian Critique of Kantian Morality', in Marcia Moen and Bernard den Ouden (eds.), *New Essays on Kant* (New York: Peter Lang, 1987).

AVINERI, SHLOMO, *Hegel's Theory of the Modern State* (Cambridge: Cambridge University Press, 1972).

BEISER, FREDERICK C. (ed.), *The Cambridge Companion to Hegel* (Cambridge: Cambridge University Press, 1993).

BENHABIB, SEYLA, 'Obligation, Contract and Exchange: On the Significance of Hegel's Abstract Right', in Z. Pelczynski (ed.), *State and Civil Society: Studies in Hegel's Political Philosophy* (Cambridge: Cambridge University Press, 1984).

BENN, STANLEY I., *A Theory of Freedom* (Cambridge: Cambridge University Press, 1988).

BERLIN, ISAIAH, *Four Essays on Liberty* (Oxford: Oxford University Press, 1969).

BITTNER, RÜDIGER, *What Reason Demands*, trans. Theodore Talbot (Cambridge: Cambridge University Press, 1989).

BOCK, GISELA, SKINNER, QUENTIN, and VIROLI, MAURIZIO (eds.), *Machiavelli and Republicanism* (Cambridge: Cambridge University Press, 1990).

BROD, HARRY, *Hegel's Philosophy of Politics* (Boulder, Colo.: Westview Press, 1992).

CHRISTMAN, JOHN (ed.), *The Inner Citadel: Essays on Individual Autonomy* (New York: Oxford University Press, 1989).

—— *The Myth of Property* (Oxford: Oxford University Press, 1994).

—— 'Distributive Justice and the Complex Structure of Ownership', *Philosophy and Public Affairs*, 23/3 (1994), 225–50.

COHEN, G. A., 'Capitalism, Freedom and the Proletariat', in Alan Ryan (ed.), *The Idea of Freedom: Essays in Honour of Isaiah Berlin* (Oxford: Oxford University Press, 1979).

COHEN, JEAN L., and ARATO, ANDREW, *Civil Society and Political Theory* (Cambridge, Mass.: MIT Press, 1992).

CRANSTON, MAURICE, *Freedom: A New Analysis*, 3rd edn. (London: Longmans, Green & Co. Ltd., 1967).

CROCKER, LAWRENCE, *Positive Liberty* (The Hague: Martinus Nijhoff Publishers, 1980).

DICKEY, LAURENCE, *Hegel: Religion, Economics and the Politics of Spirit, 1770–1807* (Cambridge: Cambridge University Press, 1987).

DWORKIN, GERALD, *The Theory and Practice of Autonomy* (Cambridge: Cambridge University Press, 1988).

FEINBERG, JOEL, 'Autonomy', in John Christman (ed.), *The Inner Citadel: Essays on Individual Autonomy* (New York: Oxford University Press, 1989).

FICHTE, JOHANN GOTTLIEB, *Beiträge zur Berichtigung der Urteile des Publikums über die Französische Revolution*, in *Johann Gottlieb Fichtes sämmtliche Werke*, ed. Immanuel Hermann Fichte (Berlin: Veit & Co., 1845–6), vi.

—— *Grundlage des Naturrechts*, in *Johann Gottlieb Fichtes sämmtliche Werke*, ed. Immanuel Hermann Fichte (Berlin: Veit & Co., 1845–6), iii.

FRIEDMAN, MILTON, *Capitalism and Freedom* (Chicago: Chicago University Press, 1962).

GADAMER, HANS-GEORG, *Truth and Method*, ed. Garrett Barden and John Cumming (London: Sheed & Ward Ltd., 1975).

GELLNER, ERNEST, *Conditions of Liberty: Civil Society and its Rivals* (London: Hamish Hamilton, 1994).

GOUGH, J. W., *The Social Contract*, 2nd edn. (Oxford: Oxford University Press, 1963).

GREEN, LESLIE, *The Authority of the State* (Oxford: Oxford University Press, 1988).

HARDIMON, MICHAEL O., *Hegel's Social Philosophy: The Project of Reconciliation* (Cambridge: Cambridge University Press, 1994).

HARRIS, H. S., *Hegel's Development, i. Toward the Sunlight 1770–1801* (Oxford: Oxford University Press, 1972).

—— *Hegel's Development, ii. Night Thoughts. Jena 1801–06* (Oxford: Oxford University Press, 1983).

HAYM, RUDOLF, *Hegel und seine Zeit* (Berlin: Rudolf Gaertner, 1857).

HILL Jr., THOMAS E., 'Kant's Argument for the Rationality of Moral Conduct', *Pacific Philosophical Quarterly*, 66 (1985), 3–23.

—— 'The Kantian Conception of Autonomy', in John Christman (ed.), *The Inner Citadel: Essays on Individual Autonomy* (New York: Oxford University Press, 1989).

INWOOD, MICHAEL, *Hegel* (London: Routledge & Kegan Paul, 1983).

KANT, IMMANUEL, *Kants gesammelte Schriften* (29 vols.; Deutschen (formerly Königlichen Preussischen) Akademie der Wissenschaften, Berlin, Walter de Gruyter (and predecessors), 1900–42). (*Grundlegung zur Metaphysik der Sitten* is in vol. iv; *Kritik der praktischen Vernunft* is in vol. v.)

—— *Groundwork of the Metaphysics of Morals*, trans. H. J. Paton as *The Moral Law* (London: Unwin Hyman, 1948).

—— *Critique of Practical Reason*, trans. Lewis White Beck (New York: Macmillan, 1956).

—— 'Metaphysical First Principles of the Doctrine of Right', in *The Metaphysics of Morals*, trans. Mary Gregor (Cambridge: Cambridge University Press, 1991).

—— *Political Writings*, trans. H. B. Nisbet and Hans Reiss, 2nd edn. (Cambridge: Cambridge University Press, 1991).

KAUFMANN, WALTER (ed.), *Hegel's Political Philosophy* (New York: Atherton, 1970).

KELLY, GEORGE ARMSTRONG, *Idealism, Politics and History: Sources of Hegelian Thought* (Cambridge: Cambridge University Press, 1969).

—— 'Notes on Hegel's Lordship and Bondage', in Alisdair MacIntyre (ed.), *Hegel: A Collection of Critical Essays* (New York: Doubleday, 1972).

KIERKEGAARD, SØREN, *Fear and Trembling*, trans. Walter Lowrie (Garden City: Doubleday & Company, 1954).

KNOWLES, DUDLEY, 'Hegel on Property and Personality', *Philosophical Quarterly*, 33/130 (1983), 45–62.

KNOX, T. M., 'Hegel and Prussianism', in Walter Kaufman (ed.), *Hegel's Political Philosophy* (New York: Atherton Press, 1970), 13–29.

KORSGAARD, CHRISTINE M., 'Kant's Formula of Universal Law', *Pacific Philosophical Quarterly*, 66 (1985), 24–37.

—— 'Scepticism about Practical Reason', *Journal of Philosophy*, 83/1 (1986), 5–25.

—— 'Morality as Freedom', in Yirmiyuhu Yovel (ed.), *Kant's Practical Philosophy Reconsidered* (Dordrecht: Kluwer Academic Publishers, 1989).

KRIEGER, LEONARD, *The German Idea of Freedom* (Boston: Beacon Press, 1957).

LOCKE, JOHN, *Two Treatises of Government*, ed. Peter Laslett, 2nd edn. (Cambridge: Cambridge University Press, 1967).

LOSURDO, DOMENICO, *Hegel et les libéraux*, trans. François Mortier (Paris: Presses Universitaires de France, 1992).

MARX, KARL, *Critique of Hegel's 'Philosophy of Right'*, trans. Annette Jolin and Joseph O'Malley (Cambridge: Cambridge University Press, 1970).

MILLER, DAVID, *Anarchism* (London: Dent, 1984).

MONTESQUIEU, CHARLES DE SECONDAT, *The Spirit of the Laws*, ed. and trans. Anne Cohler, Basia Miller, and Harold Stone (Cambridge: Cambridge University Press, 1989).

MUNZER, STEPHEN R., *A Theory of Property* (Cambridge: Cambridge University Press, 1990).

NEUHOUSER, FREDERICK, 'Freedom, Dependence, and the General Will', *Philosophical Review*, 102/3 (1993), 363–95.

NEUHOUSER, FREDERICK, 'Fichte and the Relationship between Right and Morality', in Daniel Breazeale and Tom Rockmore (eds.), *Fichte: Historical Contexts/Contemporary Controversies* (Atlantic Highlands, NJ: Humanities Press, 1994).

O'NEILL (NELL), ONORA, *Acting on Principle: An Essay on Kantian Ethics* (New York: Columbia University Press, 1975).

—— 'Ethical Reasoning and Ideological Pluralism', *Ethics*, 98 (1988), 705–22.

OPPENHEIM, FELIX, *Dimensions of Freedom: An Analysis* (New York: St Martin's Press, 1961).

PARKINSON, G. H. R., 'Hegel's Concept of Freedom', in Michael Inwood (ed.), *Hegel* (Oxford: Oxford University Press, 1985).

PELCZYNSKI, Z. A., 'The Hegelian Conception of the State', in Z. A. Pelczynski (ed.), *Hegel's Political Philosophy: Problems and Perspectives* (Cambridge: Cambridge University Press, 1971).

—— 'Political Community and Individual Freedom in Hegel's Philosophy of the State', in Z. A. Pelczynski (ed.), *State and Civil Society* (Cambridge: Cambridge University Press, 1984).

—— (ed.), *State and Civil Society* (Cambridge: Cambridge University Press, 1984).

PINKARD, TERRY, *Hegel's* Phenomenology*: The Sociality of Reason* (Cambridge: Cambridge University Press, 1994).

PIPPIN, ROBERT B., *Hegel's Idealism* (Cambridge: Cambridge University Press, 1989).

—— 'Idealism and Agency in Kant and Hegel', *Journal of Philosophy*, 88/10 (1991), 532–41.

—— *Modernism as a Philosophical Problem* (Oxford: Blackwell Publishers, 1991).

—— 'You Can't Get There from Here', in Frederick C. Beiser (ed.), *The Cambridge Companion to Hegel* (Cambridge: Cambridge University Press, 1993).

—— *Idealism as Modernism: Hegelian Variations* (Cambridge: Cambridge University Press, 1997).

PLANT, RAYMOND, *Hegel: An Introduction*, 2nd edn. (Oxford: Basil Blackwell, 1983).

POCOCK, J. G. A., *The Machiavellian Moment: Florentine Political Thought and the Atlantic Republican Tradition* (Princeton: Princeton University Press, 1975).

RAWLS, JOHN, *Political Liberalism* (New York: Columbia University Press, 1993).

RAZ, JOSEPH (ed.), *Authority* (Oxford: Blackwell, 1990).

—— 'Government by Consent', in *Ethics in the Public Domain* (Oxford: Oxford University Press, 1994).

RIEDEL, MANFRED, *Between Tradition and Revolution: The Hegelian Transformation of Political Philosophy* (Cambridge: Cambridge University Press, 1984).

RILEY, PATRICK, *Will and Political Legitimacy: A Critical Exposition of Social Contract Theory in Hobbes, Locke, Rousseau, Kant and Hegel* (Cambridge, Mass.: Harvard University Press, 1982).

RITTER, JOACHIM, 'Person and Property: On Hegel's *Philosophy of Right*, Paragraphs 34–81', in *Hegel and the French Revolution: Essays on the Philosophy of Right*, trans. Richard Dien Winfield (Cambridge, Mass.: MIT Press, 1982).

—— *Hegel and the French Revolution: Essays on the Philosophy of Right*, trans. Richard Dien Winfield (Cambridge, Mass.: MIT Press, 1982).

RORTY, RICHARD, *Objectivity, Relativism and Truth: Philosophical Papers Volume I* (Cambridge: Cambridge University Press, 1991).

ROSEN, MICHAEL, *Hegel's Dialectic and its Criticism* (Cambridge: Cambridge University Press, 1982).

ROUSSEAU, JEAN-JACQUES, *The Social Contract*, trans. G. D. H. Cole, with revisions by J. H. Brumfitt and John C. Hall (London: J. M. Dent & Sons, 1973).

RYAN, ALAN, *Property and Political Theory* (Oxford: Basil Blackwell, 1984).

—— *Property* (Milton Keynes: Open University Press, 1987).

SARTRE, JEAN PAUL, *L'Existentialisme est un humanisme* (Paris: Les Éditions Nagel, 1967).

SCANLON, THOMAS, 'A Theory of Freedom of Expression', *Philosophy and Public Affairs*, 1/2 (1972), 204–26.

SCHACHT, RICHARD L., 'Hegel on Freedom', in Alasdair MacIntyre (ed.), *Hegel: A Collection of Critical Essays* (New York: Doubleday, 1972).

SIDGWICK, HENRY, *The Methods of Ethics*, 7th edn. (London: Macmillan, 1967).

SIEP, LUDWIG, 'The *Aufhebung* of Morality in Ethical Life', in L. S. Stepelevich and D. Lamb (eds.), *Hegel's Philosophy of Action* (Atlantic Highlands, NJ: Humanities Press, 1983).

SILBER, JOHN R., 'The Ethical Significance of Kant's *Religion*', in Immanuel Kant, *Religion Within the Limits of Reason Alone*, trans. Theodore M. Greene and Hoyt H. Hudson (New York: Harper & Row, 1960).

SIMMONS, A. JOHN, *The Lockean Theory of Rights* (Princeton: Princeton University Press, 1992).

—— *On the Edge of Anarchy: Locke, Consent and the Limits of Society* (Princeton: Princeton University Press, 1993).

SMITH, ADAM, *The Wealth of Nations* (Harmondsworth: Penguin Books, 1982).

SMITH, STEVEN B., *Hegel's Critique of Liberalism* (Chicago: University of Chicago Press, 1989).

Stillman, Peter G., 'Property, Freedom, and Individuality in Hegel's and Marx's Political Thought', in J. Roland Pennock and John W. Chapman (eds.), *NOMOS XXII: Property* (New York: 1980).

Taylor, Charles, *Hegel* (Cambridge: Cambridge University Press, 1975).

—— *Hegel and Modern Society* (Cambridge: Cambridge University Press, 1979).

—— 'Atomism', in *Philosophy and the Human Sciences: Philosophical Papers 2* (Cambridge: Cambridge University Press, 1985).

—— 'Kant's Theory of Freedom', in *Philosophy and the Human Sciences: Philosophical Papers 2* (Cambridge: Cambridge University Press, 1985).

—— 'Cross-Purposes: The Liberal–Communitarian Debate', in Nancy Rosenblum (ed.), *Liberalism and the Moral Life* (Cambridge, Mass.: Harvard University Press, 1989).

—— *Sources of the Self: The Making of the Modern Identity* (Cambridge, Mass.: Harvard University Press, 1989).

—— 'Hegel's Ambiguous Legacy for Modern Liberalism', in Drucilla Cornell, Michel Rosenfeld, and David Gray Carlson (eds.), *Hegel and Legal Theory* (New York: Routledge, 1991).

Theunissen, Michael, 'The Repressed Intersubjectivity in Hegel's *Philosophy of Right*', in Drucilla Cornell, Michel Rosenfeld, and David Gray Carlson (eds.), *Hegel and Legal Theory* (New York: Routledge, 1991).

Tugendhat, Ernst, *Self-Consciousness and Self-Determination*, trans. Paul Stern (Cambridge, Mass.: MIT Press, 1986).

Tunick, Mark, *Hegel's Political Philosophy* (Princeton: Princeton University Press, 1992).

—— 'Hegel's Nonfoundationalism', *History of Philosophy Quarterly*, 11/3 (1994), 317–37.

Waldron, Jeremy, *The Right to Private Property* (Oxford: Oxford University Press, 1988).

Walsh, W. H., *Hegelian Ethics* (London: Macmillan, 1969).

Walzer, Michael, *Spheres of Justice: A Defence of Pluralism and Equality* (Oxford: Blackwell, 1983).

—— 'The Civil Society Argument', in Chantal Mouffe (ed.), *Dimensions of Radical Democracy* (London: Verso, 1992).

Westphal, Kenneth, 'The Basic Context and Structure of Hegel's *Philosophy of Right*', in Frederick Beiser (ed.), *The Cambridge Companion to Hegel* (Cambridge: Cambridge University Press, 1993).

Wildt, Andreas, *Autonomie und Anerkennung* (Stuttgart: Klett-Cotta, 1982).

Williams, Bernard, 'Internal and External Reasons', in *Moral Luck* (Cambridge: Cambridge University Press, 1981).

WILLIAMS, ROBERT R., *Recognition: Fichte and Hegel on the Other* (Albany, NY: State University of New York Press, 1992).

WOLFF, ROBERT PAUL, *In Defense of Anarchism* (New York: Harper & Row, 1970).

WOOD, ALLEN, *Hegel's Ethical Thought* (Cambridge: Cambridge University Press, 1990).

INDEX